Praise for

My Fighting Family

"This is a surprising book, a moving book that's a love note to Campbell's family, Black American resilience, Canada, music, and football. It's not really about fighting as much as it is about how families can lose and sometimes find themselves in spite of everything that seeks to tear them apart: old grudges, bitter disappointments, and property. In this memoir, Campbell mixes poignant memories of his whirlwind childhood with perceptive analysis that only age and wisdom can bring. He elevates it with humour, wit, and empathy for people who aren't necessarily empathetic. An impressive work that I'd recommend to anyone who wants to make sense of who they are and why."

—Joel Anderson, Slate

"*My Fighting Family* offers a glimpse into a Black experience that is rarely discussed—what it was like for those who went so far north that they left the United States. That, plus the candid look at his own family, makes Morgan Campbell's memoir worth reading."

—Bomani Jones, *The Right Time*

MY FIGHTING FAMILY

MY
FIGHTING
FAMILY

BORDERS AND BLOODLINES

AND THE BATTLES THAT MADE US

MORGAN CAMPBELL

McCLELLAND & STEWART

Library and Archives Canada Cataloguing in Publication
Title: My fighting family : borders and bloodlines and the battles that made us /
Morgan Campbell.
Names: Campbell, Morgan, author.
Identifiers: Canadiana (print) 20230159311 | Canadiana (ebook) 20230482570 |
ISBN 9780771050190 (hardcover) | ISBN 9780771050206 (ebook)
Subjects: LCSH: Campbell, Morgan. | LCSH: Journalists—Canada—Biography. |
LCGFT: Autobiographies.
Classification: LCC PN4913.C36 A3 2024 | DDC 070.92—dc23

Book design by Lisa Jager
Jacket art: front cover photographs courtesy of the author
Typeset in Adobe Garamond by M&S, Toronto
Printed in Canada

McClelland & Stewart,
a division of Penguin Random House Canada Limited,
a Penguin Random House Company
www.penguinrandomhouse.ca

1 2 3 4 5   28 27 26 25 24

Penguin
Random House
McCLELLAND & STEWART

To Jeanie and to Pete,
who both taught me how to make every word count.

Contents

A NOTE ON CHARACTERS AND DIALOGUE

All these stories are true, but I've changed some names to protect some folks, and accept that many of the old family tales included here may have grown taller in the retellings. In some cases, I distill processes into distinct events and acknowledge that I can't always know what was said in my absence. Some of these conversations are dramatizations, recon-structions rooted in fact, and what I do know about the people and the situations. I have some leeway to be creative, but it's still non-fiction.

All these stories are true.

I Don't Know Any Campbells

Every morning, I sensed her eyes on me when I boarded at the city transit terminal in downtown Windsor. As the bus rumbled through the tunnel to Detroit, I could feel her stealing glances. We'd unload quickly on the U.S. side to funnel through customs, then back on the bus for the loop around downtown. I'd hop off at Washington and Lafayette. Short walk from there to the *Detroit News*, where I was working an internship. She'd exit a few stops earlier, closer to Congress, after she'd peeked at me a few more times. At twenty-two, I knew an appraising look when I received one, and this woman's eyes said she wanted to know something about me.

Certain details, we could each glean from routine. We both lived in Windsor and worked in Detroit, like everybody making their morning commute on the Transit Windsor Tunnel Bus. She was Black by racial category, light brown by phenotype, high yella by vernacular. Lighter than a paper bag but darker than coffee creamer, and still looking at me like a piece of a puzzle she needed to solve.

She was at least forty-five. Probably closer to fifty. Whatever she wanted with me, it certainly wasn't *that*. I figured she was trying to profile me the way I had profiled her.

Growing up near Toronto, if I met a medium-to-fair-skinned Black person old enough to be my parent but who spoke without an accent, they were usually old-school African-American Diaspora Black Canadians, from Nova Scotia or southwest Ontario. My uncle Ken had a knack for attracting folks like those into his circle. He used to play softball with a trio of brothers, caramel-coloured, last name Chase, born and raised in Windsor. The oldest, Rick, worked with Uncle Ken, driving buses for the TTC. Another was into judo. The youngest, John, was an actor and singer who sometimes hosted *Polka Dot Door* on TVO. If they needed a sister to complete their set of siblings, they could have drafted the woman from the Tunnel Bus.

As for me, I walked around downtown Windsor, looking like I belonged, which is probably why she paid attention. I was young enough to be her son, but wasn't. I was *somebody's* son, though, and she wanted to know whose.

After about three weeks, we exchanged eye contact and greetings. She lobbed a softball conversation-starting question, and we were off: talking about her office job in Detroit, and my summer gig at the *News*. When she told me she grew up in Windsor, I asked if she knew the Chase brothers.

"Ricky and Johnie? Of course I know them," she said. "We all came up together. They lived on Mercer Street. Right downtown. How do you know them?"

"They're friends with my uncle," I said. "They come to his birthday party every summer. John used to tell me all his football stories."

"Are you guys from here?"

"No," I said. "I'm from Mississauga."

"Oh," she said. "What's your last name?"

Only four words, but so many layers to that question. In Mississauga, where most of the Black kids I knew were first-generation Canadian with Caribbean immigrant parents, it had several permutations.

Which island are you from?

Where are your parents from?

Where are you really *from?*

Sometimes people asked out of good-faith curiosity, but often the question carried undertones. They weren't just seeking information, but a way to categorize me. Windsorites wanted my last name. Torontonians wanted to know my island. These were bigger questions of belonging. Different cities, different ways of asking, "Are you one of us?"

The woman on the bus figured I was, which made sense. Her family and community had more history in Canada than my folks did, but we shared Black American roots. Her folks were as likely as my sisters and I were to have been baptized in an AME church, or have grandparents who attended a segregated school, just on opposite sides of the border. So she asked my last name and probably expected to hear an answer she recognized—Shadd or Shreve or Hurst or McCurdy, something that would mark me as a descendant of the fugitive slaves who came to Canada via the Underground Railroad. My family *did* cross into Canada at the Detroit River's narrowest point; we just did it four generations later, in a car, and kept driving, all the way to Toronto. I was one of them, but not quite.

"My last name's Campbell," I said.

"Oh," she said, looking puzzled. "I don't know any Campbells."

I could empathize. I didn't know many Campbells, either.

My dad had a wide network of relatives across the U.S., with hubs in Chicago and Detroit and Grand Rapids. Annual family reunions filled hotels and city parks, but only featured a handful of Campbells—my parents, their kids, Granny Mary. My dad's late father was a Campbell, but *his* mom was a Wilson. My dad's half-brother's last name was Brazil, and most of the cousins on the Campbell-Wilson side were named McClinton and Jennings.

Among the general population, the Campbell name was way too common to tell my family, without further context, whether somebody was kin. So Dad never suspected Earl Campbell from the Houston Oilers was a distant cousin, nor Luther Campbell, aka Luke Skyywalker, the 2 Live Crew's ringleader. The actress Tisha Campbell, who played the light-skinned love interest in the movie *House Party* and Gina in the '90s sitcom *Martin*? With her build and skin colour, she could have tripped my dad's sensor, and maybe passed as a big sister to my big sister Courtney, or strolled into a McClinton-Jennings family reunion without folks questioning whether she belonged.

One afternoon in the late 1980s, my dad dragged me to Square One, the sprawling shopping mall in central Mississauga, and we headed to HMV, the newly opened music superstore. I trailed him past all the rock and pop albums on the main retail floor to the back room, where they kept the jazz and blues records. Dad found a column of LPs and flipped through them and saw a name that grabbed him.

Delbert McClinton.

"Hmph," he said. "Might be one of your cousins."

He pulled the record up from behind the partition and looked at the cover. Delbert would have stood all the way out at a gathering of my dad's McClintons. White guy, black T-shirt. Light tan, shallow wrinkles. Dad frowned and put the record back, shrugged; McClintons came in all shades, including white. None of my immediate family was biracial, but we had plenty of white blood. Picked it up from slave masters; same place most of us got these English/Scottish/Welsh/Irish surnames.

"Sheeit," he said. "He still might be your cousin."

Similar dynamic in Granny Mary's bracket. Her maiden name was Gibbs and her mom was a Donald, but *her* mother had the last name that gave us away: Gaddis. Even now, when I see that surname in real life or on social media, I start questioning people, the same way people—sometimes white, but usually Black—used to cross-examine me growing up.

Where are your parents from?

And their parents?

And their parents?

If you answer any of those questions, "Sumter, South Carolina," congratulations, we're cousins. I don't know if I'm welcoming you to the family, or if you're welcoming me. Either way, it's great to meet you.

People who know my mom's family often tell me I look like a Jones, usually because they know me and have met my mom. Maybe they've also seen my uncle Jeff. The three of us together look exactly like family. When I tell those same folks I've probably got more Campbell in me, they don't believe it. But if I show them pictures of Courtney and my other sister, Dana, and then a photo of my dad, then they get it.

When regular folks tell me I resemble the Joneses, it's a harmless observation, meant as a compliment. But when Granny Mary would say it, like she would occasionally, when I was grown enough to understand subtext, it was a judgement. A jab.

"You look like a Jones."

She said it to me a couple years before she died, a few decades too late to succeed at rebuilding the boundary between the two families. My two sisters and I would always bridge them, whether or not people on opposing sides wanted to accept it. Nobody else was a Campbell *and* a Jones by blood. Only Courtney, Dana, and me. Granny Mary could try to stack bricks, but she couldn't build a wall around Pete and Jeanie Campbell's three kids.

"You look like a *Jones*," she said.

Granny Mary had known the Joneses since before she started high school, and didn't like them. She couldn't understand why a Black family in Chicago, in the 1930s, would *choose* to live in all-white West Pullman, on the far South Side. Stuck up, Granny Mary figured. She thought the Joneses felt they were better than the working-class Black folks, who, like her, mostly lived a little farther north. When she enrolled at Fenger High School, the same year Claude Jones did, they already knew and couldn't stand each other.

The Joneses were, in reality, a blue-collar family, just like the Gibbses. West Pullman was white, but working class. My great-grandfather got a job at a lumberyard in the neighbourhood and rented a house from the company. None of those details paint the Jones family as bougie. Yet, my grandfather still found Granny Mary off-putting, common, and a little bit country.

Claude Jones and Mary Jane Gibbs weren't that different. Both were the first in their families born up north. Mary's parents came from South Carolina, but had her in Trenton, New Jersey. Claude's mom was from Ruston, Louisiana, and his dad from Marshall, Texas, where they met and where, in 1915, their daughter, Edith, was born. A few years later, they moved to Chicago and here came Claude. He married Margaret at eighteen, and their first child, Jeanie, was born seven months later.

Claude and Mary both also craved attention and control and, as adults with grown kids, would become common denominators in family fights. And, as parents of young adults, they both agreed that Mary's son, Pete, should not marry Claude's daughter, Jeanie. Claude even issued a threat wrapped in a warning.

"When this marriage falls apart—and it will—don't come running back to me," he said.

Pete and Jeanie got married anyway, August 7, 1965, in Claude and Margaret's big apartment on Paxton Avenue at 70th Street in South Shore, and had three kids: Dana, the oldest, a glass-shattering soprano who never outgrew looking exactly like my dad; Courtney, a magician of a chef who communicates the way her father did, with short answers and long silences; and me, talkative like my mom, moody like my dad, and looking like both of them in ways most people could see.

Except Granny Mary, when she felt miffed or slighted. Then . . .

"You look like a Jones."

A soft excommunication from the clan. Some get-back for all those years, after my dad died, that I never called. I had a good reason. My dad didn't have a will. Granny Mary cased his apartment while he was dying and looted it after his funeral. Hauled all his belongings back to Chicago and never even called us to say she was leaving.

She knew why I stayed away, just like she knew "You look like a Jones" was a lie. I looked like my dad, who looked like his dad. She had the Campbell name, but I had the DNA.

The name still matters, though. That's my public-facing identity, and the hook people use to try to connect me to something bigger than my immediate family. I've had white Canadians, for example, ask how I got this Scottish surname. A natural question for anybody who looks at me and surmises, correctly, that my folks aren't from Inveraray. But the better question for the white folks, based on the number of Black people I see named McKnight and McKenzie and McFadden and Harris, is why so many Scottish people, when they arrived on this side of the Atlantic, bought so many slaves. We weren't Campbells or McClintons when they snatched us from Africa. That happened over here.

Once, during a conference at a university, my last name attracted the attention of a Black Canadian Studies prof, Canadian with Jamaican parents. She didn't tell me I was Jamaican, but she didn't ask, either— just slid it into our small talk as a given. I told her my folks were both from the South Side of Chicago, and we fell into a familiar rhythm.

"What about their parents?"

"From Chicago, too," I said, because I didn't feel like explaining how that generation of ancestors straddled the Great Migration, and how my mom's mom—birth name: Bebe Norma Miller—came from a town too small to appear on maps. If this prof wasn't buying Chicago as a launching point for my family, what could I tell her about Bunn, Arkansas? That it sat in the south-central region of the state, almost exactly halfway between the Mississippi River and the Oklahoma border? That the nearest big city was Carthage, six miles northwest, population 558, according to the 1930 census? Carthage dwarfed Bunn, which was home to a few white people, a few Black people, and Pickett Creek, where they all caught catfish. Bebe moved to Chicago, eventually, and lived with Grandma Carrie, her deeply Catholic aunt, who renamed her Margaret Theresa. Eventually she picked up a nickname that stuck: "Deeer." She grew up in Englewood, on the South Side, west of State Street, heart of the city. But her actual hometown was no bigger than a rumour. She used to say it was just a wide spot in the road.

"Don't be so sure," the prof said, still skeptical about my family's background. "The first wave of Jamaican immigrants came to the U.S. in the early 1900s."

Cool, except I had a handle on family history that far back. Unless some part of Jamaica bordered on Tennessee, these Campbells weren't from there.

"Thanks," I said. "I'm sure."

I didn't doubt that a lot of Jamaican Campbells existed; still didn't make me one of them. But the prof profiled me the way I pigeonhole Gaddises. It's normal. If you grew up Black in Toronto, and paid attention, you'd figure out how closely surnames mirrored a kid's parent's country of origin. I'm not talking about the obvious ethno-linguistic ways that transcend racial categories—the way the name Kim says Korea, or Mirkovic says Serbia, or Frempong says Ghana. I mean, specifically, those of us descended from folks hauled across the Atlantic, chained together in the cargo holds of slave ships, sold like merchandise across colonies, and saddled with the English language.

I don't know enough about each island and enclave to ascertain why some surnames concentrated in certain places, but growing up around Black folks in Toronto taught me that if I met a Barrett or a Webley or a Whyte, they were probably Jamaican. If I encountered a Braithwaite, their folks were most likely from Barbados, unless they were from Guyana. But they weren't from Nova Scotia, where names like Cain and Beals and Provo told stories older than Canada itself. That first wave of Black Loyalists transplanted to Nova Scotia after fighting for the British in the Revolutionary War. Another cohort after the War of 1812. Black labourers imported from the U.S. and Caribbean to toil in coal mines.

In contrast, the names in my immediate family hid more than they revealed. My mom was a Jones and my dad was a Campbell, and those names appear in big numbers almost anywhere people speak English. As labels, they're much too general to say anything specific.

My mom had a brother, government name Claude Robert Jones, nickname Bobby, whom she called the Phantom, because one day, when Courtney and I were toddlers and Dana was in grade school, he vanished—for the first time. By choice, so don't worry, but from then on, like clockwork, he would disappear for fifteen-year intervals, materializing long enough to check in for a few months before fading away again. Eventually he resurfaced for good—we think—just west of Kalamazoo, a mile and a half south of a stretch of I-94 we travelled every time we drove to Chicago.

But in those intervening years, he could hide in the open, mostly in suburban Los Angeles, because his real name gave him more cover than an alias ever could. Even if we could have, in the late '80s or early '90s, procured a Los Angeles phone book, who was going to call every number listed for Bob Jones? Nobody in this family had that kind of time.

But if Bob Jones *had* wanted to adopt a creative alias, he had options on my mom's side of the family, which contained Kennedys. If Bob Slaton was too plain, he could have tried Slayton.

Last names on Dad's side of the family also had alternate spellings. The phenomenon was probably common for families that, like ours, lived through a series of post–Civil War transitions. From bondage to Reconstruction to life under Jim Crow. From forced illiteracy during slavery to separate but allegedly equal schools after emancipation. From speaking our names to finally, legally, writing them down.

People in my dad's family, for example, loved the name Prentice, pronounced the way people do. The first *E* so short, it sounds like an *I*, and the *T* is just a notion. You would only pronounce it if you also pronounced the *E* as written, which would give you "Pren-tiss." Prentice. But nobody said it that way. In that branch of the family, *Prentice* rhymes with "Guinness." And the first person to write the name down put it together phonetically.

P-R-I-N-E-S

Prines.

It's my dad's name. His dad's, too.

No, Prines does not rhyme with Shines. Break it in half. Prin-es. Still rhymes with "Guinness." My mom says that name runs like a river through my dad's extended family in Mississippi and Arkansas, where you might even find women named Prinestine. If you can imagine the pebble-in-your-shoe level of annoyance that comes with a lifetime of explaining that pronunciation to folks, you'll know why my dad just went by Pete. And if you're wondering whether my dad even liked his given name, note that Prines Jr. did not beget Prines III.

Granny Mary's family had folks named Gaddis and Geddis, and Geddes and Gathers, and Geddies and maybe Geathers. If I've missed your spelling, please mark yourself as present. And if you have people in Sumter—again, I'm thrilled to have found another cousin.

But if you're a Bonner, then you know we spell it B-O-N-N-E-R, and if that's your last name, I'll assume we're related on Mom's dad's side unless you prove we're not.

To be clear, Bonner was nobody's slave name.

My great-great-grandfather was born a slave named Penn Brooks, somewhere in Virginia, sometime around 1844. We might never reclaim the details of his early life. Did his owners sell him deeper south? Did he choose to relocate post-emancipation? And if teaching slaves to read was illegal—and in most cases it was—how did Penn Brooks learn enough to notice the name he would adopt as his own?

What we do know is he arrived in Ruston, Louisiana, sometime after the end of the Civil War, with a wife named Ann, maiden name Banks. According to family folklore, Penn Brooks saw *Bonner* on a sign somewhere in Ruston, and decided right then on his new name.

Penn Brooks Bonner.

Not just a name change, but a reinvention that would echo for generations, across state lines and national borders. Half James Gatz rowing alongside Dan Cody's yacht and introducing himself as Jay Gatsby, and half Cassius Clay, a name change as a Black man's act of self-determination, a new identity for a new stage in life. Muhammad Ali: Activist. Muslim. Heavyweight champion. Penn Brooks Bonner: Husband. Father. Free man.

Penn and Ann must have known the name would spread. They raised thirteen kids in their farmhouse; within a generation and a half, the Bonner Diaspora had extended well beyond Ruston. If you attended or worked at Grambling State University, six miles west of Ruston, and you had a professor or classmate or colleague named Bonner, that was one of us. Bonners have sprouted everywhere from Chicago to Texas to California. I'm not sure Penn and Ann envisioned their grandson, Claude Jones, growing into a jazz pianist whose playing would get him recruited by talent scouts from Toronto, or that Claude's career would lead to the name reappearing in Canada, like a long-dormant recessive gene. But all that happened, too.

Unless you're old enough to have hung out at the Scotch Mist or the Blue Note in Chicago, or the Inn on the Park or the Hyatt Regency in Toronto, you haven't heard Claude Jones play jazz. He performed six nights a week, nearly every week, for almost fifty years, but almost never recorded. At least not with his own ensemble, the way Oscar Peterson or Ahmad Jamal or other jazz pianists you've heard of did.

But you *have* heard Claude Jones. By day he played sessions at Chess Records and other studios with R&B acts, landing on some classics that still get radio play. You've heard "It's in His Kiss" by Betty Everett. If you don't know the title, you know it's the "shoop shoop song." That's my grandpa on piano. The first notes you hear on "I'm So Proud," that ageless ballad by Curtis Mayfield and The Impressions? The song playing at the end of *A Bronx Tale*? That's Claude Jones on the celeste. And the last notes you hear as the song fades out? Same guy, same instrument.

In Chicago, he was well-known but never famous, already a professional musician by the time he married Margaret, who was sixteen and pregnant with my mom, in that storefront church downtown, with one of Scott Joplin's nephews as his best man. Claude and Margaret made a handsome couple at every age. His hair turned white; hers never did. By his fifties, he could have donned a pair of shades and passed as Ray Charles, and she could have served as Diahann Carroll's understudy.

They raised four kids: Jeanie, Phantom, Peggy, and Jeff. My grandfather's decision to leave Chicago for Toronto shaped their lives, and the lives of a long list of other folks, some who loved him and some who couldn't stand him. But no matter how you felt about him, if you liked your life in Canada, you owed my grandpa thanks or a handshake or a pat on the back for making this place an option for you.

My grandparents came to Toronto in the summer of 1966. So did my uncle, Jeff Jones, a bass guitar player and Black rock music pioneer, whom some of you know. He has JUNO Awards and platinum records. If you didn't know him from the gospel rock band Ocean, you might recognize him from Infidels, the nearly-all-Black rock band that won a JUNO in 1991. But most likely, you saw him with Red Rider. Go back and look at those old album covers. Four white guys with feathered hair, and a Black dude with a short 'fro and a mustache. I'll let you guess which one's my uncle. He's still collecting royalty cheques from "Lunatic Fringe."

My uncle Phantom moved to Toronto in 1967, along with his wife, my aunt Eileen, whom we all call Cheeky. After Uncle Phantom vanished for the first time, she remarried. Ken Morgan was her teenage sweetheart from the West Side of Chicago, and the uncle I grew up with.

My parents moved at the end of 1969 because they wanted to raise kids, and they wanted to do it someplace integrated and safe. In

Chicago, my mom always told me, they might have had one kid, but no more.

I was number three.

My full name: Morgan Peter Bonner Campbell.

My dad chose Morgan and Peter, and handed Campbell down to me; my mom picked Bonner to honour her paternal grandmother, Penn and Ann's youngest child. Her given name, like my mom's, was Eugenia, but we all called her Gram, and she loved the idea of a baby boy Bonner. That's thanks to my mom, thinking fast like her great-grandfather, figuring out how to make me a Bonner, not just in the genes but on paper, with a name that also sent a signal to folks who knew to look for it.

One afternoon in July of 2009, I checked in for a flight to Tampa, and stopped in with a U.S. border agent, because when you fly to the States from YYZ, you clear customs *before* you board. I'd call the agent a sister, but she was more of an auntie. Black and American, seconded to this post in Canada. Short hair, long nails. Younger than my parents but older than me. Old enough to analyze me the way the lady on the bus in Windsor used to.

I handed her my passport, and she stared at it a long time. Too long. It didn't have issues. I had just picked it up from the U.S. Consulate and never used it before that day.

"Who is Bonner?" she asked.

"Excuse me?"

"Morgan Peter Bonner Campbell. I like that name. Bonner. Where'd you get it?"

"Oh yeah," I said. "It's my great-grandmother's maiden name."

"See, I knew it," she said, smiling and handing me back my passport. "I saw that name and knew you were named after *some*body."

"You right," I said, smiling back.

I thanked her and wished her a safe weekend. There was a longer story, but I didn't have time to tell her.

My Fighting Family

I come from a fighting family.

We didn't get into shoot-em-up feuds with other clans, like the Hatfields and McCoys. And we weren't pugilists like the Mayweathers, though thirteen-year-old me did meet thirteen-year-old Floyd Jr. at a family reunion during a summer trip to Grand Rapids with my dad. He wore a T-shirt with super-short sleeves, his hair shaved into an impressive flat top, and introduced himself as "Floyd Mayweather," as if his full name already meant something. Maybe, among thirteen-year-olds in southeast Grand Rapids, it already did.

"My dad's Floyd Mayweather, too," he announced within a minute of meeting me. "He fought Sugar Ray."

"You guys related to Roger Mayweather?" I asked because I was already a *Ring*-magazine-reading boxing nerd. I knew Roger as a miniature Thomas Hearns—long jab, deadly right cross, shaky chin.

"Yeah, that's my uncle," Floyd said.

Where the Mayweathers traded punches for a living, the Jones-Campbell specialty was the Family Fight, where a perceived slight ignites an all-out, sides-choosing rumble that splits kin into bitter factions before settling into a cold war lasting years, sometimes outliving its participants.

There was always *somebody* to set them off.

Like when my sister Courtney got into it with our uncle Jeff's father-in-law over rent money. The old man was the landlord, a lax record-keeper who preferred that his tenants pay in cash. Courtney said she paid him on time every month. He said he couldn't find the money and accused Courtney of stiffing him. They could have worked it out as adults, but somebody jumped in on the father-in-law's side, concerned the conflict would cost the family a white person's esteem. My mom and I had to back Courtney, and we all said stuff we had to apologize for later. Barack Obama was a state senator from Chicago when that fight started; he was finishing his first campaign for president when it ended.

Or when, the morning my dad died, *somebody* who had never liked him wanted to hang around his hospital room. My mom forbade him, and then came the blowup, followed by a long stalemate. I was a high-school senior when this one began, and had earned a bachelor's degree by the time folks agreed to a ceasefire. Midway through this conflict, about a month before my sister Dana's wedding, she and my mom convened a family meeting to try to broker a truce so the whole family could see her marry. In response, *somebody* kicked them out of his apartment and told them to go to hell.

It was always the same somebody. My Grandpa, Claude Jones, who functioned like the first guy to rush the field in a bench-clearing brawl. If anybody's fighting, *everybody's* fighting—and he never aimed to settle the dispute. He came to escalate it. The sloppier and more chaotic, the better. Except baseball fights end, and my Grandpa's often didn't. He'd hold a grudge until you gave in, then claim victory. And if he couldn't defeat you, he'd disappear you.

He made my mom vanish for a few years.

Ray and Jeri Carter lived nine floors directly below my grandparents in the same high-rise on Bloor Street in Mississauga. Jeri's parents were among the Caribbean immigrants trickling into Canada in the late 1910s. Her dad's fair-skinned upper-class family cut him off when he married Jeri's dark-skinned working-class mother, so they fled St. Kitts and landed in downtown Toronto, near Dundas and Bathurst, where most of the city's Black residents lived back then.

Ray came later, following a friend from Pittsburgh to Toronto in the early 1950s, when that friend married a woman from Jeri's neighbourhood. He met Jeri and fell in love, and only ever returned to Pittsburgh to visit. Ray stayed in Toronto, and like a small but significant number of other African Americans who came before and after him—Underground Railroaders, CFL players, railway porters, Vietnam War draft dodgers—he stuck around. He and Jeri married and moved to Mississauga, raised two kids, and, as seniors, became neighbours to Claude and Margaret.

The four of them could have been better friends, if only because meeting other African Americans in Toronto is so rare. It's like a tax refund—always welcome, but you wish it came more than once a year. For my grandparents, having the Carters downstairs should have been like found money. Grandma got along beautifully with them, but Claude and Ray never clicked.

It was strange. They both loved baseball and jazz. Ray idolized Erroll Garner and Oscar Peterson; Grandpa was a retired jazz pianist, and friends with Erroll and Oscar in real life. They had both served in the U.S. Army, and both felt charmed by Toronto's clean streets, friendly people, and a life not circumscribed by segregation, either Jim Crow or de facto. So, they both stayed and grew roots.

Those details alone should have propelled Claude and Ray into a deep, late-life, shame-we-didn't-meet-sooner friendship like my Grandpa had with the white guys at the seniors' centre where he played cards twice a week. They could have become buddies who teased each other lovingly, like Jack Lemmon and Walter Matthau in *Grumpy Old Men*. Instead, they just grated on each other like grumpy old men.

Really, they were too alike to get along. Claude was the oldest and played the age card to win friendly debates and family fights. Ray, meanwhile, had moved to Canada fifteen years before Claude and Margaret did, and liked pulling rank as the longest-tenured Canadian among their crew of immigrants. They both knew everything about everything, so neither could tell the other anything.

"Ray's always pontificating about something," Claude said to me once, after pontificating about something. "Gets on my nerves."

Ray and Jeri welcomed me tenderly when I first met them in the spring of 2001. I was midway through my internship at the *Toronto Star*, working on a feature about African Americans in Toronto. Ray sat for a long interview about what drew him to Canada, and how Black folks in Toronto lived before a surge of immigration from the Caribbean changed the face of the city. He and Jeri told me their story, and then Ray asked for mine.

"So are you Peggy's son," he said, "or Jeff's?"

Strange way to frame the question, I thought. My grandparents had four kids, but Ray only gave me two options, as if my mom and Uncle Bobby didn't exist.

"I'm Jeanie's son," I said.

"Who," Ray asked, "is Jeanie?"

"Their oldest kid."

"Oh . . ." Ray said, looking puzzled. "I thought Peggy was the oldest. Your folks told us they had two kids: Peggy in Chicago, and Jeff in Toronto."

"No, Mr. Carter," I said. "They have four kids: Jeanie, Bobby, Peggy, and Jeff. Jeanie has three kids. I'm the youngest."

Ray sat silent as he digested these new facts, and we both pondered the revelation that the sweet retired couple from upstairs had told such a bold and fundamental lie. That this man, denied by his grown daughter the chance to worm his way into a hospital room to gawk at his former son-in-law's dead body, in turn banished her from the family. And that, seven years later, among new friends, he would still pretend his first child was never born. And the lie might have survived even longer, except that her son tugged at a loose string and pulled the whole story apart.

Most people wouldn't deny their own children over a fight, but most people don't fight like Claude Jones.

—

To extinguish the deadliest race riot in the city's history, Chicago mayor William Hale Thompson urged the governor to summon the National Guard, and within hours of the order, soldiers flooded South Side streets. By July 30, 1919, several thousand troops, bayonets fixed, lined up along Wentworth Avenue, a central thoroughfare on the city's South Side and a border between its Black and white residents. They came to complete a straightforward yet daunting task: keep white people on the west side of Wentworth, and Black people on the east side.

The previous three days had been bloody and ugly, and full of the racialized violence Black migrants thought they had escaped when they flocked to Chicago from across the South. White rioters set Black people's homes ablaze. Black soldiers just back from the Great War suited up in uniform and patrolled Black neighbourhoods police refused to protect. White thugs lynched a Black cyclist. Black vigilante snipers picked off white marauders. By mid-week, the *Chicago Tribune* reported twenty-six people dead—eleven white and fifteen Black—and more than three hundred injured. And Thursday morning, armed National Guardsmen intervened to stop one group of whites from hanging a Black man from a telephone pole, and another from attacking a Black family whose house they had just tried to burn down.

Four days of deadly violence sparked by one harmless act: Black people showing up at the 29th Street Beach.

Chicago wasn't necessarily segregated by law, but it was by custom and habit, and by a caste system that advantaged whites, who defended their privilege with deadly force. So when, on a sweltering Sunday afternoon, a few Black bathers drifted a little too far south into the whites-only section, rocks and bottles flew. One stone thrown by a white assailant crashed into the forehead of a Black swimmer named Eugene Williams. The fourteen-year-old sank beneath the surface and drowned, the first casualty of that infamous race riot, and a stark lesson on the steep price of integrating anything in that city.

So, if you're wondering how the incumbent residents of all-white West Pullman welcomed the neighbourhood's first Black family—Claude and Eugenia Jones, their daughter, Edith, and, later, their son, Claude Jr.—they did it warmly by the standards of 1920s Chicago. They didn't form a lynch mob or raze the big wooden house at 11848 South Halsted Street, where Claude was born in 1923. They didn't fire bullets through the windows or spray-paint racial slurs on the lawn. But they did circulate a petition, white neighbours co-signing on a resolution that the new Black family should move out.

And if you're wondering how my great-grandparents' family dodged that petition, and housing covenants, and the other tricks racists used to keep Black people from buying homes in white neighbourhoods—the Joneses never bought that house. The Sterling Lumber Company owned it, along with several other homes in West Pullman, and employed many of the neighbourhood's breadwinners. When the company hired my great-grandfather, it offered him the chance to rent the house, and Gramps accepted. Less time commuting meant more time with his family, even if it also meant dealing with white folks.

According to family folklore, the lumber company's owner went to the local bank when he learned of the petition and threatened to withdraw all his money if racist West Pullmanites forced Claude Jones Sr. and his young family to leave their new home. Whether it actually happened that way, or whether the white folks weighed the risks of pissing off their boss and decided on their own to back down, West Pullman's first Black family stayed.

Before *tolerance* became a buzzword in discussions about multiculturalism, West Pullman and its lone Black family practiced the principle daily. These days, white folks use *tolerance* as a synonym for *acceptance*, to imply that all cultures and skin colours are welcome everywhere. But *tolerance* is really just another word for *endurance*— your capacity to suffer something unpleasant. How much pain can you take before you ask for an epidural? How many blows can you absorb before your corner throws in the towel? How many Black neighbours will you accept before you surrender the fight and run to the suburbs?

And so West Pullman and its only Black family tolerated each other. My great-grandparents endured racism for the sake of a short commute and better public schools. Local white folks held their bigotry in check for the sake of staying employed. Few of them liked having a Black family move in. Many of them hated it. They all lived with it.

———

Freshman year at Fenger, Claude Jones Jr. tried to join the Reserve Officers Training Corps, which most people call the ROTC—a cadets-style program that teaches high schoolers how to become military officers. The director rejected him. Fenger's ROTC "didn't accept coloreds," he said. Claude went back on a different day and got the same answer. The school was integrated, as many Chicago institutions were, technically, but the ROTC was for white students only.

Fenger had a small but stable Black population. Claude had fewer Black classmates than his kids would when they would attend Fenger in the late 1950s, but more than his big sister Edith did when she graduated in the early 1930s. The Black student body was big enough to permeate some school clubs, and active enough to prompt white people to make up rules excluding them from other stuff. That teacher knew nothing in Fenger's regulations prevented Black students from joining the ROTC, but he also knew he had the power to enforce segregation on a whim. No Black kid was going to challenge his authority.

Except this was a fight now, and Claude intended to win. He went to the principal, and when the principal backed the ROTC director, Claude did something that would have terrified his humble, deferential Southern parents.

He went downtown.

He knew they wouldn't have approved, so he didn't tell them until months later. One morning, instead of heading to school, Claude took the bus to the school board to file a complaint against Fenger High School for keeping him out of the ROTC. Fenger would either have to admit an eligible freshman to the ROTC, or explain to their bosses at the school board why they were enforcing a rule that didn't exist.

Soon after Claude's complaint, the phone calls started, from the school board to Fenger and back. Not long after that, the director changed his mind and decided Black boys could, in fact, join the ROTC at Fenger High, starting with Claude Jones Jr.

When Claude would tell us the story of how he single-handedly integrated Fenger High School's ROTC, he emphasized the value of keeping important projects to yourself. If he had told his parents about his plan, they'd have forbidden him from following through. Where they grew up, you didn't antagonize white folks like that, lest they, in anger, crack down on the whole Black community. He stressed the importance of going over the head of any gatekeeper who fails to give you the response you want.

But the idea of fighting was embedded in every layer of the story of Fenger High School's first Black ROTC member. Claude fought the school and the racism of its daily routine. He fought his parents' programmed deference to white folks when he took his complaint to the school board. And each retelling of that story reinforced a central lesson about growing up in the U.S., and why he came to Canada.

If you were Black and American and wanted something—anything—you would have to fight. Voting rights, a spot in the ROTC, a place to raise your kids. Freedom, sanity, breathing room. White people weren't giving you any of it. You'd have to fight to create it for yourself.

———

A generation later, the neighbourhood's Black presence had more than doubled. All the new arrivals were Joneses—the original four, plus my grandmother and the kids, Jeanie, Bobby, Peggy, and Jeff.

After World War II, West Pullman's white population underwent some subtle changes, too. A few immigrants from eastern Europe moved in, seeking the same new start my great-grandparents wanted when they came north, but thankful America's racial hierarchy would ensure they always outranked someone. These new neighbours grappled with the language, but they soon mastered two words.

Dehrtee neegehr.

Or there was the pair of white country bumpkins, new to Chicago and too poor to rent a room, so they moved into the garage of a home on 118th Place, only to peer across the street and see a Black family living in an actual house. Wherever they were from—Kentucky? Tennessee? Missouri? Downstate?—Black people didn't one-up white people like that. Back home, Black folks either knew their place, or learned it.

So they introduced themselves to the neighbourhood by throwing stones at the Joneses' house. Their accuracy, from across Halsted, was erratic. They hit the side of the house, mostly, with rocks and even a fragment of a brick. A few projectiles did hit the front of the house, and it became clear that they were targeting, but couldn't connect with, the big windows on the main floor.

But their aim was specific: to terrorize whoever was home. That night, it was Margaret and all four kids, plus Claude Sr., Jean, and Edith.

Everybody except Claude Jr., who was downtown at the Scotch Mist, playing piano, unaware his family was under attack.

The next day, the grown-ups plotted countermoves. Margaret's aunt Inez, whom everybody called Mike, was friends with a few Black police officers. She offered to recruit one of them to park outside the house overnight. If not, she had a revolver that fit in her purse.

Claude Jr. freelanced as a portrait photographer, so he kept a set of powerful lights at home. He gathered some studio lamps and rigged them to the front of the house, so they could illuminate the yard and any troublemaker trying to cross it after dark. Then he headed to work, his mind still on the trouble at home.

At the Scotch Mist, Claude played for the usual mix of newcomers out for a night on Rush Street and regulars, like the little Sicilian guy with the cauliflower ears, perched at the bar. He topped out at five feet tall, and part of him loved conflict, which explained the ears; as a teenager, his main hobby was boxing. But with Claude, he was always warm and curious. He loved listening to Claude play and drawing him into conversations, like he did tonight, craning his neck to make eye contact. Claude stood five-foot-six, a giant in contrast to Marshall Caifano.

Few people who recognized the name of that notorious mob enforcer would describe the man as sensitive, but he read Claude's mood and figured out, correctly, that something wasn't right.

"What's bugging you, Jonesy?" he asked.

Claude sighed, reluctant to bring his personal problems to work.

"Nothing big," Claude said, finally. "Just some neighbourhood trouble."

"Really?" Marshall said, placing his drink on the bar. He knew about trouble. Claude had all his attention now. "What kind of trouble?"

Claude grimaced, shrugged. He knew a certain class of powerful Chicagoan could enlist Marshall Caifano to solve their problems. Like when the Chicago Outfit needed Bugsy Siegel dealt with. It's understood that Caifano was present when Siegel was shot to death in a Beverly Hills mansion, just before a bookie named Gus Greenbaum showed up at Siegel's Flamingo Hotel in Las Vegas and announced that the Chicago mob was taking over.

It's also understood that Caifano made sure Estelle Carey never testified in the extortion trial of his associate, Nick Circella. They found her body, burned and beaten and jabbed with an ice pick, at a building on the North Side, a few blocks east of Wrigley Field.

And then there's Theodore Roe, the Robin Hood of the South Side, a Black man who got rich running a numbers racket and rebuffed the Italian mob's efforts to take over the illegal lottery business. Roe shot and killed one of the two mobsters who tried to kidnap him in 1951. The dead guy was Caifano's brother. Roe beat a murder charge by arguing self-defense. The next year, a pair of guys gunned him down on Michigan Avenue, near 52nd Street. Caifano was suspected and questioned, though never charged.

Marshall Caifano tended to go to prison for stuff like extortion and fraud, but it was understood that murder was his real racket, just like music was Claude's. Maybe Caifano thought of Claude and himself as peers. They were both multi-instrumentalists. Claude could play piano and Hammond B-3 and a little upright bass; Marshall used ice picks and shotguns and car bombs. When he died in 2003 at age ninety-two, the *Chicago Tribune* sent a columnist to his funeral. The next day's headline: "Unlike his many victims, hit man dies quiet death."

Claude knew what Marshall did for a living and didn't want a guy with his résumé knowing too much about life at the Jones household. But Marshall was relentless.

"I can tell it's something, Jones," he said. "Can I help?"

Claude took a heavy breath. Whether Marshall Caifano was acting as an enemy, a creditor, or a concerned music fan, when he wanted something from you, you gave it to him. Claude didn't need Marshall's help, but he didn't need the stress of trying to hide the truth, either. So he opened up about everything: the hillbillies and the flying stones, the nagging fear that bad things could happen to his parents *and* his wife and kids while he was out at work.

He finished talking, and the two men eyed each other in silence. Claude dropped his head. Marshall laughed and grabbed his drink.

"Is that it?" Marshall asked.

"Is what it?"

"These two guys throwing stones? That's the big problem?"

"Yeah, well, it's a hell of a problem," Claude said.

"Jonesy," Marshall said.

"Yes?"

"If you say the word, we'll take care of this, and nobody will ever connect you to it," Caifano said. "They'll never find the bodies."

Claude stood there, silent, too stunned and too smart to ask any follow-up questions.

"Oh," he said, finally. "You don't have to go and do all that."

Nobody ever found out whether the hitman really visited the hillbillies, but we know the actual police did knock on their garage door and remind them about the Second Amendment. The people inside the house they used as target practice had a right to bear arms, and permission to defend themselves with whatever force necessary. Even here in Chicago.

So maybe that information, coming from white men in uniform, swayed them.

Either way, all that stone-throwing stopped.

For good.

—

Years before the rednecks showed up, though, Jeanie already knew white people's violence didn't just occur in newspaper pages or her grandparents' stories from back home. It was in the environment, like bad weather or a flu virus. One more hazard to guard against. So when, at eleven years old, she saw the shadows of those three white boys behind her, and heard their footsteps closing the gap between them, she tightened her grip on the strap of her knapsack and kept marching east on 119th Street. She didn't need to see their faces to know they were white. This was West Pullman in 1954.

Only four short blocks to school.

The taunting started when they crossed Union and headed toward Lowe. Not too loud. Sing-songy, but constant.

"Taaaar Baby!" one of them kept saying. "Taaaaaaar Baby!"

"Herrrrrrshey Bar!" another started. "Heeeeeershey Bar!"

Jeanie couldn't match voices to faces. Doing that would mean looking back at the three boys stalking her; she was too terrified and, even as a sixth-grader, too cagey with racists to make that mistake. Looking back would mean acknowledging the taunts, and giving bullies recognition means they win. When you and your siblings are the only Black kids in a white neighbourhood in 1950s Chicago, you learn that lesson early. So Jeanie did her best Jackie Robinson impression. She tuned out the taunts and kept walking.

"Taaaaaaar Bay-bee!"

"Herrrrrrrrshey Bar!"

To them, it was a game: race-baiting as risk-free entertainment on the way back to school after lunch. Three boys against one little girl. If, somehow, this turned into a fistfight, it would quickly devolve into a beating. Three *white* boys against one *Black* girl. Even if it came to that, who would the authorities believe? One Black girl, or three white boys heading to a white school in a white neighbourhood? The boys had Jeanie outnumbered and outflanked, and they knew it.

"Taaaarrrrrr Bay-bee!"

"Herrrrrrshey Bar!"

Louder. Closer. Bolder.

They continued east along the sidewalk on the south side of 119th Street, traffic to their left and plate-glass storefronts to their right.

Jeanie tried to ignore them, but she didn't want to block out their voices. She needed to hear them, to gauge the situation. To assess the level of danger. If she could just cross Wallace, she'd be able to see the school and maybe a teacher would scare the boys into falling back. She kept track of the distance, counted down the steps, yard by yard.

"TAAAAAR BAY-BEE!"

"HERRRRRRRSHEY BAR!"

Maybe the boys were counting steps, too. Maybe they aimed to escalate this conflict before they reached the schoolyard, where teachers could defuse it. Their sneers assumed a menacing edge.

"*TAAAAAAR BAY-BEE!*"

More obnoxious. More contemptuous. More privileged.

Jeanie still hadn't turned to look at them, but she knew they were close enough to touch her. She could hear it. She could sense it with the skin on the back of her neck.

"*TAAAARRRRR BAY-BEEEEE!*"

They crossed Wallace.

"*HERRRRRRRSHEY BAR!*"

Enough.

Jeanie squeezed her right hand into a fist.

She stopped walking, planted her right foot, and pivoted . . .

. . . A quick story from Jeanie's future helps explain what happened next.

My sister Dana, leafing through a stack of my mom's old photos, finds a picture from prom night. Junior year at Fenger. Jeanie's hair is freshly permed and her glasses firmly in place. Thick lenses and thicker frames. She's in the hallway of that house on Halsted, a little younger than my sister Dana was the night she found the photo. She's in a pink strapless dress, smiling wide, standing with her back to a wall-mounted mirror. You can see the back of her head and the top of her dress and the exposed skin in between.

"Mom, what's going on with your shoulders?" Dana said. "Look, Morgan. Look at Mom's shoulders."

"Yeah, Mom, what's happening back there?" I said. "What are those lumps?"

"What lumps?" my mom said, not even looking up from her needlepoint. "What are you fools talking about?"

"Oh wait," Dana said.

"What?" my mom said.

"Wait, those are your muscles? Morgan, look at Mom's muscles."

"Jeez, Mom," I said. "You were ripped."

My mom just shrugged, still busy with the thread and needle.

"I guess."

If the white boys had accosted her on prom night, maybe they'd have noticed Jeanie was as compact and powerful as a stick of dynamite and decided against lighting the fuse. But they couldn't see those muscles under her school clothes and didn't realize they had picked the wrong target until her right fist crashed into the biggest kid's left jaw.

The force of the punch spun him sideways and sent him stumbling. The impact turned his legs to jelly. In a boxing ring he would have landed face-first, like Roberto Duran did against Thomas Hearns. But on 119th Street, he careened headlong into a storefront, his forehead bashing it so hard the plate glass nearly shattered. As the window wobbled, all four kids stood frozen, contemplating their next moves.

Jeanie could have turned and sprinted for the safety of the schoolyard. If she had a head start, those white boys wouldn't outrun her; none of the white girls at West Pullman could do it, even when she spotted them a yard.

But she didn't move. She just stared at the big kid, who didn't know whether to rub his aching jaw or his sore forehead, and at his two friends. They had all shut up as they calculated the cost of carrying on. Jeanie didn't know if she could beat up all three white boys, but after what she had just done to the lead bully, the white boys weren't sure she *couldn't* manhandle them. Whatever they thought they would get out of ganging up on a little Black girl on the way back to school, none of them saw the caper ending with her tossing the ringleader aside like a dirty sock. So they stayed put, too, eyeing Jeanie as she eyed them, all four kids hoping someone else would break formation first.

Jeanie took a step back. Then another. Eyes on the white boys, all still too stunned to move. She backpedalled a few paces, then turned and walked east on 119th Street, toward school and her afternoon classes.

The white boys regrouped and trailed her all the way back to West Pullman Elementary.

In polite silence.

At a respectful distance.

Living with Music

Claude Jones Sr. and his wife, Eugenia, must have felt pride that day in 1933 when their oldest child and only daughter, Edith, graduated from Fenger High School. More than pride, they probably felt validation. Edith Jones joined a sprinkling of other Black kids attending Fenger, a large and well-regarded high school on Wallace Avenue at 112th Street. The school's Black enrolment expanded a little each year, as African American residents edged farther south, pushing in from the fringes of Fenger's boundary. But they were still a tiny minority of students, who faced racism daily but stuck together, stuck it out, and made good grades. In graduating, Edith and her Black classmates proved a basic truth they already knew but that the white people around them needed to see: if you made the playing field anywhere close to level, Black kids could compete.

Fenger's existence helped make all-white West Pullman tolerable for the Joneses. When they first moved to Chicago from Marshall, Texas, Claude Sr., Jean, and Edith landed on the South Side, on Wabash Avenue in Bronzeville, alongside thousands of other migrants fresh from the Deep South. Claude Jr. was born on November 25, 1923, emerging from his mom's womb wrapped in an amniotic membrane.

Born in the caul, they called it.

Old folks said it was a good omen, and that caul babies were destined for something special.

By then, Claude Sr. had scored a job at a lumber mill in West Pullman and moved his family to the far south side of Chicago, to the big wooden house he rented from the company. Of course, the Joneses butted heads with racist white neighbours, but they hung around and gained access to some of the same perks white Chicagoans enjoyed.

White people, for example, could trust the city to fund local infrastructure, so potholes got filled—quickly. You also knew the city would pick up your trash every week, as long as you got it to the curb on time. A lot of Black folks in segregated cities couldn't take those services for granted, but living in a white zip code made your neighbourhood a priority. You could also count on decent public schools with clean halls, newish textbooks, and smaller class sizes. If a quality education gave your kids a head start on A Better Life, moving to a white neighbourhood gave the Joneses a chance to hand that advantage to their kids—provided Edith and Claude could survive regular doses of up-close racism and focus on their studies.

But Edith didn't just survive Fenger: she blazed a trail for her younger brother, and graduated with good enough grades to make plans for the following school year. She had modest ambitions: junior college, an associate's degree, and a quiet career as a librarian. Otherwise, like a lot of working-class Black women in 1930s Chicago, she knew racism and sexism would team up to limit her options. She could find work as a domestic, or maybe cleaning hotels, or some other job with long hours, low pay, and a lower upside. A lot of people tolerated that kind of work to pay bills and feed families, and a lot of people settled for it because of factors they couldn't control. But with that degree, Edith could give herself some choices and do something she loved.

For her parents, that was a problem.

Claude Jr. had recently begun piano lessons, and the Joneses couldn't afford to keep him enrolled *and* pay Edith's junior college tuition. For a different family in a different time, there would be no dilemma: you send your daughter to college and shunt your son into a cheaper hobby. But race and money and the prospect of upward mobility complicated the equation for the Joneses. They came north from Texas to create opportunities for themselves, their daughter, and their future kids, chasing the same American Dream that brought white people over from Europe. Why move all the way to Chicago just to fix a lid on your daughter's ambition and funnel her into a job she wouldn't love, in a field already full of Black women who had accepted a similar shitty bargain? Why have two kids just to choose between them?

But the decision, for Eugenia and Claude Sr., was still obvious. Edith might have wanted a degree and a career, but she didn't need them. She was, after all, they figured, a woman. She could settle for any job, then hope to marry a man who made real money. But ten-year-old Claude Jr. would lead a household one day. He wouldn't just need a job—he'd need a trade. A ticket. And piano might be it.

And so the Joneses chose their son. Not a huge surprise, if you knew them. When he was a toddler, they took a pair of his recently outgrown infant shoes and had them bronzed. The youngest child and the only boy? No way Claude Sr. and Eugenia weren't going to spoil their son. Eugenia would hover over his plate before he ate, cutting his meat so he wouldn't have to—*as a grown man.* So imagine him as a bright and talented ten-year-old, bewitching his parents with his wits and his cuteness.

A year or so before he died, Claude Jr., my grandfather, summoned me to the small office he had fashioned out of the second bedroom at his and Margaret's apartment. He had just printed a black-and-white photo, which he held in his trembling right hand, of a group of Black school boys arranged in front of a schoolhouse they had just built. It was taken in Marshall, Texas, in the early 1900s, and had survived as a hard copy until Claude was able to scan it into a digital file, which he could print for whoever wanted it.

The boys looked proud but didn't smile; with primitive cameras and their long exposure times, you couldn't. Twitch a facial muscle and you risked wrecking the whole picture. But some of them scowled to fend off the midday sun. It reflected off their foreheads anyway.

"That guy right there," Claude said, pointing his left index finger at an unsmiling boy down front, "is my father. Your great-grandfather."

"Cool," I said, leaning closer to the photo.

"And the guy next to him is Scott Joplin's nephew."

"Really?"

"Yep. You know who Scott Joplin was, right?"

"Of course," I said. "Ragtime pianist. Didn't he write 'The Entertainer'?"

"Yes!" Claude said. "That's his nephew. He and my father were best friends, and his son was the best man at my wedding."

Scott Joplin might have been the biggest pop music star of the first part of the twentieth century. Along with "The Entertainer," he wrote "Maple Leaf Rag" and an opera called *Treemonisha*. His music influenced new generations of piano players, and it survived on the paper rolls that make player pianos work. His peak paralleled Jack Johnson's, and Joplin might have been just as famous as the heavyweight champ, just half a degree of separation from Claude Sr.

Plug that info back into the equation and the decision to invest in Claude Jr. over Edith looks just as cruel but more logical. Claude Sr. had seen up close what mastering the piano could do for a Black boy from a humble family.

Having a caul baby enthralled with the piano must have seemed, to Claude Sr. and Eugenia, like the fulfillment of a prophecy. Maybe Edith had potential, but Claude Jr. wasn't just a ten-year-old piano novice. He was promise.

PART II | PLAYING OPPOSITE

One night in Indianapolis, late 1950s, Claude Jones in a packed jazz club, on a stool, at the bar, sipping water. On the stand, Oscar Peterson and the second incarnation of his trio, and they're swinging. *Hard.* Ray Brown laying down bass lines, heavy and thick and deep, a big round sound you could feel in your chest, and Ed Thigpen setting the tempo on drums, playing his ride cymbal with a rhythm so crisp, you'd know it was him with your eyes closed. When Oscar first hired Thigpen to replace Herb Ellis as the third member of the trio, Claude's wife, Margaret, told him he had made a mistake. Ellis kept impeccable time on guitar and gave the crew the airy sound that allowed Oscar's piano so much room to breathe that the trio didn't need a drummer. At the time, Margaret didn't know Ellis needed to leave the trio to treat his alcoholism, but she did know music and which players sounded best together, and how you couldn't possibly upgrade from a guitarist like Ellis.

Then she heard Ed Thigpen play.

Then she understood.

Oscar was Montreal-born-and-raised, but already a worldwide star by the late 1950s when he and Claude crossed paths in Indianapolis. Oscar had long arms and meaty hands, a heavyweight boxer's reflexes and a surgeon's digital dexterity. A blues soul with a classical virtuoso's touch. Go listen to "A Waltz for Debbie," or "Reunion Blues" from the album the trio cut with Milt Jackson. You'll hear those solos and have to remind yourself it's just one man playing all those notes.

Claude caught the trio in Indianapolis at everybody's peak. This was the musical equivalent of Satchel Paige pitching to Josh Gibson. Three geniuses, thinking with one brain. The intuitive familiarity of longtime partners. Great as individuals, but together elevating their music from art to epiphany. The audience, entranced. Claude, on his stool, tapping his thumbs on the bar, appreciating—back then he still enjoyed music for music's sake—but trying to focus on his own work.

The set climaxed with a roof-raising ovation. People stood and clapped and whistled, and begged Oscar, Ray, and Ed to keep playing. Oscar pushed back from the keyboard, stood, and raised those massive hands to wave to the audience. Then he pulled a folded white handkerchief from his pocket and dabbed at the sweat beading on his forehead.

Over at the bar, a different player might have gathered sheet music before climbing off his stool and striding toward the stand. The room still buzzing, Claude just collected his thoughts. If you needed to read the song off a page, you weren't really playing it. Claude kept his whole repertoire—twenty thousand songs and counting—in his head.

Oscar weaved through a thicket of well-wishing audience members and inched toward the bar as Claude waded past people toward the stand. They made eye contact, and Oscar broke into a wide smile and stuffed his handkerchief back into his pocket. When they reached each other, they slapped hands and traded pats on the back. They were occasional co-workers and professional peers, but also friends. Both loved taking photos—Oscar as a hobby and Claude as a side job. And both owed their careers to their older sisters. Daisy Peterson first taught Oscar how to play, and Edith Jones skipped college so her folks could afford to keep Claude in piano lessons at the Calumet Conservatory of Music.

"Been a minute, Oscar," Claude said, acknowledging that following Oscar tonight was impossible. "Thanks for warming up the crowd for me."

"Aw shoot, Claude," Oscar said. "I knew you were playing tonight. I *had* to set the bar high."

"Is that what you call it?"

Oscar laughed and clapped a massive hand on Claude's shoulder.

"I missed you, man," he said. "Now get up there and do what you do. I'll be listening."

It's pointless to compare Claude and Oscar as pianists. Oscar was the best, period. If the audience in Indianapolis that night expected Claude Jones, solo pianist, playing opposite the headliner, to match the Oscar

Peterson Trio's volume and intensity, they were just setting themselves up for disappointment. But this crowd knew music. They knew better.

Claude and Oscar had different skills. Oscar didn't sing; Claude did. Claude also spent his adolescence playing the Hammond B-3 organ, which had a set of pedals to play notes that, to less-educated ears, sounded like they came from an upright bass. They're the reason organ trios usually consisted of the organist, a drummer, and a sax player. You could add a guitar or trumpet to form a quartet, but you never needed a bassist. Those pedals and a B-3 expert like Jimmy Smith made a bass player redundant. On the job, Claude often used a Lowrey Organo, a contraption you could attach to a piano to make it sound like an organ. He kept a set of Organo bass pedals and they travelled with him to every job, turning his solo act into a one-man trio—piano, bass, and vocals.

And he was a southpaw. A lot of pianists work their whole careers to strengthen a lagging left hand, but Claude could pick and strum and stride at the bottom end of the piano, easy as a reflex. His right hand had no choice but to catch up, because it plays the melody of every song, ever. If the right hand built the house, the left laid the foundation. Claude said a left-handed pianist was like a left-handed batter—always an extra step closer to first base.

The bench at the piano on the stand was still warm with Oscar's body heat when Claude sat and perched his hands above the keys. He didn't always trust nightclub pianos—the only instrument that didn't travel with the person playing it. And they often belonged to people who didn't know enough about music to keep them clean and tuned. But this machine felt as sturdy and sounded as crisp as the concert-sized Steinway in his living room. If it had some sour keys, he'd have heard them during Oscar's set.

He saw Oscar in his peripheral vision, getting comfortable at the bar. Famous as Oscar was, he still liked to listen to the guys playing opposite him. As a practitioner, not a critic. As a fellow professional who still loved the craft.

From the stand, above the hum of conversation, Claude heard a small stirring at the back of the room, near the entrance. He looked up and saw a crowd forming around a white man he recognized as George Shearing. George couldn't see, which explained why he strutted into this dark night club wearing shades and holding a white cane. But he could play piano. He played with as much soul and swing as any other pianist in Claude's circle, and spent the 1950s cranking out albums for Savoy and Capitol and MGM records. Claude dismissed a lot of players as hacks, or glorified hobbyists, or Great White Hopes—but not Shearing.

If you asked Claude to set his ego aside and name the three greatest pianists of his generation, the guys he would have spent time and money to listen to, Shearing made the cut, one spot behind Erroll Garner. Number one had just finished his set and would play some more after Claude finished.

"Oscar was," Claude said years later, on a rare day when he felt like talking music with his grandkids, "perfection."

But right now, Oscar was a spectator. And now here came George Shearing, who had burrowed his way through a small crowd of admirers to find a seat in the middle of the room. He, too, wanted to sit and listen to Claude Jones.

Claude took in a deep breath, the air full of second-hand smoke and nervous energy, then exhaled and curled his left hand over the keys. With his right, he pulled the mic toward his mouth and addressed a crowd still abuzz at the presence of two legends.

"So," Claude said, peering out at the room, nodding toward Shearing's table before turning back to the mic. "Who wants to buy this gig for five bucks?"

Oscar and Shearing both cracked up. They knew how their presence in the crowd might rattle a pianist, even a veteran like Claude Jones, whom they had both made a point of seeing that night. The audience laughed, too, in on the joke. Claude even chuckled to himself. Back then, in certain settings, he still knew not to take himself too seriously.

Then he crouched over the keys and leaned into his work. The lavish bluesy intro kept the crowd guessing. If you knew the music as deeply as Oscar and Shearing did, you might have suspected where all these notes were headed—a hunch confirmed when Claude eased into the first few bars of "How Long Has This Been Going On?"

Shearing, at the table mid-room, smiled and nodded. Oscar, on a high stool at the bar, sipped his drink and listened. Claude didn't upstage the headliner, but in this set, he did what he always did.

He didn't just hold his own.

He played like a pro.

PART III | HOMEWORK

Bernice Williams rang the doorbell at 11848 South Halsted, exchanged greetings with Margaret when she opened the door, and walked upstairs to the living room with four guys trailing behind her. They were singers, allegedly. Not kids, but young enough to fantasize about getting rich making music. Not grizzled grown-ups, but old enough to know better.

The living room at the Jones home doubled as a recording studio, one of several places Claude made a living. By night he played clubs and lounges; if you can think of an old-time downtown Chicago jazz spot, Claude Jones probably performed there. The Blue Note. The Scotch Mist. He didn't just work the piano bar at the Playboy Club on Michigan Avenue, at the top of the Magnificent Mile: he *designed* it and played there the night it opened. Somewhere among his thousands of photos is a snapshot of him at the keyboard, smiling as a waitress—white and blonde with bunny ears on her head and boobs spilling out the top of her black bustier—leans over his shoulder. He loved that gig. Margaret didn't.

And by day, he recorded. Sometimes with jazz and blues artists in sessions at Chess Records, sometimes backing R&B acts on pop songs you'd hear on the radio. And other times he worked from his home office, on the recording equipment hooked up to the big Steinway, helping people record their demos or coaching them on their vocals.

Claude rigged that setup, and his record player, to a series of speakers on the second floor, where he and Margaret and the kids lived. He wanted to be able to listen to his music anywhere in the dwelling, but the setup also let people in other rooms hear his recording sessions. Margaret and the kids would retire to the kitchen once work started, but Claude would activate the speakers if that day's singer sounded remarkable.

Sometimes remarkable meant outstanding, like Amanda Ambrose, the young singer-pianist who stopped by sometimes to work on stuff. Over the decades, she would flirt with fame as a cabaret singer and blues artist, put out some albums, get written up in *The New York Times*. She would even, like Claude and Margaret, wind up living in Toronto. Back at Claude's house, she would make that Steinway sing, and could even play Irish folk songs, like "Sweet Molly Malone," with gospel soul. A true talent.

But remarkable could also mean atrocious. Laughably bad. Like the woman who showed up one day calling herself a singer in need of some coaching. Looked in her late twenties, Black, with medium skin, a medium build, and glasses. Nobody remembers her name, but they'll never forget what she did to "September in the Rain." If you can hear Sarah Vaughan's rendition in your mind's ear, try to imagine the opposite. A voice at once bland and tuneless and joyless *and* loud. A vocalist with no sense of rhythm, who, if you asked what key she wanted to sing in, could easily have answered, "Several."

> *The leaves of brown came tumbling down . . .*
> *That September, in the raaaaaaain*

Years later, if Margaret wanted to make her kids laugh, she would imitate the lady in glasses, and her futile search for the low note at the end of each stanza, on "rain," and every word that rhymed with it. Claude had to give the woman a "maybe music isn't your hustle" talk, and she never came back. But among the Joneses, she was already immortal.

People like September in the Rain Lady presented a dilemma. Claude would turn on the speakers so Margaret and the kids could laugh, but if they cackled too loud, he would have to pause the session, march into the kitchen, and banish them. They could head downstairs, where his parents lived or out of the house entirely. But laughing too loud, too long, risked messing up his money.

Still, some of these folks were too hilarious to ignore.

Some serious musicians passed through that living room, of course. The kids might come home from school to find Erroll Garner playing around on the Steinway, or Oscar Peterson chatting with Claude and Margaret while Ray Brown bounced their little brother, Jeff, on his knee.

In between those visits, all kinds of dreamers drifted through the living room, at various stages of the cycle of singing, recording, pitching, waiting, and wishing in pursuit of a record deal. Because Claude was also a photographer, he could take their headshots and do mock-ups of hypothetical albums. One-stop shopping for hopefuls and the hopeless.

Like the guy who showed up looking to cut a demo of a song he wrote. He looked in his late forties and just knew he had a hit. "Dog O' War," which he pronounced "*Dawg* uh *Waw*." The title not a metaphor or figure of speech, but a headline. An actual song about a dog named Rover who was gallant and well-trained, and expert at searching out terrain. Except *gallant* came out as "gallatin," and *terrain* as "terrange."

> *He didn't bark*
> *And he didn't whine*
> *He took his position*
> *Right in the front line*
> *He was a Dawg uh Waw*
> *He was a Dah-awg uh Waw!*

It never advanced past the demo stage, but Peggy can still recite it, word for word, note for droning note. Recording a demo required a few hours and dozens of takes. Peggy and Jeanie heard more songs than they could count, good and bad alike, etched into their memory through sheer repetition.

Then there was Bernice and this quartet who showed up with chord charts and lyrics, crude harmonies and hope. Jeanie and Peggy and Margaret busied themselves in the kitchen, ready to wait out another forgettable session. Claude tried not to frown when he looked at the song on the page, imagining how it might sound. They were paying for this session, so he'd play and record and wish them luck, but he already knew this crew was about to sing themselves into a brick wall.

A few bars into take one, the song sounded even worse than Claude thought it would. Boring and tuneless, with clumsy chord changes and dumb lyrics. The B-team vocalists Bernice brought with her didn't help, but Claude couldn't think of a singer skilled enough to save this song from itself. Not Joe Williams or Dinah Washington. Not Lurlean Hunter. So this group of stragglers wasn't going to dress up this half-assed melody and whole-assed lyrics. But rent was always due. Claude had two kids in college. He kept playing, and they kept singing.

This song was too bad not to share. Claude flipped the switch to pipe the sound into the kitchen. On the other side of the door, Margaret, Jeanie, and Peggy perked up when they heard the speaker crackle. They were about to hear a future star or a disaster. No in-between. Then those lyrics floated through the room . . .

Jeanie nearly lost it. Margaret and Peggy, too. A fourth-grader could have written this stuff. And these guys thought they were turning this mess into a record contract? It was entertaining, Jeanie and Peggy thought. As comedy. Unintentional.

In the living room, Claude played on, and the quartet kept singing. In the kitchen, Peggy grabbed Jeanie and led her in a tango across the kitchen floor. A parody of a dance for this mockery of a song.

We'll walk through my dukedom
And a paradise we will share

"Dukedom" did Peggy in.

She yelped, and because laughter spreads like a bug, Margaret and Jeanie wanted to crack up. Tried to stifle it. Almost succeeded. They knew the cost of cackling too loud. When the take ended, they heard footsteps approaching. The kitchen door swung open to reveal Claude looking peeved. No need to guess what came next.

"You guys," he said, "are gonna have to leave."

Margaret gathered her car keys and her daughters, and they headed out. A little disappointed they couldn't hear more, but they understood. Fun is fun, but Claude's career was serious. Plus, they had already heard plenty. "Duke of Earl," future member of the Jones Family Living Room Bad Music Hall of Fame, just like "Dog O' War" and the September in the Rain Lady.

Claude headed back to the piano for take three.

Duke, Duke, Duke, Duke of Earl . . .

The song didn't sound any less ridiculous later that year when Jeanie and Peggy started hearing it on the radio. The four scrubs weren't singing this time, though; a local vocalist named Gene Chandler had recorded it and, against everything Peggy and Jeanie and Claude and Margaret thought they knew about songwriting, had turned it into a hit. Jeanie and Peggy told a few close friends about the afternoon in the kitchen, but certainly didn't brag to people that they had laughed the Duke of Earl crew out of their house.

The song hit number one in early 1962, and the first cover came the following year. Another in 1967, from a Jamaican band called The Supersonics. A remake from the U.K. in the late 1970s by The Darts. Another from Australia in the late 1980s by a choral group named The Dukes of Earldom.

By 1991, Cypress Hill, who only ever rapped about getting high and shooting people, sampled "Duke of Earl" for their song "Hand on the Pump." That song was about shooting.

In 2002, the song that barely survived the Jones family recording studio was inducted into the Rock & Roll Hall of Fame.

But it's like that when you grow up like they did, with all-stars and journeymen alike traipsing through your living room. You hear a lot of singing and a lot of playing, and you learn to appreciate great music, even if you can't always recognize a hit.

PART IV | AWAY GAMES

Winter of 1966, Claude's agent called with a question.

"What do you think of Canada?" she asked.

"I don't think of Canada," he said.

"Well, maybe you should."

Claude preferred long engagements at home to life on the road. Once he and the club's management could agree on a price—well above union scale, because this was Claude Jones—and the length of his run, Claude could concentrate on his job. Packing and unpacking, hauling suitcases to hotel rooms, scouting out restaurants that served Black people—all that was the unpaid work of an itinerant musician, and Claude had lived that life in his twenties. But now, at forty-two, without fame but with a decent-sized following in Chicago, he had trimmed his job duties to the things that paid: making music and making connections, every night, Monday through Saturday. After two or four or six weeks, he could bounce to his next engagement, bringing listeners with him or leaving them at the old spot, missing him until he returned. Which he would, eventually—at a higher price, of course, once he'd proven he could draw an audience and keep them spending money at the bar.

"I'm not talking about putting you back on the road," she told him. "These Canadians have been calling. They're interested. They're not talking dives and one-nighters. They're talking Ritz-Carlton, Waldorf Astoria, places like that. Same kind of money you're making in Chicago."

"I understand," Claude said. "But I'm really not interested."

Whenever Claude said "really," he put equal weight on each syllable, and extra stress on the whole word. You could almost hear it in italics, so the listener would know how deeply he meant it. "Really not interested" meant exactly that. "*Ree-lee* not interested" meant please don't bug me anymore. Why would Claude hop a plane to snowy Canada? He was a proven pro, with steady work and options in snowy Chicago.

By the time the Canadians started ringing his agent's phone, Claude's playing style, up-market jazz but rooted in the blues, and repertoire, heavy on standards, sprinkled with soulful bebop, was somewhere between old-school and outmoded. Jazz had evolved over his two decades as a pro. Now a lot of serious listeners preferred Coltrane and Mingus and others on the avant garde, stretching the genre in new directions. Claude respected those players, but found their music bloodless and abstract and noisy. He understood about pushing music's boundaries and playing outside the restraints of man-made concepts like "time" and "tune."

He and his musician buddies had made sounds like that all their lives, running up and down the keyboard with both hands, some scattershot banging on the drums, some foghorn blasts from the saxophone. Called it AJFA music.

Aw, Just Fuckin' Around.

They would do it as a warm up then laugh about it before they started playing for real. None of them imagined people would pay to listen to it, yet folks were putting it on vinyl, and avid jazz fans started sneering at dinosaurs like him, who didn't play that way in public.

If people paid to hear him, he might play "See See Rider," that grimy blues tune Ma Rainey first made famous in the 1920s. It's gritty and funky, and more suited to a juke joint than a jazz club, but Claude could dress up songs like that and make them work in any setting. For that, you needed rhythm and a strong left hand to keep those bottom-end notes moving. You also needed a feel you can't learn in music school. It's easy to say Black folks have that kind of soul naturally, but talent alone won't have you playing those songs like Claude. You still had to listen and learn and practice.

Or he would play "Prelude to a Kiss," with the soft touch of a watercolour painter. That was Margaret's favourite song when they first met. To the extent that sixteen-year-old Claude could envision his ideal woman, those early conversations, where she confessed her love for that Duke Ellington ballad, told him Margaret was it.

Figure: Slim.

Skin: Soft and flawless.

Taste in music: Sophisticated.

If record-buying jazz snobs didn't appreciate the range Claude showed every night, the Canadians looking to book talent did, and let his agent know every time they called. He didn't realize it, but these Canadians knew better than to waste his time.

The Canadians had no way of knowing that, after four decades in Chicago, Claude was getting burnt out on the city. Professionally he still had options there, but personally he was tired of the place. He had lived his whole life on the South Side, navigated systemic segregation and one-on-one prejudice, the kind of stuff that grinds on Black folks' nerves just about everywhere we live. But maybe another city would be different. Claude had been itching to find out.

Perhaps his agent told the Canadians that he spent the summer of 1964 playing in San Francisco; he needed a new scene, and fresh relationships in a different city, to figure out if he wanted to live there. San Francisco hadn't captured him, though, and he returned to Chicago in August. But Claude still thought of leaving his hometown for good.

Maybe the Canadians' research led them to Claude Jones's formative years as a pro musician. His apprenticeship with Eddie South, the violinist, was public record. Claude played piano on Eddie's *South Side Jazz* album. Eddie taught Claude how to tie a Windsor knot, and took him on gigs in

a string of midwestern cities. In Springfield, Ohio, they stayed in a rooming house in the Black part of town because hotels downtown only accepted
white guests. Up north, postwar, didn't matter. The law said Ohio was
integrated. Local custom said Black and white didn't mix in public.

They almost certainly didn't know about the union grievance
Claude had filed a decade previous against Stuff Smith, another legendary violinist and mentor to Claude, but an ex-friend by the time
the grievance hit. Stuff had a small ensemble; Claude played piano,
and in the evenings they played local clubs in Chicago. One afternoon
a week, they also formed the core of the house band on radio deejay Al
Benson's TV show. Stuff and Al got to jaw jacking one time, and
nobody thought to step between them because none of them figured
two middle-aged men with careers and reputations would throw hands
on live TV. But hands flew, in both directions, and Stuff, naturally,
lost his job before his first punch landed. When Stuff saw Claude on
TV the next week, playing piano for Benson's big band, he fired
Claude from the quartet, which prompted the call to the union.

Whatever it was, the Canadians had profiled Claude as somebody
they could lure to Toronto for a while. Not famous, but well-known.
Not rich, but making a living. A pro, but not a celebrity—he would
already be one, if that were his destiny. The industry wasn't minting
new stars playing Claude Jones's style of jazz. Whatever he thought
he'd get from the rest of his career, the big break most performers
dream of wasn't happening in the mid-1960s for a tuxedo-wearing,
singing pianist in the Nat King Cole mold.

You couldn't get a Nat Cole–sized star to Toronto on their budget.
But Claude Jones? He was in play, even if he wouldn't acknowledge it.

Yet.

The Canadians kept calling, and the agent kept relaying the mes-
sages. Claude still didn't accept any offers, but he was listening.

Margaret ironed one of Claude's tuxedos one afternoon as he sat at
the dining room table, sipping coffee and reading the *Tribune*. A

crack-of-dawn ritual for most people, but 2 p.m. felt like sunrise on Claude Jones's body clock. He mentioned the Canadians, which meant he was softening. Most of what happened at work stayed there. Claude certainly didn't give Margaret play-by-play recaps of the women who fawned on him at the club, and the ones he indulged. Sometimes she'd find out anyway, but never because he volunteered it.

He mentioned his agent's insistence that he do an engagement in Toronto and his polite but stern rejection.

"What's the problem?" she asked.

"It's Canada," he said, unfolding the sports section. "Too cold for me, Mag."

"It'll be summer, Claude," she said without looking up from the ironing board. "And it can't be any colder than Chicago. You live here just like I do."

"Well, there's no Black people up there."

"How's that different from West Pullman?"

"It just is," he said. "You know what I mean."

"Oscar's Canadian, so there's one," she said. "He has two parents, so that's three. Wasn't Duke Ellington's wife from Canada? That's at least four other Black people, right there."

Claude sipped his coffee and went back to his sports page, scrolling through his list of reasons not to travel to Canada.

"It's far, Mag."

"Claude," she said, placing the iron on its butt, wisps of steam curling from the soleplate. "Remember when Oscar came to see us driving that red Mercedes? Said he drove here in five hours."

"I don't speed like Oscar does, Mag."

"Yeah, well, it's still a hell of a lot closer than San Francisco."

"I know," Claude said. "But it's another *country*."

"We're in Chicago, Claude," she said. "We can cross Wentworth and feel like we're in another country."

"I . . . I just don't know, Mag."

"Yes, you do."

She went back to her ironing board, and he returned to his sports page.

"You come home every night talkin' about you're tired of Chicago. You spent the whole summer in San Francisco last year. We drove to *Niagara Falls*, Claude. That's as close to Toronto as Chicago is to Milwaukee."

"I know."

"So quit acting like they're trying to get you to play in Alaska."

"But it's so *different*."

Margaret grabbed the iron again and returned to work on the crease in his right pant leg. She leaned on it, her weight plus the heat squeezing out the wrinkles and making a crease sharp enough to cut butter. Claude stared at the baseball box scores a few silent moments, his eyes on the numbers but his mind on what Margaret just said. He mentioned the offer from the Canadians hoping she would give him an excuse to reject it outright. Instead, she talked sense to him.

Still, the conversation felt unfinished. They hadn't resolved the topic. They had simply stopped talking. But Claude knew. He drank the last drop of coffee in the bottom of his mug, folded the sports section back into the rest of the paper, and tossed it on the table. Then he pushed back in his chair and walked toward the living room. On the way, he paused near Margaret, who didn't look up from her ironing, and said two words he almost never used together.

"You're right," he said.

He walked out of the dining room and down the hall and into the bedroom to lie down a while and think about work.

———

Claude Jones loved Toronto. His first booking came in late winter. He fell for the city fast, just like he had for Margaret when they first met as teenagers. Big and busy and next to a Great Lake, just like Chicago. Except Toronto had clean streets and friendly people. It was overwhelmingly white, but integrated. The few Black and Brown people he saw seemed to know their place—anywhere in the city they pleased. This was new and alluring.

When the agents booked him at another glitzy downtown venue, he returned to Toronto, this time bringing Margaret and Jeff.

Daytimes the three of them would walk downtown streets near his hotel, strolling Spadina Avenue, on the western edge of the University of Toronto's sprawling campus. Jeff became infatuated with crosswalks, and the idea that any person could slap a button, activate flashing lights, and stop traffic so he could cross the street. Chicago drivers would ignore a signal like that and would commit vehicular homicide before they'd ever pause for a pedestrian. But in Toronto, everybody stopped and waited, no matter how slowly you crossed.

Margaret couldn't believe they kept a city so big that sparkling clean, or that Canadians could treat each other so kindly, so much of the time. When a bus stopped, for example, people would line up and climb aboard, single file. In Chicago, people just crowded the door, and elbowed each other aside.

When they reached College Street, they stopped to wait for a walk signal. As cars puttered past, Margaret turned to her husband.

"I could live here," she said.

In July 1966, Claude, Margaret, and Jeff Jones moved to Toronto for good. Peggy stayed in Chicago; she jumped straight into the workforce after her freshman year at Loyola rather than move to Canada. Jeanie stayed in South Shore; she and Pete had been married less than a year, settling into their big apartment at 69th and Oglesby. Bobby and Eileen still lived within walking distance of them.

But Claude and Margaret had decided to become Canadian, and so they made Jeff's choice for him. Their apartment search landed them in Thorncliffe Park, near Don Mills Road and Eglinton Avenue, where construction had just begun on the Ontario Science Centre, twenty minutes northeast of downtown. Claude lived in Canada three years before he realized "Don Mills" referred to mills on the Don

River, and not to some superman after whom Torontonians named roads and schools and car dealerships.

But more than the result, the process of finding a place to live stood out to Claude and Margaret.

In Chicago, you couldn't make a decision on moving without weighing a neighbourhood's racial makeup. Were racist white people keeping Black folks out? Happened all the time. That was West Pullman, where Claude grew up.

Were white people fleeing because too many Black people had moved in? Just as common. That was South Shore, where they lived before coming to Canada—90 per cent white in 1960 and 50 per cent Black by 1970.

In Chicago, all those factors influenced who lived where, and how much they paid. But they didn't seem to arise in Toronto. Claude and Margaret liked the building and the neighbourhood, and they could afford the rent, so they signed the lease. An everyday act for most folks, but for my grandparents, a sort of liberation. Where de facto segregation still constricted options for most Black folks in Chicago, in Toronto the Jones family was free to live wherever their income would allow. In a few years, Jeff would be free to date or marry whomever he wanted. And visiting the doctor? That was free, too. A thrilling experience, but still a little jarring, like stepping from quicksand onto solid ground. You know you're better off, but you still have to learn to move without restrictions. You're using a different set of muscles.

This was 1966, and Claude and Margaret were both in their forties. They were still landed immigrants, but starting fresh in Toronto made them feel, for the first time in their lives, like full citizens.

This Ain't No Got Damn Jamaica

The fistfight between Pete Campbell and Jamaican Karl started with a conflict between their two daughters—my big sister, Dana, and Jamaican Karl's little girl. Karla was a little older than Dana, noticeably larger, and easing into playground bully habits: shoving, mean-talking, snatching stuff. Dana told Pete, who marched up the street for a dad-to-dad chat with Jamaican Karl, who wasn't interested in talking. By the time Jeanie ran over to try to defuse things, Pete and Jamaican Karl were toe-to-toe and forehead-to-forehead on Jamaican Karl's lawn, exchanging punches the way good neighbours trade greetings.

Pete went upside Jamaican Karl's head with a left hand, which, given the girth of Pete's forearms and the width of his fists, must have felt like a brick. Jamaican Karl went upside Pete's head with an actual brick and left a small scar that would never fully fade. Jamaican Karl's wife, whom we'll call Shelly-Ann, arrived at the fight just as Jeanie did, carrying a two-by-four and a grudge against her Black American neighbours.

Shelly-Ann wasn't familiar with Jeanie's history, and had no way of knowing Jeanie, at eleven, had cold-cocked that big white boy for calling her a Tar Baby. She might have acted differently if she were aware of Jeanie's punching power. Like old-time light heavyweight champ

Archie Moore's, it transcended weight classes. If Jeanie hit you, you hit the floor. Smart money stayed out of punching range. I know I did. Shelly-Ann would learn.

She'd also never seen Jeanie rifle through her purse to retrieve her lipstick and keys before sprinting out the door before work each morning. If she had, she'd have noticed Jeanie's hands were Olympic champion-fast. Ever see that clip of Sugar Ray Leonard shoe-shining Marvin Hagler's bald head, when they fought in 1987? Fast like that. But Shelly-Ann didn't know that, either, so she could only stand empty-handed and wonder how someone as small as Jeanie could dispossess her so quickly of the two-by-four she intended to crack over Pete's head.

Shelly-Ann turned to her daughter, who couldn't have foreseen simple my-daddy-is-stronger-than-your-daddy posturing devolving into a brawl, and a string of assaults with improvised weapons. But it had, and empty-handed Shelly-Ann, unhappy with Karl's progress, had a task for her daughter.

"Get the knife," she said.

Not "Get *a* knife." Then Karla might have retrieved any knife. Pocket. Swiss Army. Butter. Shelly-Ann said, "Get *the* knife," as if they kept one at home specifically for shanking neighbours.

Karla moved toward the house, and Jeanie blocked her.

"Girl, don't come back here with a knife unless *you* wanna get cut."

Karla might have possessed a perspective her parents lacked. Within a minute, the fight had escalated from fists to bricks to two-by-fours, to a call to fetch the special neighbour-slashing blade. Maybe she sensed that, whatever the original conflict was with Dana, it didn't merit all this.

Or maybe she watched Jeanie disarm Shelly-Ann and figured this threat wasn't just talk. So she defied her own mom, who thought deadly weapons belonged in low-grade neighbourhood spats, and obeyed Jeanie, who might actually have fileted her to restore peace to our street. Imagine bringing a knife to a fistfight and getting sliced your damn self. Not Karla, who stayed put and watched the wrestling match between the dads peter out. The knife remained wherever Jamaican Karl's family stored it, waiting for the next fight to erupt.

Pete and Jeanie made the short walk home feeling closer than they had in years. Inside, Jeanie helped Pete patch a scrape on his forehead. Pete lashed an ice pack to his left hand. They were both exhausted, but energized and united after repelling a threat to the family, fighting side-by-side against a common enemy outside their marriage.

The fight happened a decade after Pete and Jeanie had moved to Canada, following her parents across the border, and three years after they became citizens. Later on, in the ugliest moments of their divorce, Pete would threaten to move back to Chicago, but he never meant it. He wasn't going to leave his three kids. He had ties to Canada now. Deep enough to withstand the body blows a divorce would inflict.

Jeanie embraced Canadianness in ways she never needed to. Multi-culturalism, after all, wasn't just a feature of life near Toronto. It was official federal policy. Immigrants weren't merely allowed to bring old-country cultural norms with them; the government encouraged them to do it and add to Canada's cultural mosaic. But Jeanie was born in the U.S. and grew up in the Melting Pot, where immigrants were expected to adapt quickly to their new country. So, she adjusted to Canadian life with the gusto of a newcomer to the U.S.

Each morning from Victoria Day in May until Labour Day in September, she would unfurl a Canadian flag and hang it in front of our small brown townhouse, and every night she'd roll it up and store it just inside the front door. She adopted Canadian spellings, like *labour* instead of *labor*, and Canadian pronunciations, like "shedgle" instead of "skedjool." She never assimilated enough to bake pumpkin pie, but if you had Thanksgiving dinner with us in October, and you needed to wipe your mouth after eating a piece of her sweet potato pie, Jeanie wouldn't hand you a napkin. She'd offer you a *serviette*.

Maybe Canada wasn't the Promised Land, but for Jeanie it was a land of promise, and the best place on earth for Black folks to blossom. She harboured Josiah Hensonesque fantasies of Black Americans crossing the border en masse, to discover what we could achieve with free healthcare, cheap higher education, and a less deadly strain of racism than her generation had fought their whole lives. If the racism she knew in the U.S. was like stepping on a landmine—violent, debilitating, deadly—the racism she encountered in Canada felt like treading on a pile of dog poop. Unexpected and unpleasant, but not enough to ruin your life. Not even enough to wreck your day if you clean it off quick and keep moving forward.

Pete, meanwhile, embodied the cultural mosaic. He loved his new country, but that didn't mean he'd Canadianize his whole life. On weekends, he'd drink a Labatt beer, and if Tony McKegney or Grant Fuhr was playing, he'd watch the occasional hockey game. But for him, "route" would always rhyme with "spout," and if you messed up you said "sah-ree," not "soary." He also kept his car radio tuned to WBLK, the Black station from Buffalo—not for the traffic or the weather, but for the culture.

If Black Americans had a neighbourhood in Toronto, like Little Italy or Portugal Village, he'd have gladly moved us there, or at least brought us on weekends. But my folks didn't come to Canada as part of mass migration, like the one that brought their own relatives to Chicago from across the South, or even a small one, like the recruiting drives that drew Black American and Caribbean railroad workers to Canada in the early twentieth century. The Campbells were just part of one family that trickled across the border a couple of members at a time, with few ways to plug into a larger community the way Italians or Portuguese or Jamaicans could.

So Pete was always going back home. Sometimes he'd bring us back to Chicago or Grand Rapids for something specific, like a funeral or a family reunion. Other times he'd invent a reason.

"I gotta get back to Chicago," he'd say. "I'm losing my accent."

Pete lost a lot living in Canada.

When sales of the De Havilland Dash 7 or Dash 8 slowed, he would lose his job at the plant in Downsview until business picked up and the company summoned workers back to the factory floor to produce more turboprops. Once, he lost his wallet on a weekend jaunt to Niagara Falls with his girlfriend; he lost his marriage over that stunt, and the countless other small acts of bad husbanding preceding it.

But actually losing the accent?

Never came close.

Even before I started grade school, I recognized three syllables that could precede a stern warning, or serve as one.

You bet'not . . .

Years before *The Wire* and Clay Davis, we knew Pete could use the same word as an interjection, a rumination, or an invitation to fill in the blank.

Sheeeeeit.

And long before these rap N-words made the issue mainstream, and thousands of think-pieces numbed our brains to it, I knew the meaning of the N-word depended on speaker, audience, context, and consent.

My cousin LaRue? That lil nigga could run.

I learned all this just listening to Pete talk. Linguists call it African American Vernacular English, but it was just the way people spoke in Pete's home and neighbourhood. Pete left the South Side of Chicago for good at twenty-seven, but the South Side never left him.

———

When Pete saw the first cockroach skitter across the kitchen floor, we knew we had a problem. Our townhouse was less than five years old in a tidy neighbourhood deep in the suburbs. Other townhouse complexes nearby weren't much older than ours, and the detached homes across the park had wide and well-trimmed lawns. Falconer Drive didn't profile as a cockroach hotbed, yet here came this bug.

Then the second roach appeared. If you've seen two roaches in the light, you know there's a colony in the shadows and damp spots and crevices of your dwelling. It would have been a headache in better times, but Pete's mom, Mary, was scheduled to visit. She and Jeanie never got along. Mary would always resent Jeanie for taking her son and grandbabies to a strange country. Bring Mary into a home with a roach problem, and tense relations could turn combustible.

The roaches grew bolder and more numerous. They'd trot through the kitchen midday or saunter across the thin brown carpet in our living room. It had become a crisis, and Pete thought he had a culprit.

"You slackin' on this housework, Jeanie," he told her one day. "We wouldn't have all these roaches if you kept this place cleaner."

"Pete, I don't know where these bugs are coming from," she said. "But it's not me."

Pete hated two things: cockroaches and Kentucky bourbon.

He hated bourbon because his dad drank it. Copiously, every weekend.

Friday nights, after his last shift at Inland Steel, Prines Campbell Sr. might get buzzed at home, then wander out to another drinking spot. Or he might climb into his Oldsmobile to go visit a mistress. He wrecked more than one family car and kept a lawyer on retainer for the DUIs. Or he might just drink in the living room and hurl insults at his wife. Fists, too. Or, one time, a bullet. Yes, a bullet. It missed Granny Mary and hit a china hutch, where it stayed lodged forever.

As an adult, Pete would drink beer or rum or Seagram's gin. But he never touched Kentucky bourbon. The smell made him want to vomit.

And the roaches?

He hated them just for being roaches, and because they symbolized so much unsavoury stuff. Not poverty, necessarily, but neglect. Poor upkeep. A lack of respect for yourself and your home. And they summoned ugly memories he'd never fully articulate to his kids about his time in Jacksonville, where he was stationed in the Navy, and where Jim Crow ruled even as the rest of the country integrated; where white people called him "colored" and worse, and where the roaches were the biggest he had ever seen.

Nothing about the Campbell house made it a breeding ground for vermin. Sometimes it was disorganized, in the way homes become when they contain three kids younger than ten, and one parent who sees housework as the other parent's job. Dirty laundry might pile up outside the linen closet at the top of the stairs, and grown-ups might have tripped over kids' toys left on the living-room floor, but nobody made the kinds of festering messes that drew pests. No food left out to spoil. No crappy diapers abandoned in the hallway.

Still, Jeanie kept cleaning and the roaches kept coming. They arrived in such big numbers, it became clear nothing in our house was attracting them. For the roaches to go this feral, this fast, something had to have introduced them to this new environment.

Or some*one*.

New next-door neighbours, for example. Like, say, a man named Willie and his wife and kids. Just arrived from Jamaica.

At first, Pete was just happy to have Black friends. In suburban Toronto, in the late 1970s and early 1980s, running into other African Americans was strictly a function of luck. My sister Courtney wound up in junior kindergarten with Damon Ealey, my future little-league football teammate, whose folks were Black Ohioans who stayed in Mississauga after his dad retired from the Canadian Football League.

Years later, while running track in high school, I met Mace and Leila Freeman, whose dad—birth name: Joseph Pannell—was a brilliant, intense, low-key hilarious man who grew up in Washington, D.C. His Canadian origin story isn't mine to tell in full, but elements of it made headlines. Racial profiling and a violent showdown with a white cop in Chicago. The cop ended up with some bullets in his arm. For Pannell, an arrest and the prospect of a long prison sentence. He made bail and then vanished before his trial, resurfacing in Montreal, in 1974, as Douglas Gary Freeman, before moving to Mississauga.

That name, of course, was also a nod to the fugitive slaves who found freedom in Canada before the Civil War. And to the extent that you can make generalizations about people like us, those families—Ealey, Campbell, Freeman—covered three types of African Americans most likely to relocate to Southern Ontario: athletes, entertainers, and people on the run.

But we could never actually plan on meeting other African Americans, and my family had no cultural ties to neighbourhoods like Eglinton West, where many Caribbean immigrants, like the parents of the Black kids I went to high school with, often landed before fanning out to the suburbs. Out where we lived, half an hour from downtown Toronto, on the Streetsville-Meadowvale border in northwest Mississauga, you didn't meet enough Black people to act picky over what type of Black person they were. If you saw one, you said hi. If you became neighbours, you tried to make friends.

When the Campbells lived in a townhouse complex on the west side of Falconer Drive, they befriended the Bishops. These were Jeanie's kind of people. Black and Nova Scotian. Several generations deep in Canada, with American roots beyond that. They ate cornbread and collard greens but still considered Canada home, just like Jeanie.

In November 1976, Pete and Jeanie closed on a new townhouse on the east side of Falconer, brown with three bedrooms and two bathrooms. They still shared walls with next-door neighbours, but these houses were a little roomier than the ones across the street, and they all had garages. From there, you could build some equity and maybe save some money and, in five years or so, sell the townhouse and move your family around the corner to Kenninghall Boulevard. Those houses looked like the one on *The Brady Bunch*—big and angular with broad lawns and long driveways and double-wide garages. The new townhouse brought the Campbells a quarter mile east and a big step closer to the North American dream.

Eventually the Bishops moved away, but we had some Black neighbours in the new complex, immigrants like Pete and Jeanie, with Jamaican names like Ralston and Karl, the neighbour-turned-sparring partner. They weren't too different from Pete—hard-working fathers with blue-collar jobs who liked to tinker with cars and drink beer and talk shit. And they were all Black in Canada and living on the same street in the late 1970s, so they coalesced into a crew.

They all got along until they didn't.

After a decade in the country, Pete and Jeanie knew better than to think skin colour was enough.

When they were brand new to Canada and living in a high-rise apartment at Graydon Hall, just south of the 401 and just west of the Don Valley Parkway, they'd sometimes see another couple in the elevator and exchange warm smiles. They were all young and married and the same café au lait shade of beige. One day, conversation progressed past "hello," and they heard Pete's accent, which nobody anywhere ever mistook for Caribbean. His speech was Black and American, and when the couple heard it, their smiles faded. They stepped off the elevator at the ground floor and never spoke to Pete and Jeanie again.

At times, growing up, I'd get that same cold shoulder, under similar circumstances. A kid with Caribbean parents would learn my folks were American, then decide I didn't measure up. Most of the Black kids I knew clung to their parents' backgrounds and identified as Jamaican or Trini or Bajan or, in my unicorn of a case, American. Hardly anyone identified as Canadian. But we were all Canadian and Black and mostly first generation, trying to force those identities to coexist.

People our parents' age were all from where they were from. They all were brand-new immigrants at some point, and unsure how much room to make for each other's back-home customs in a country where they were all newcomers.

In our little townhouse complex, it sometimes caused friction. Small disagreements exploded into fistfights, like the one between Pete and Jamaican Karl. Or neighbourly relations blew up the way Pete and Willie's did when Jeanie finally pinpointed the source of the roaches.

We all lived in the suburbs, but Willie and his kids were country.

Correction.

These. Folks. Were. Country.

They removed the panes and screens from their windows, so they just had holes in the side of their house. I don't know what they did when it rained, but they seemed not to care about getting wet. If Willie's kids owned shoes, we didn't see them. And if their house had indoor plumbing like everybody else's, nobody told Willie Jr., who used the asphalt in front of their lawn as his personal urinal.

Nobody had seen a roach in our complex before they moved in, and Pete, once he figured out Jeanie wasn't the cause, came to recognize the exact kind of roach they were confronting. They weren't the mid-sized roaches he had seen in Chicago . . . in other people's houses, not his—get that straight. No, these were full-sized, well-fed, warm-weather roaches like the ones he had seen in Jacksonville. They came from someplace hot.

And now the roaches needed to go.

Fast.

Mary was still planning to drive up from Chicago, and now wanted to bring her new boyfriend, Marcel, *and* his teenage daughter, Michelle. One townhouse couldn't fit a family of five, three guests, *and* a roach colony.

Mary hated roaches, too, and loved needling Jeanie about the way she raised my sisters and me. We were always too soft, too lazy, too ungrateful, too white, or too something else, and it was always Jeanie's fault. She nagged Jeanie about living in Canada, with so few other Black folks around, and about bringing us to visit her so infrequently. A roach infestation would add one more exhibit to her ongoing case that her son had married the wrong woman.

We've got roaches back in Chicago, Pete. You all didn't have to move up here for this. Might as well come on back. I'll straighten those kids out, too, since your wife won't.

Nobody needed that fight.

The roaches had to go.

Jeanie located the source one afternoon while small-talking with Willie's wife. She asked if their family had also suffered an invasion of cockroaches recently, and Willie's wife answered that the roaches weren't invaders. They had roaches in Jamaica, and the bugs had come with them to Canada, stowing away in the family's furniture and luggage. Willie's wife relayed this information casually, the way you'd say you had a pet goldfish or kids in swimming lessons.

And now Pete needed to deal with Willie. He strode out of our house and across the small driveway to Willie's doorstep, rang the doorbell, and waited. Eventually, Willie answered, propping his door open and inviting Pete inside. But Pete would never enter Willie's house. Roaches lived in there.

"Willie, we gotta talk outside a minute," he said.

Pete really did just want to talk, but reasonable people could have interpreted those words, uttered in his deep-chested baritone, as an invitation to throw down. Willie, though, was impervious to bad vibes and ambled happily out of his house and onto his lawn. He didn't let stuff bother him. Not cockroaches. Not moving to a new country. Not a shouting match about to pop off with his next-door neighbour. He was still grinning as he and Pete squared off on the lawn, as oblivious to the tension as his son was to by-laws against public indecency.

"You need to do somethin' 'bout these roaches, Willie," Pete said. "I'm tireda this mess."

Willie looked bewildered, as if he hadn't imagined his roaches might pose a problem to other people. They certainly didn't bother him.

But Pete was ready to explode.

Before his friendship with Jamaican Karl devolved into that brawl, he had been cool with his Jamaican neighbours and their culture. He didn't listen to reggae, but he didn't tease them about it, or bug them about eating goat. Even tried it himself. But the live-and-let-live approach to customs from the old country didn't cover cockroaches. Willie didn't know it yet, but Pete had reached his limit.

"Easy nuh mahn," Willie said. "Roo-chez hevreh weer bahk hoom. Dem like flies in Jamaica."

Wrong answer.

"NIGGA, THIS AIN'T NO *GOT DAMN* JAMAICA!" Pete boomed.

This was serious. Willie finally clued in. Pete didn't want another fight with yet another Jamaican neighbour, but if he had to pummel Willie into stemming this roach infestation, well then . . .

"Jus cool!" Willie said, raising his hands, pleading. "Jus cool, bredda."

"I ain't coolin' a got damn thing, Willie. These roaches gotta go."

"Cool, cool, cool . . ."

"*Fix it*, Willie!"

Pete went home and waited.

The whole family waited.

And we kept seeing roaches. Scrambling across the kitchen floor. Strolling through the living room. Inching along the baseboards.

Eventually Pete and Jeanie called an exterminator and paid him money they couldn't spare. He was still fumigating the place when Mary and her crew arrived, giving her one more thing to complain to Pete about.

But nobody saw any roaches after that. And Willie never even thanked us.

Floating On

From directly above the house, you'd have seen the tall trees, with deep green midsummer leaves, shading the margins of the backyard. In the middle, in full sunlight, an above-ground swimming pool and two bronze bodies, belly-up on the shimmering water.

One of them, my dad, shirtless in black swim trunks, beige skin glistening, reclining on an air mattress. His broad-shouldered and big-armed physique exuding dad strength. Solid, where abdominal muscles might once have made an outline. Not all the way out of shape, but not quite in it anymore.

The other person, Marla, in a white two-piece swimsuit. She was short and blonde and shaped like the number eight. Round on top, and rounder on the bottom. Her bikini looked even whiter in contrast to her skin, which bore the deep tan of somebody who spent plenty of hours doing exactly this.

She and my dad lay side by side, facing in opposite directions, so her left thigh aligned with his. They each placed a hand on the other's leg, so they didn't drift apart as they bobbed atop the water. Together in the centre of the pool, they rotated slowly, like the minute hand on a clock, or floating like two grown-ups sharing a lazy afternoon alone.

Except they weren't alone.

At the far edge of the pool, Dana and Courtney batted a beach ball around with Marla's nearly teenaged daughters. I dawdled along the opposite wall, closest to the house. I was eight years old, younger than the other kids, and the only one who couldn't swim. I fiddled with my water wings, not quite listening to Dad and Marla's conversation, but still hearing parts of it.

"You glad you made it?" Marla said, raising her free hand to shield her eyes from the sunlight.

"Yep."

"Sure beats working, don't it?" she said, patting Dad's knee.

"Mmm-hmmm."

As soon as the Great Skate Place opened—five minutes from our house, over the train tracks, across the Streetsville-Meadowvale border, behind the new McDonald's—the Campbells became a roller-skating family. At least three Saturdays a month, sometimes on Sunday, and, if we were caught up on our homework, the occasional Wednesday night.

My sisters and I never rented skates. Our dad didn't do cheap, and that was the only word to describe the skates that management handed out for a dollar a pair. Stiff beige leather uppers. White stripe along the heel with the size written in black marker. Dirty orange wheels and bulky toe stops. The setup was heavier than a cast, and only a touch more flexible.

Our skates came from the pro shop: trucks and wheels bolted to low-cut canvas sneakers, gleaming white wheels with matching toe stops. Skates for real skaters. Mine were blue with two yellow stripes.

Mom never made it to the Great Skate Place; Dad never missed an outing.

He could thread through slower skaters, bouncing in time to whatever roller-funk tracks crossed the border from the U.S. "Cutie Pie" by One Way, or "More Bounce to the Ounce" by Zapp. No collisions or even close calls, no matter how fast he moved or how many beginners clogged the rink. As a solo skater, Dad was all smooth strides and effortless pivots, always in rhythm.

As a couples skater, he paired up with Marla, and they would cruise to slow jams, hand in hand, body to body, and step for step. Marla had two kids and an accent from somewhere down south. She also had a husband who didn't skate, and a big house in a rich part of town with a wide lawn, tall trees, and a pool in the backyard.

They drifted together in the middle of the pool. Marla patted Dad's thigh. Dad splashed her, and they both laughed. He peeked over, then tickled her navel with his index finger.

"I can do that because you have an innie," he said. "You can't get me back. I got an outie."

I didn't watch, but I saw. Dad never touched Mom like that in front of us.

They floated some more. Dad with his black swim trunks, bare torso, and out-poking belly button; Marla with her tanned skin and white bikini and hair the colour of the straw that broke the camel's back.

I Didn't Come Here Lookin' for Trouble

The instant Number 20 from San Francisco lined up facemask-to-facemask with Willie Gault was the moment he decided, unwittingly, how this play would end.

You could play this kind of tight bump-and-run coverage against a regular wide receiver; if you couldn't stonewall him at the line of scrimmage, you could chase him down and make a play later. But against Gault, who could run 100 metres in 10.1 seconds, you wanted to do the opposite—unless you ran faster, which few humans could.

NFL teams had to invent a whole new set of defensive schemes when Bob Hayes, with his Olympic gold medal and 10.06-second 100-metre speed, joined the Dallas Cowboys in 1965. Until then, defenses assumed their cornerbacks were roughly as fast as the receivers they covered, so they played man-to-man all day. But Hayes was literally the fastest man in history. Shortly after he arrived, so did the zone defense, which coaches drew up to deal with the mismatches Hayes created. Now you could just stand back and defend an area, give yourself a buffer and a running start. Otherwise, you'd choke on Hayes's exhaust as he zoomed past. Otherwise, Hayes would do to you what Gault was about to do to poor Number 20, early in the first quarter between the Chicago Bears and the San Francisco 49ers, on October 13, 1985.

At the snap, big bodies collided along the line of scrimmage—
49ers in red and gold, and the Bears in white jerseys, pants and helmets the deepest shade of navy. Quarterback Jim McMahon hopped
back and cocked the ball in his right hand. Over near the sideline,
Gault gave Number 20 a stutter step, then sped past him. Number 20,
head bobbing, arms flailing, fought to run faster, and lost ground
with each stride to Gault, who unleashed his speed with little visible
effort. The difference between running and sprinting—between a
fast guy, which Number 20 was compared to normal folks, and an
Olympian, which Gault would have been had the U.S. not boycotted
the 1980 Summer Games in Moscow.

McMahon unspooled an arcing pass downfield. Gault hit yet
another gear, tilted his head skyward without breaking stride,
cupped his hands in front of his chest, and let the ball drop in. One
play, thirty-three yards, a first down, and a clue that the Bears had a
lot of ways to beat you. Blunt force, blazing speed, or both.

"Got eem!"

My dad, shouting from his spot on the couch, next to the end
table and the window that overlooked our small backyard. He was
more of a Walter Payton guy, but still appreciated Gault's gaudy speed,
and the space it created for the rest of Chicago's offense.

"Too bad he couldn't keep his feet." My mom, from her post, two
seats over, closer to the bookcase. "I wanted a touchdown."

I watched from my place on the floor. My folks had just replaced the
living room's original brown carpet—dull as dishwater, and threadbare as
an old sock in some spots—with something fluffy and beige and modern.
It felt like a duvet in contrast to the old rug. Before, I *had* to sit on the floor
because I was the youngest and my older sisters took the good seats. Now,
I *got* to sit on the floor, so I planted myself there and didn't complain.

"You know Willie Gault does ballet, Morgan."

Periodically, my mom would pitch ballet as an after-school hobby.
She thought it would keep me in shape and help with balance,
flexibility, and, most of all, discipline. Maybe nudge me out of my

schoolyard troublemaker phase, which, by early fourth grade, didn't look set to end. Ever. Gault gave her an opening. If NFL players could do ballet, why couldn't I?

But pro football players also played football, and I didn't, even though I wanted to and was finally old enough to sign up for the Mississauga Football League. Maybe, hypothetically, ballet could complement football, but I knew which activity I wanted to try first. The one with helmets and shoulder pads and running and hitting.

"You should think about taking lessons," my mom said.

"Okay," I said, because I couldn't say "No way."

Plus, I didn't want ballet talk distracting me from watching Walter Payton take a handoff and veer left, then churn upfield toward the 49ers' end zone. Between Payton and the goal line loomed Ronnie Lott, a six-foot, 203-pound sledgehammer of a man, who played free safety for San Francisco and had a well-earned rep for knocking ball carriers unconscious. In 1989, on a play similar to this one, he would smash Cincinnati's Ickey Woods into oblivion.

That single collision put the 49ers in control of Super Bowl XXIII, turning Woods from aggressive to tentative. Not just for the remainder of the game, but the rest of his career. Ronnie Lott hit hard enough to alter lives, and Payton treated him like a revolving door. Just pushed through him, to the other side of the goal line. A superhuman act of strength and leverage, but a routine play for Payton.

Dana hated sports and Courtney tolerated them, but they drifted downstairs and lingered a few minutes in the living room to watch the Bears lay this bruising on the 49ers. We rarely did anything as a full family. My mom never came roller skating, and Dad mostly stayed home Sunday afternoons when the rest of us went to visit my mom's parents. But on weekends when WIVB or WGRZ in Buffalo happened to carry the Bears game, you might actually find all five Campbells in one place, engaged in the same activity. My folks weren't religious, so those Sunday afternoons watching the 1985 Chicago Bears maul some other team were the closest my family had to church.

All of Chicago pulled for the Bears. South Side, North Side, West Side, downtown, the suburbs. Black, white, and all the colours in the middle. A bigger feat than most non-Chicagoans appreciate. Schools, churches, living spaces—all tended to fall cleanly along colour lines in Chicago. Only support for the local NFL team could span gaps in race and social class and rally the city around a common cause.

My parents were native South Siders and brought their Bears fandom with them to Canada. My dad would never string together four words about his feelings, but he'd talk a long time about Walter Payton, or how untouchable Gale Sayers was before he shredded his knee. He kept his game-day commentary concise and, for a hyped-up Bears fan, remarkably clean.

When the Bears defense forced Joe Montana to scramble from the pocket:

"GIDEEM!"

When Richard Dent collared Montana and slammed him to the dirt:

"*Got* eem!"

When Chicago's Thomas Sanders flattened San Francisco's kickoff returner with the kind of helmet-first hit that would get a modern player suspended:

"Knocked the taste out his mouth!"

My mom's observations hinted at just how much football she watched.

A lot.

"Payton shouldn't carry the ball in his palm like that. He needs to tuck it away."

Or:

"Why does Gault use his body to catch the ball? Those other fellas just use their hands."

Or:

"McMahon sure takes a long time to throw the ball. He winds up like a pitcher."

But by the time I could understand football, my parents, like most Chicagoans, cheered for the *idea* of the Bears, and yearned to return to what the team used to be.

Before the NFL and AFL merged, before the Super Bowl and widespread racial integration, the Bears lived near the top of the standings. From 1921 to 1963, they played ten NFL championship games and won six titles. Most of those trophies came between 1941 and 1946, when they made four straight title games and won three of them. When Chicagoans discussed the Monsters of the Midway, and rhapsodized about the broad-shouldered, smash-mouth brand of football that defined the franchise, they meant those Bears teams— the old squads, generally, but specifically the editions that straddled World War II.

Head coach George Halas directed all that success, and his name still resonates in the NFL. "Papa Bear" is a legend in Chicago, where, conceivably, a Bears player could, in a single season, practice at Halas Hall (the team's training facility), win the George Halas Trophy (for a conference title), the George S. Halas Trophy (for the league's best defender), *and* the George S. Halas Courage Award (for overcoming adversity).

Halas and his teams were also literal legends because their feats existed on the fringes of living memory. My parents didn't witness the original Monsters of the Midway. They heard about them from older Chicagoans, who inflated those stories with each retelling. By the time my generation arrived, the old folks told us Red Grange ran faster than Bo Jackson, that Halas once beat God in a game of chess, and that Sayers, with ball in hand, was more elusive than racial harmony.

In reality, for half my parents' lives, and all of mine, the Bears vacillated between bad and average. They missed the playoffs every year from 1964, their first season without Halas, to 1976, the year I was born. Another playoff drought lasted from 1979 to 1983. Lowlights included 1969, the same autumn my parents left Chicago, when the Bears won one game and lost thirteen. By 1975, my folks had settled in Mississauga and the Bears still stunk. Four wins and ten losses; 191 points scored and 379 surrendered.

That year, Payton, a twenty-one-year-old rookie running back, nicknamed "Sweetness," was a revelation. He came from Jackson State, five-foot-ten, two hundred pounds, all thighs and forearms and quickness and power. He ran around or over tacklers depending on the situation and his mood, and he gave people a reason to watch the Bears. By 1976, he had already emerged as the NFL's best running back, and the team's success increased in proportion to his workload.

He had 311 carries in 1976, when the Bears won seven games.

The next year, 339 carries, leading to nine wins and the team's first playoff appearance in fifteen years, which, in a prideful sports town like Chicago, must have seemed like a century.

Another 333 carries in 1978, then 369 the following year to carry the Bears into the postseason again. Those totals each led the NFL, a cumulative burden that would fast-forward the aging process for most running backs. But Payton kept producing: 1,460 yards in 1980, 1,421 more in 1983.

All that output triggered the familiar, sickening feeling that Payton might waste his once-in-a-generation talent on putrid teams. After Papa Bear Halas retired, the late-1960s Bears had Gale Sayers and Dick Butkus—and losing records every season. In 1984, Payton hit thirty—senior citizenship for an NFL running back—and the Bears finally made the conference title game, losing 23–0 to San Francisco. You couldn't predict their trajectory would bend upward from there, with Sweetness closer to retirement than to his prime, on a franchise with no recent record of sustained success. Would Payton, who led the NFL in career rushing yards, and whose name would later grace a Chicago high school and an NFL award for good citizenship, ever even sniff a Super Bowl?

Fair question.

But then the Bears won five straight games to open the 1985 season. No split decisions, either. Their defense would swamp you like a storm surge, force leaks in your pass protection by blitzing more people than your team could block. Linemen, linebackers, defensive backs. You could hold them back for a while, but couldn't stop them all. They didn't just beat you. They beat you up, and beat you down.

And their offense? Heavy and steady and relentless, like a river cutting through rock. They would pound you with Payton and Matt Suhey early to set the tone, or hammer you with them late to drain the clock and protect a lead. Your defense's confidence? Their stamina? Their game plans? They would all erode, eventually.

Last Sunday in September, they crushed Washington in a home game. Following week, they travelled to Tampa to trample the Buccaneers. Aggregate score: 72–29.

By the time Willie Gault dusted Number 20 to set up the opening touchdown against San Francisco, optimism was already rippling through the community of Bears fans, both at home and in the diaspora. Maybe this year the reality might match the memory. Were the Monsters of the Midway back? Was it too early to think about a championship?

Maybe not.

Two more possessions, two Chicago field goals, and a 13–0 lead after one quarter. When Chicago kicked off, William "The Refrigerator" Perry chugged down the field on coverage. Jobs like this usually went to second stringers and mid-sized players better equipped for a full-field sprint. Perry was a 300-pound defensive tackle, drafted in the first round. He didn't project as a special teams player by size or pedigree, yet there he was, chasing the play and breathing hard.

"They're so high on this Perry, but I don't know," my mom said. "I don't see it. What is he besides big?"

"Big's half the job, Jeanie," my dad said.

I sat with my legs spread-eagled on the soft new carpet, leafing through the latest issue of *Sports Illustrated* between plays, ignoring the pile of homework Mrs. Girouard had assigned. Most weekends I'd have procrastinated until about 7 p.m., after the late football game had ended, finished whatever I could before 8 p.m., and then gone to bed by 9:30 p.m. But this was Thanksgiving weekend, so I could immerse myself in football and push homework back until Monday morning.

I'd have left it until Monday night, except by then we'd have driven across town to my grandparents' place for their annual dinner party—us, them, and a few dozen of their white friends, in the pale light and stale air of their building's party room. Longest day of every year. We'd arrive before 4 p.m. and stay past 10 p.m. I hated it more than I hated the idea of taking ballet, but I didn't have a say. My grandpa set the schedule, and it didn't bother him to wait until the final phase of the last day of the long weekend to start the party. He was a musician, whose body clock said the day started at sundown. The rest of us had an extra day off and still went back to work and school exhausted. I wasn't slick enough to feign sickness and skip Thanksgiving dinner, so I let the Bears game distract me. I needed Sunday to last as long as possible.

Joe Montana lofted a pass toward the sideline. Roger Craig sprinted over and grabbed it, then fell out of bounds for a fourteen-yard gain, and the 49ers appeared, for a moment, to have solved Chicago's fearsome defense. A couple plays later, Richard Dent barrelled into San Francisco's backfield, wrapped his massive arms around Montana, and slammed the future Hall of Fame quarterback to the dirt. No opportunity to build on Roger Craig's catch. Against Chicago, a scoring chance could vanish just that fast.

"Ainno running from Dent," my dad said, before he rose from the couch and ambled to the fridge for another beer.

"Nope. Singletary either. Or Wilson. Or Marshall," my mom said. "That defense doesn't even give you time to *breathe*."

For my folks, it qualified as a long conversation. And with the Bears up by six points heading to halftime, the mood in the Campbell house felt as bright as the team's outlook that season.

I could fill pages explaining the ways the 1985 Chicago Bears shaped me. Player names burned into my mind like times tables. I can list them without glancing at a roster. Not just stars like Payton and McMahon and Singletary. Special teamers like Maury Buford and Kevin Butler. Role players like the two Dennises, Gentry and McKinnon. Backups and *their* backups, like Thomas Sanders and Calvin Thomas, Dave Duerson, Todd Bell, and Shaun Gayle.

By high school, when I had shed my preteen fat and grown into some speed, and they finally let me play tailback, I should have tried to run like Barry Sanders—to daylight at all costs, but for big gains because I could squirt through small openings and sprint away from pursuit. But I was raised on Payton, so I tried to run like him—around tacklers if possible, but straight through their chest plate if I had to, and often because I wanted to. Gaining yards mattered, but sometimes the message mattered more. Seven yards for me, and a bruised sternum for you. I'd take that tradeoff.

In the autumn of 1985, we built our schedules around Bears games. By then my parents' marriage was limping. They knew it, even if their kids didn't. My mom had figured out who my dad was meeting at the the Great Skate Place—same woman who went with him on those weekend excursions to Buffalo. He might have known she knew, but it didn't stop him. People have habits and need hobbies, and the affair, for my dad, was some of both.

Chicago Bears football gave our family a gravitational centre, an example of what you could achieve when you put your team before your pride. Without Suhey and Gault, Payton could have carried the ball more; Suhey could have racked up more yards if he wasn't always blocking for Payton; Gault would have caught more passes if the Bears didn't run so much. Instead, they all shared the ball, and the responsibility, so the team could prosper. Simple idea, but difficult to implement in pro sports, on a squad full of alpha males, where the team needs to win, but the big money flows to individuals who stand out.

Still, the 1985 Bears managed it. And if this collection of egos and interests could cohere into the NFL's best team, why couldn't a husband and wife do something similar? A successful NFL squad needs more than fifty people on the same page. A solid marriage only needs two.

My uncle Bobby and his wife, Eileen, moved to Toronto in 1967, the year after my mom's parents did, but my parents stayed behind in Chicago, still hopeful. Mom had a degree from Simpson College in Iowa, and a job downtown at Blue Cross Blue Shield. Dad finished his four years in the Navy, took some metallurgy courses at the Illinois Institute of Technology, then dropped those to drive a city bus. Back then, the move made some sense. A union job with good pay and benefits. And when he drove the southbound bus on Lafayette Avenue, he could hop out at 92nd Street to say hi to his folks if they were home.

My parents also had an apartment in South Shore and could walk to the lake in less time than it took a pot to boil. Proximity to the water and the quick drive to the downtown core should have made the neighbourhood one of the city's most desirable, but property values cratered as white residents fled to the suburbs. Panic-selling spread among petrified whites, and more Black families moved in. By the mid-1960s, people paying attention could recognize the cycle of integration and re-segregation.

My folks liked to escape Chicago, too, one weekend at a time. Friday afternoons, my dad would drive downtown in his gas-guzzling gold Corvette and meet my mom at the office after work. Then they would head east on I-94 and arrive in Toronto before midnight. They'd spend Saturday exploring the city, and on Sunday they'd pack the car for the sprint back to Chicago. The drive might take most people nine hours, but my dad and his Corvette covered it in closer to seven.

My parents loved that type of childless couple freedom, but they still wanted kids. Actually, they wanted several. My dad had two half-siblings but grew up as an only child, and always envied the full-house feel at the Jones home. But by the mid-1960s, with the Vietnam War escalating and the Civil Rights Movement turning militant and cynical, my parents found all the uncertainty unsettling. Why raise a son just to have the Army draft him, then ship him overseas to die fighting for a country that treated Black people's rights as an afterthought? It took 102 years to get from the Emancipation Proclamation to the Voting Rights Act. How much longer until society caught up with the law and treated Black people as equals? Another century?

Why raise kids with targets on their backs?

If other possibilities existed, why not explore them?

My parents wrestled with those big questions as they debated where they'd want their kids to grow up, and whether they'd have children at all. April 4, 1968, they got some answers.

Early that evening, Dr. Martin Luther King Jr. was shot through the neck while standing on a balcony at the Lorraine Motel in Memphis. His friends dragged his limp body back into his room and tried to stanch the bleeding, but he died within minutes.

Almost immediately, Cleveland, Buffalo, Cincinnati, and dozens of other American cities ignited in riots. Chicago did, too. Mostly on the West Side, home to more Black neighbourhoods, and the anger that festered after decades of systemic neglect.

Over on the South Side, my parents felt gutted, demoralized, and betrayed, resigned to second-class citizenship in their native country. That a Black man who made peaceful protest the organizing principle of his work could die by violence told my parents nearly everything they needed to know about the United States and their place in it as Black people. When James Earl Ray assassinated Martin Luther King Jr., my parents' hope that America could cure its racism died, too.

Richard Nixon's victory in the 1968 presidential election ensured at least four years under the leadership of a Republican Party that swung hard right in response to the Civil Rights Movement, and it pushed my parents closer to a reckoning.

They could have stayed and awaited a great awakening, a nationwide epiphany inspiring white Americans to shed personal prejudice and dismantle the systemic racism that benefitted them. But those

same white people had just elected Richard Nixon. Those same white
people ran to the suburbs when people like my parents moved to South
Shore. White people would rather drive an hour each way to work,
burning extra gas and precious time, than live near Black folks.

My parents could have chosen a different city. Detroit. Grand
Rapids. Cleveland. Buffalo. But de facto segregation ruled in those
places, too, and so did the cycle of fitful integration, white flight, and
disinvestment that turned thriving neighbourhoods into ghettos.
None of that was changing—at least not on my parents' timetable.

So they started calling immigration lawyers. And they called my
mom's relatives in Toronto and told them to get ready. By Christmas,
my parents had decided.

They were moving to Canada.

So, about ballet . . .

My mom liked the notion of a non-violent method of teaching
coordination and discipline and all that. I preferred the current way:
three classes a week at Mugen-Do Karate in Erin Mills, where I picked
up some of the values my mom thought ballet could provide. I learned
to tolerate the discomfort of knuckle push-ups and light taps with a
kendo stick from the sensei. I memorized kata and perfected my
movements: horse stance, cat stance, fighting stance; front kick, side
kick, roundhouse. Karate gave me a framework for self-discovery, and
a chance to explore cause, effect, and the link between hard work and
achievement. The satisfaction of earning a yellow belt, and then an
orange one. The thrill of winning a trophy at a tournament.

The byproduct of all that practice?

A repertoire of moves I could use on kids I didn't like.

I used to butt heads with a loudmouthed ginger named Jimmy
Bradford, on our street, in the park, and one day in fourth grade, in the
outfield of a baseball diamond at Meadowvale Village Public School.
Most days, we just jabbered and shoved. This day, he pushed me extra

hard and lobbed the exact insult you'd expect an obnoxious white boy to hurl at one of the few Black kids in the school.

When I heard "nig," I clenched and chambered my right fist, next to my hip, just like the sensei taught me. My knuckles hit his face the instant he finished "ger." I didn't even let him savour the taste of the word. Just dropped him with one shot. He hopped up and ran toward the school, holding his face and crying about a chipped tooth. If he ever said "nigger" again, he didn't say it to me.

Danny challenged me one morning at the bus stop. We were playing British Bulldog and one of us tagged the other too hard. Chest-bumping ensued. He pushed me, and I pushed back. He balled up his fists. I eased into a southpaw stance, right foot forward, but with my body turned sideways, like Bruce Lee.

When Danny charged, I timed him. Shuffle step with the left foot, side kick with the right. My foot in his gut, and Danny on his butt. The other kids laughed, and I smiled. Danny jumped up and rushed me again, and caught another side kick to the belly. One more trip to the pavement, with a crash-landing on his backside.

More laughter from the other kids. Danny scrambled to his feet once more, his face even redder than before.

"It's not *fair*!" he said, pointing at me and turning to appeal to the crowd that had formed around our little fight. "He's using his *karate*!"

Of course I was. My parents weren't sending me to piano class. I hoped to goad him into one more side kick, but the bus arrived.

So when Edward barrelled toward me one day at school, I figured I'd impale him on my deadly right foot. He advanced at a full sprint, and I waited in my Bruce Lee stance. When he neared striking distance, I gauged his speed and shifted some weight to my left leg, so I could shuffle, step, and jam a side thrust kick into Edward's belly.

Nine-year-old Morgan didn't understand the physics of this situation. Whatever I weighed, Edward weighed double, even at the same height. His body didn't offer flat surfaces, like Jimmy's face or Danny's belly, that I could dent with a punch or a kick. He was a boulder of a boy—as heavy at the bottom as he was up top—and round all around, and rumbling all his bulk toward me as I stood stationary, waiting. Mass times acceleration equals force, all three working together for Edward.

Shuffle, step, kick . . . my foot hit his chest a split-second before my own right knee hit my chin. In open space, Edward would have knocked me for a back somersault, but I stood between him and the wall of the school building. Worked out well for Edward's face, spared a full-speed collision with solid brick, but poorly for my spine, my knee, my chin, and my pride, all compressed under the crushing weight of Edward's momentum.

A teacher saw this all unfold and sped over to comfort Edward as I lay on the pavement, dazed and moaning in pain. From there, consequences cascaded because Edward wasn't Danny or Jimmy, whom even grown-ups found annoying. Teachers might have thanked me for smacking Jimmy, just so they wouldn't have to. People lost their jobs for that stuff, even in the 1980s.

But Edward was a Mode III student, among the best of the best performers on the standardized tests the school boards employed to separate the dullards from the normals from the bright kids from the geniuses. Mode III meant genius, so Edward and his classmates had special status in our school, the human equivalent of the fine china your parents displayed but never let you touch. He had done some acting and been written up in the *Toronto Star*, a student whom school officials liked and valued and strove to showcase.

And me?

A regular at the principal's office. They should have just moved my desk to the hallway outside to shorten the trip for everybody. In kindergarten, I kicked Mrs. Foster in the shin, and I *liked* her. The next year, when Mrs. Lynch tried to drag me by the collar away from some ruckus I started, I spat on her slacks. I liked her, too. I hit my sister Courtney with a backpack because she took the seat I wanted on the school bus. I tossed a pebble across the schoolyard that hit another girl in the head. She wasn't injured, thankfully. Just hurt. I didn't throw the pebble at her, but was old enough to know it would hit something or someone in a crowded playground.

And those are just the incidents that stand out among the more mundane trouble I caused most days. So, when the teacher saw Edward squash me against the wall, who do you think went to the principal's office: the kid featured in the *Toronto Star*, or the one who hopped onto a moving trolley to escape his teacher during a class trip to the zoo?

I can't say whether this particular fight triggered the Decision. I landed in the principal's office so often, and my mom fielded so many calls from the school detailing my bad behaviour, it's impossible to determine which specific act prompted the school to make the move. It's like asking which blade of grass makes a lawn.

Eventually we would learn this bad behaviour didn't spring from something outside our home. My friends didn't turn me into a trouble-maker, and neither did the Streets. Whatever caused my meltdowns would have done it to me anywhere. Mississauga or Toronto, Chicago, Detroit or Buffalo. But if my eruptions were a constant, then the variables, where and when all this happened, they mattered.

My parents didn't move to Canada thinking they could outrun racism forever. When you're Black and live in a country that's mostly white, you're going to wrestle with it somewhere on the spectrum between interpersonal and systemic. Maybe everywhere. Still, my sisters and I didn't have to contend with rednecks pelting our house with stones, or live in a city that spelled out, either by law or custom, where we, as Black people, had to live.

My folks also knew that racism didn't stop at the border. Like a police speed trap or bird shit on your windshield, it could show up anywhere, out of nowhere. Sometimes white people would sell you short because you were Black; you solved that problem by asserting yourself, and by being twice as good. And if somebody lobbed an N-bomb . . . Jimmy Bradford's dentist can tell you we were ready for that, too.

But Canada gave my parents a chance to live someplace where racism didn't seep into every aspect of their lives and shape where we lived or shopped or attended school. Which is to say, Canada gave us a chance.

I don't know where this story would have turned if it had unfolded in 2020, when the Ontario government published a report detailing systemic racism at the Peel District School Board and called the situation "dysfunctional." In the time between my experience at Meadowvale Village Public School and the release of that report, we don't know how many Morgan Campbells were steered into remedial programs or had their behavioural problems met with punitive solutions. Maybe they would have called the cops if I kicked Edward in 2020. Or maybe they'd have stashed me wherever they stuck bad-acting kids until I grew old enough to become some other institution's problem.

But we know the school-to-prison pipeline is real in racially segregated, class-stratified American cities. Later, on the other side of my hell-raising phase, my mom could point to 1985 and 1986 as a cluster of months that justified the move to Canada. Otherwise, what would have happened to a bad-acting, stone-throwing, karate-kicking Black kid in a place like Chicago? Tough to contemplate, but easy to imagine. Straight from the principal's office to the Pipeline, most likely. No margin for error, no digging for the root of the problem.

But at Meadowvale Village Public School, in the fall of 1985, school officials didn't let my skin colour, and chronic misbehaviour, blind them to the numbers. The standardized tests that put kids like Edward in a privileged class within our school also said I performed several years above my grade level. So, the same people dragging me to the office twice a month managed to see talent in a troublemaking Black boy. Instead of being scared enough to call the cops, they cared enough to call the school board, which had access to a network of psychologists.

Then they called my parents to ask how they would feel about sending me to therapy.

—

My dad and I met the first specialist early on a Saturday morning in the fall of my fourth-grade year. The facility could have passed for a pre-school: low-roofed with a small playground on a tiny street; east of Keele and north of the 401, a few minutes' drive from the De Havilland plant where my dad worked. The woman looked as plain as the building itself, white and skinny with frizzy brown hair pulled into a ponytail. She greeted us, then directed my dad into a waiting room, where he sat and opened a thick science-fiction novel. My dad's books changed, but until he discovered John Grisham in the early 1990s, they were different iterations of a similar type—bulky and set in another galaxy.

Then she ushered me into the room where we would work—cold, with white tiles under bright-coloured play mats. Tables and chairs ringed the edge of the floor, and one corner had boxes full of toddlers' toys, coloured balls and numbered blocks and shape-and-cutout puzzles. The therapist pulled some toys from the box and placed them on a table, then put me in a chair and sat across from me.

"Now, Morgan," she said slowly, as if English wasn't my first language. "Can you tell me which of these shapes is the square?"

I pointed to the blue cube in front of me.

"That one."

"Good," she said, her demeanour about as warm as the white tile floor. "Now, can you put the square in the square hole on this board?"

I did it, wondering why but saying nothing.

"Good," she said. "Now what about the triangle?"

I found it and slotted it into its spot on the board before she could ask me to. We continued like this for the rest of the session, her assigning me tasks that might not challenge a four-year-old, then congratulating me for completing them. I placed a ball in a basket on the floor, then sat with a pencil and copied a few pages from a big picture book about dinosaurs. None of this stuff required as much brain power as my schoolwork, or karate class, but the therapist with the frayed brown ponytail treated each feat like an accomplishment.

After the session, she directed me back to the waiting room, where my dad closed his novel and stood up. He thanked her, then led me out to the parking lot, where we loaded into his car, eased back out onto Keele Street, and headed farther north.

Dad didn't say much. He never did. But he seemed annoyed in ways I would come to understand as a grown-up. None of this stuff fit his budget. Not the money to pay two therapists, or the time carved out of his Saturday mornings to shuttle me to back-to-back appointments. Courtney and Dana had activities. The leaky kitchen ceiling needed repairs. So did the creaky garage door. And so did my parents' rickety marriage. My folks couldn't really afford all these psychologists, but they couldn't afford to let me keep messing up, either. My temper, the attention it drained from Dana and Courtney, all those phone calls from the school to my parents at work—those cost, too.

Dad and I turned left somewhere north of Sheppard Avenue. We rounded a few more corners and pulled into the driveway of a beige bungalow. In the living room, Dr. Gloria Yablo conducted therapy sessions with troubled kids like me, and in the foyer she had built a waiting room, where my dad sat with his thick sci-fi novel while Dr. Yablo started to try to figure out why I couldn't behave.

She looked older than my parents but younger than *their* parents, tall with curly greying hair. When I saw her, I thought of Dorothy from *The Golden Girls*. She smiled at me. Conveyed more warmth in thirty seconds than the first therapist had in a whole hour, which made sense. Dr. Yablo got paid to get me to talk—or at least draw.

She showed me to a box of toys in the living room and asked me to grab what I wanted and start playing. I picked up a pair of puppets tricked out with boxing gloves and had them spar for a few minutes while Dr. Yablo watched. Felt self-conscious, but I kept going until she brought me to a table where she had laid out some salmon-coloured construction paper and black markers.

"Draw a picture of what happens in your house," she said.

"What happens in my house?"

"Yes," she said. "Just on a typical day, what's happening? Who's there? What are you guys doing? Things like that. Can you put it in a picture?"

"I think so."

"Good."

"But I'm not very good at drawing," I said.

"That's fine. It's not art class. Just draw what you can."

My penmanship was as poor as my behaviour, which explained how I landed with that first therapist. Later I learned that my teachers thought my sloppy handwriting might signal motor control problems. In therapy, we all learned it signalled nothing. In terms of my body's ability to carry out my brain's orders, I was fine. I just wrote like a doctor.

Artistically, I never graduated from stick figures, but I fashioned a crude sketch, a cross-section of our house that I thought depicted daily life at home. Dr. Yablo returned after about ten minutes and asked me to explain what I had drawn.

"Who are these two?" she asked, pointing to the long-haired stick figures in an upstairs compartment of the house.

"Those are my sisters," I said. "They're fighting."

"Okay," she said, then pointed to two more stick figures, one tall and one short, that I had placed just outside the townhouse. "Who are these two people?"

"That's me and my dad," I said. "We're in the front yard, play-fighting."

"Interesting," she said. "And who's that last person inside the house?"

"That's my mom," I said. "She's with our dog, watching TV."

For the rest of the hour, I played and talked and drew, and Dr. Yablo watched and listened and asked intermittent questions. Afterward, she led me back into the foyer, where my dad closed his novel, then thanked her and brought me back out to the car for the thirty-minute drive home. The next few Saturdays followed that rhythm, an early wakeup and a long morning split between two therapists. Expensive and inconvenient and time consuming, but it at least left Sundays free for football.

So, about football . . .

In my mom's family, it opened wounds that never healed. Her brother, my uncle Bobby, the Phantom, wanted to join the team at Fenger High School, but their parents wouldn't sign the forms. Too small, they said. And he *was* tiny. Not much taller than my mom, who wasn't much taller than a fire hydrant. But my mom was also strong as steel; Uncle Bobby's limbs were about as thick as Duke Ellington's mustache. If he didn't have Willie Gault speed, his football career could have been short and painful.

His folks never let him play, and he never forgave them. When he vanished to California in the late 1970s, my mom wondered whether, all those decades later, her brother was still bitter over football. And when he materialized for a few months in 1991, he made sure we knew that both his young sons played.

My dad, six feet tall with broad shoulders and big fists at the end of thick forearms, was built for sports, but never pursued them. Part of him had an aversion to sweating or struggling or stumbling in public, all of which happens to every athlete eventually. Only way to ensure nobody ever saw him bruised or breathing heavily was to remain a spectator, so Pete Campbell left sports alone.

He also lived with an old-fashioned maternal grandmother who, when she discovered he was left-handed, spent his grade-school years working to convert him. She would tie his left hand behind his back and force him to write with his right. If she caught him using his left hand to raise a fork or scratch his cheek, she'd put a pocketknife in his right hand so he could go to the yard, find a tree, and cut the switch she would use on his backside. Of course, Grandma Lillie's home remedy for left-handedness failed. It just made my dad the opposite of ambidextrous. He wrote poorly with both hands and laboured to play catch with his son. He threw harder, but I threw straighter.

But football, like thorny personalities, ran in my dad's family because they were from the Midwest, where everybody knew somebody who took the sport seriously. My dad's half-brother, Ernest, was a standout high school quarterback in Grand Rapids, born a generation before most colleges up north would put a Black person under centre. Dad also had a cousin named LaRue, short and stout and shifty and fast, who played running back in high school and scored a scholarship to Marquette University in Milwaukee.

Both my parents learned early the difference between a good high school player and a future NFL star. They sat in the bleachers at Gately Stadium and cheered for Fenger as Dick Butkus single-handedly strangled their school's ambitions. City titles, state playoffs—the path to that stuff went through Chicago Vocational, which meant it went through Butkus, and nothing went through Dick Butkus, middle linebacker. Not NFL players during those years he spent with the Bears. Not Big Ten players during his All-American career at the University of Illinois. And certainly not high schoolers whose parents signed permission forms, not realizing they had consented to letting Dick Butkus body-slam their sons all afternoon.

By 1965, the year Butkus and Sayers joined the Bears, picked back-to-back in that year's draft, Butkus had already become a claim to fame for people like my parents. You see that guy manhandling NFL running backs? The one making the sad-sack Bears defense respectable by his damn self? We saw him play in high school. He kicked our asses.

After my parents moved to Canada, they supported the Bears from across the border. But my aunt Peggy, the lone Jones child still living in Chicago, cheered in person from Soldier Field's metal benches. She and her buddy Denise bought season tickets in 1981, and renewed the next season, and the season after that, even as the losses mounted and it looked like Payton's career would end like Sayers's and Butkus's had. Brilliant individual highlights. Zero team success.

The muggy summer air at preseason games in late August was suffocating, but at least a weather forecast could warn you about it. Nothing prepared Aunt Peggy for the Soldier Field spiders—hairy and black, fat-bodied and long-legged. They would sneak out from under the bleachers and inch over your shoe tops, or crawl along your limbs or up your back. Bold little creatures, but it made sense. They lived at the stadium. Football fans were just visiting.

Peggy and Denise survived late season games with help from their stadium neighbours, white guys from northern Indiana who smuggled orange liqueur into the park and shared it with people sitting nearby. Tasted strange but it helped keep you warm during those frigid games between Thanksgiving and Christmas, when the windchill might hit negative double digits.

But after three years, between the spiders, the cold, and the racist fans complaining about Vince Evans, the Black quarterback who lasted a season and a half as the Bears' starter, Peggy tapped out. After the 1983 season, she let her subscription lapse.

Payton was still producing, but about to turn thirty. That's young in real life, but the age NFL running backs break down and rust out like old cars. If you couldn't count on Payton to improve, then you also couldn't assume the team he carried would play any better next year. Somebody else could fight the heat and the spiders and the soul-shattering cold eight Sundays a year. She would watch the Bears from her couch.

Two seasons later, those losing teams morphed into *The 1985 Bears*, a team as tough and proud as the city they represented. The offense pounded you with Payton and Suhey, then sliced you wide open with Gault and McKinnon. And the defense overwhelmed you with co-ordinator Buddy Ryan's aggressive schemes, and hard-hitters at every level.

Singletary. Fencik. Wilson, Marshall, Dent.

Or William Perry, the rookie defensive tackle who weighed 300 pounds, which, by 1980s NFL standards, made him a giant. His college teammates at Clemson had nicknamed him "The Refrigerator," because he put away so much food, and in Chicago, he fleshed that character out. He spoke with a slight lisp and had a wide gap between his two front teeth. Sometimes his jersey, Number 72, rode up in the front to reveal his navel, and a belly that jiggled a little when he moved. In public, he embraced the Affable Fat Guy archetype. William Perry, the Fridge. Half man, half mascot.

But Perry was also nimble and strong, and fast for his size. Less a refrigerator than an actual bear. By trade, he played defensive tackle, but as the season progressed, Ditka would deploy him in the offensive backfield, either alongside Payton or instead of him. Always as a novelty, but also with intent.

He carried the ball twice against San Francisco. The next week, against Green Bay, Perry lined up as running back again, but I didn't see those plays. It was a Monday night game, with a 9 p.m. start that bumped up against my bedtime. I slunk to the living room floor just before kickoff, and tried to disappear into the carpet, hoping my folks would forget where I was. They did not and sent me upstairs at 9:30. Ten hours later, as we each moved through our morning routines, my mom saw me in the kitchen and recapped the action with the zeal of a teenage boy.

" . . . and then they put the Fridge in the backfield," she said as she dumped a spoonful of Horlicks malt into her chocolate milk. "I couldn't believe Ditka did it, but he did. The Fridge bashed through there and opened up a big hole, and Payton just walked into the end zone."

I poured hot water on my instant oatmeal and squirted some extra maple syrup into the bowl because I liked porridge that tasted like pancakes. After a splash of evaporated milk, I took my spoon and mixed the oatmeal till it thickened. Mom kept talking.

"Next time down the field, they put the Fridge back there again, and they gave him the ball."

"What happened?"

"What do you think?" she said. "Green Bay wasn't gonna stop that big galoot. Three hundred pounds with a running start? Shoot."

Bears 23, Packers 7.

From there, Chicago stomped Minnesota, then throttled Green Bay again. Then they hosted the Detroit Lions and pummelled them, too. The Bears totalled sixty-seven points in those three games. Their opponents managed twenty-two.

The next Sunday, another road game and another lopsided win over an opponent that was supposed to pose a challenge.

Bears 44, Dallas Cowboys 0.

We watched that game together, my parents at opposite ends of the big couch and me on the floor next to Bandit. Even my sisters came down from upstairs to check in. I should have spent the afternoon preparing a presentation for Monday morning at school. Each week, a couple of students had to give the class a short speech on a topic of their choosing. Good students treated it like homework and showed up with cue cards and a peppy delivery. I viewed it as a nuisance and procrastinated until I blew it off. When I stood up in front of my class on Monday, I hadn't prepared a damn thing, so I talked about the Bears, their perfect record, and their one-sided thrashing of the Cowboys in Texas. I talked Payton, of course—my first favourite football player—and Mike Richardson, who intercepted a Danny White pass and glided through a throng of Dallas tacklers to score a touchdown.

I closed by reminding my class that the Bears hadn't lost all season, and that they would probably finish the regular season undefeated, and then win the Super Bowl. I didn't know if they liked football, and I didn't care. The Bears meant more to me than the assignment had, so the whole class had to endure my ode to them.

Optimism bubbled up from Chicago and wafted across the border to my parents. A Bears toque showed up at our house. And then a headband. And then some non-licensed Monsters of the Midway sweatshirts that deftly omitted the team's logo or proper name. Either my folks had ordered that gear, or relatives just sent it. Beyond our house, consensus was building that the 1985 Bears weren't just good, but ready to make NFL history. Ten games into the 1985 season, the

Bears had ten wins and few prospects of losing. Only one team had finished the NFL regular season undefeated and gone on to win the Super Bowl—the 1972 Miami Dolphins. The 1985 Bears looked set to do it next.

Amid all that winning, the Bears cut a rap song called "The Super Bowl Shuffle," and spent one of their scarce in-season days off recording a video. They didn't all rap. Solo verses went to a handful of standout players whose rhyme skills, like the drum machine and synthesizer-driven instrumental track, were a crude parody of rap you might actually listen to. The songwriters fashioned verses from the two main components of rudimentary early '80s rap: couplets and arrogance.

The video shows hulking players crowded onto a stage, in their navy jerseys and shiny white pants but without pads, the starters rapping and two-stepping up front, the role players in back filling out the chorus and the band. Payton rhymed first, Perry rapped last. Shaun Gayle on bass, Maury Buford on the cowbell. Broad-shouldered fullback Calvin Thomas strutting around with an alto saxophone, looking about as comfortable as Cannonball Adderley would blocking for Payton. But these guys didn't claim to be musicians or even rappers. Between verses, the featured guys and the chorus would serve up a refrain:

> *We're not here to start no trouble,*
> *We're just here to do the Super Bowl Shuffle*

———

My dad stomped on the accelerator, and his off-white Hyundai Stellar shot forward as we merged onto the eastbound 401. Mom, riding shotgun, gripped the door handle. Courtney, in the back seat behind her, sat with her hands folded across her lap, straight-faced, as if Dad's stop-go-and-swerve charge through rush hour traffic didn't jolt us like a roller coaster ride. Dana peered out the rear driver's side window, her head bobbing each time the car jerked to a stop or sprung into motion. Between them, nine-year-old Morgan, the youngest and still the smallest, but too big to fit comfortably between my two sisters. I barely needed a seatbelt. Wedged like a sardine between Courtney and Dana, I wasn't moving. The car's rear end sagged. The engine growled. Dad pressed the accelerator again and ripped through the gears.

He hated arriving late, and we had a 7 p.m. appointment in Downsview with Dr. Yablo for an exit interview. After several weeks of Saturday afternoon play therapy, she would update me and my folks on what she had learned and lay out a game plan to make me less of a hellraising, bad-tempered brat. My parents still didn't know why all of us needed to attend. I visited the principal's office more often in one term than Courtney and Dana did all year, every year, combined. Either way, my dad aimed to arrive on time, which, for him, meant five minutes early. But none of the other drivers clogging the 401 knew his schedule. They dawdled and he tailgated. They puttered. He dive-bombed between lanes and lectured.

"C'mon now," he said to the driver of the Ford van, muddling along in the passing lane. "Drive your car, man!"

"The doctor's not going anywhere, Pete," Mom said. "We'll get there either way. Don't mess around and get a ticket."

Dad eased off the throttle.

A touch.

We had a tight timetable. First Monday in December, Bears versus Dolphins with an undefeated season and all that history at stake, starting at 9 p.m. If we lingered too long at Dr. Yablo's or lollygagged in traffic, we might miss kickoff. In the fall of 1985, the Campbells didn't gamble like that. But if we showed up early and talked fast, we could arrange ourselves in the living room in time to watch some of the pregame hype on ABC.

No normal family would force those priorities to compete. Debriefing with the therapist who could help reprogram your son's bad behaviour should justify missing the beginning of a football game. But we weren't a normal family, and Bears-Dolphins wasn't a normal game. Nobody left on the schedule could even give the Bears a headache; it was the last real obstacle between Chicago and a perfect record.

Our parents herded us into Dr. Yablo's house at minutes to seven. My sisters and I peeled off our jackets and scarves and piled onto the couch. Mom and Dad occupied the loveseat across from Dr. Yablo, who sat, legs crossed, in her chair, holding a notebook and pen. She had my parents describe their daily routines and how we all interacted, knowing she could already guess the answers based on our conversations and my stick-figure sketches. Me and my dad doing one thing, my mom doing something else, not with us. My sisters, either playing together or bickering. Courtney and Dana listened. My attention drifted. Dr. Yablo and I covered this stuff every session.

She wrote in her notebook as my parents described the families that raised them. Mom shared details we already knew about growing up with her parents and grandparents in that big wooden house, the lone Black family in a white neighbourhood. Dad introduced new information about his family. I knew he had two parents at home, and a half-brother in Grand Rapids, but beyond that he never volunteered details, and I wouldn't have known which questions to ask.

"My daddy liked to drink on the weekends," he said. "Sometimes he'd hit my mama."

At nine, I didn't recognize all the ways my dad was falling short as a partner. Didn't husbands sometimes take weekend trips without their wives? But the stuff he described about his own dad was unambiguous, even to a fourth-grader with no real idea how healthy marriages worked.

Dr. Yablo closed her notebook and laid it on the coffee table, then placed her pen on top. She folded her hands and looked at my parents. Mom made eye contact. Dad glanced down at his watch, then up at the ceiling.

"The problem with Morgan's behaviour isn't Morgan," she said. "Fundamentally there's nothing wrong with him. He's smart. A good student when he's motivated. He doesn't have any behavioural disorders that make him act up."

I looked at my parents, then at Dr. Yablo, then back at my hands in my lap. Courtney and Dana stared straight forward. My mom turned her head to look at my dad, who finally engaged Dr. Yablo.

"So what's the problem?"

"Not Morgan," she said. "It's you two. Your marriage. As far as I'm concerned, Morgan's done here. He'll be fine as long as you two fix your marriage. But your marriage needs work. It's in trouble."

If Dad wasn't happy with his marriage, he never verbalized it. But he didn't need to. The time and energy he invested at the Great Skate Place, and on those dates with Marla that started Friday night and ended Sunday morning, made it plain. Even if Mom didn't know everything, she knew enough. And if she hadn't known their marriage was *the* problem, she recognized it as *a* problem. The current setup couldn't last. Either they would fix their partnership, or it would keep splintering until it disintegrated. Mom knew which option she wanted, and felt vindicated when Dr. Yablo told them to mend their partnership. Maybe the therapist's warning would be the boot to the backside my dad needed to start putting his wife first.

"I understand about the marriage," Mom said. "God knows we're scuffling. But what does that have to do with Morgan acting up?"

Dr. Yablo explained that even if I couldn't put words to the tension between my parents, I felt and reacted to it. Every temper tantrum and every stunt that landed me in the principal's office was actually aimed at them, a child's attempt to force co-operation between spouses who barely spoke. Mom leaned in and listened. Dad sat there, still except for the clenching and unclenching of the muscle in his jaw.

"So what now?" my mom asked.

That, Dr. Yablo said, was up to them. If they wanted to fix my behaviour, they needed to fix their marriage.

Dad glanced back at his watch, that jaw muscle still working. Mom placed a hand on his forearm.

"What about it, Pete?"

Dad said nothing, as usual, at first. He had spilled a week's worth of words describing his dad's drinking and spousal abuse and didn't have much talk left over for this question.

"Well?" Mom asked.

"We'll see," he said.

"Think about it," Dr. Yablo said. "It's not convenient. It's work, but it's worth it."

Dad looked at his watch again. Minutes ticked toward kickoff.

"We'll see."

Half an hour later, my dad backed the car into our driveway, hopped out to open the passenger-side door for my mom, and hurried into the house. Courtney and Dana headed upstairs to get ready for bed. I followed my parents into the living room. Digital clock on the new VCR said 8:58. Two minutes until the broadcast started and nine minutes until kickoff, enough time for me to scurry to my bedroom, change into my PJs, and sprint back downstairs.

Dad turned the TV to ABC and found his spot on the couch. Mom made herself a cup of hot chocolate and sat at the other end. I dashed back to the living room and splayed out on the floor, hoping to stay below my folks' line of sight, feeling the way I would years later, at the start line before the 100 metres, or at the five-yard line, waiting to receive a kickoff. Aroused. Eager. Amped. I would settle down once the Bears wrestled Miami into submission, which I figured would happen sometime in the second quarter. Until then, I'd have to grapple with nerves.

When Miami quarterback Dan Marino connected with wide receiver Mark Duper on a pass play that saved the Dolphins from third-and-26, I dismissed it as a fluke. Miami couldn't make those plays all night. Not if the Bears kept manhandling them on first and second down.

A few plays later, Marino fired a quick pass to Nat Moore, who caught it near the left sideline. From here, a skilled cornerback, trailing the play by a quarter step or less, would arrive a split second after the ball and either bat it from Moore's hands or wrap the receiver in a bear hug and drive him out of bounds.

But the Bears didn't have a skilled cornerback shadowing Moore, who caught the ball and turned to face Gary Fencik, a slow-footed free safety who hit hard, but treated man-to-man coverage like a chore. Moore's jab-step toward the sideline left Fencik lurching, and opened the alley through which Moore accelerated, past Bears defenders and into the end zone.

Miami 7, Chicago 0.

My dad: "*Sheeeeeit.*"

My mom: "Hmph."

Me: silent, so my parents would forget I hadn't gone to bed already. If I slunk low enough, and stayed quiet enough, maybe I could stay up to see Chicago take the lead.

"Morgan," my mom said. "It's past your bedtime."

"But can't I just watch the first half?"

"No."

"But how will I know who won?"

"I'll tell you in the morning."

"But what—"

"*Morgan.*"

Dad, with authority. Voice deep as a bass line. He wasn't negotiating.

"*Git.*"

So I got—up off the floor, out of the living room, and upstairs to bed. I didn't know what my folks said to each other after that, whether they discussed Dr. Yablo's warning or just focused on the football game. I just knew that when I woke up Tuesday, Dad had already left for work, and Mom was stirring Horlicks malt into her chocolate milk when I walked into the kitchen to make my oatmeal.

"Hey, boy," she said. "Bears lost."

"No!"

"Yep."

"What was the score?"

"38–24."

I couldn't process it. The Bears hadn't coughed up thirty-eight points combined in all the games I had seen that season, but Miami did it in one night? The numbers didn't compute.

How?" I asked.

"They couldn't stop that Mark Duper," Mom said. "Or Clayton. Or Nat Moore. And McMahon got hurt, so Fuller had to play quarter-back. I'm surprised that fool's even *in* the NFL. I can throw a football farther than he can."

I filled a mug with water, placed it in the microwave, and pressed a few buttons. The machine hummed and I tilted my head down, reminding myself that I was too old to cry over a football game I didn't even play in. Mom heard me sniffing.

"It'll be fine, Morgan," she said. "It happens sometimes. They just lost."

Dr. Yablo created an opening. When Mom tried to sneak through, Dad closed it the way Mike Singletary shut down running lanes—with non-negotiable force.

"So what do you think about counselling, Pete?" she asked him later, sometime after the Bears lost to the Dolphins. "I think we should do it."

"Nope."

"You heard what she said. We need counselling."

"Which one of us got marriage counselling money?"

"Why does that matter? We can't afford to let Morgan keep acting up like this, Pete."

"If *you* want to go to counseling, you can go," he said. "Ain't nothing the matter with me."

Our family had one driver's licence and one car, and my dad owned them both. Was Mom going to take the bus from Streetsville to Downs-view every week? That's at least four hours round-trip, not counting the hour spent with Dr. Yablo. Nobody had that kind of time, especially not a working mom with three kids and a limping marriage. Telling her *she* could go to counseling was telling her nobody would go. If Dad had a better plan for reviving this partnership and keeping me out of trouble, he didn't share it.

A month later, Sean Landeta held the ball in both hands out in front of him, waist high, part of the process preceding the perfect punt. Catch the ball, extend your arms, and turn the ball on a slight diagonal. Step with your left foot and let the ball drop. Swing your right leg to meet it. Hit the ball right and it'll rocket off your foot and fly fifty or sixty or seventy yards downfield, in a spiral so tight it'll look like you threw it.

But Landeta, just a few steps from his own goal line, in the first quarter of a playoff game between the New York Giants and Chicago Bears, didn't hit it right. He didn't hit it, period. A gust of frigid wind sideswept the north end of Soldier Field and blew the ball off course before it could reach Landeta's right foot. He missed everything, like a batter swinging through a curve ball. Like he was Charlie Brown, with Chicago's infamous wind playing Lucy. Bears fans afterward nicknamed him Sean "Let Me Kick the Ball" Landeta.

He played twenty-one years, won two Super Bowls, and made three All-Pro teams, but my mom never let go of that one moment. The rest of his career, playing for the Giants, Eagles, Rams, or Packers, whenever my mom saw him on her TV, she'd react the same way.

"Hey, there goes 'Let *Me* Kick the Ball'!" she would say. "I'm surprised he's still playing."

The ball hit the turf. Shaun Gayle scooped it and trotted five yards to the end zone, giving the Bears their first points in a game they would win 21–0. A predictable, one-sided drubbing before a conference title game against the Los Angeles Rams.

They worried me a little, mainly because of Eric Dickerson, their prototype of a tailback. Like Payton, he embodied a mid-'80s Black athlete aesthetic. Both built better than anything a human could engineer—fast and nimble as a Ferrari, yet as durable as an Army Jeep. Except that Dickerson, at six-foot-three and 220 pounds, towered over Payton. Where Payton accented his Jheri curl with a bright white headband, Dickerson complemented his with Kareem-style sports goggles. And, like Payton, he ran hard enough to make defenders calculate the cost of tackling him. You could get him to the ground, but, like your parents would lament at spanking time, it would hurt you more than it hurt him. Dickerson rushed for 2,105 yards in 1984, a single-season record. If he treated Chicago's defense like Payton treated everybody else's, I thought he could cause problems.

I thought wrong. Seventeen carries, forty-six yards. That's all the Bears allowed him, which meant Dickerson performed better than the Rams did overall. The entire squad managed just 130 yards of offense. Against lesser defenses, Dickerson could produce that much on his own.

Against the Bears, the Rams could only sputter until they stalled. In the fourth quarter, Richard Dent barged into the Rams backfield and flattened quarterback Dieter Brock, knocking the ball from his hands. Wilber Marshall grabbed the fumble and sprinted toward the Rams' end zone. Dickerson chased him down and grabbed him by the collar. Marshall brushed him off like dandruff. Dickerson hit the turf as the first flurries of a cold afternoon fell, and Marshall ran to the end zone for the game's final touchdown. The whole 1985 season in one play. Chicago's defense breaking the opponent's will like a brittle bone. The city and its weather imposing themselves like a twelfth player. Another one-sided win.

Bears 24, Rams 0.

Our parents didn't tell us whether they would start marital counselling, like Dr. Yablo advised. After that meeting in December, our lives just slid back into familiar rhythms. Work and errands for my parents. School, choir, and karate for my sisters and me. Dad would drink beer with Dave, his buddy from up the street, struggling to keep his own marriage upright, and sometimes he would still step out to the roller rink. I never saw my parents leave the house together for counselling, or date night, or anything else couples do to keep their marriages healthy.

One afternoon, Mom sent me to fetch something from her bedroom and I saw a book on the dresser, slim with a mustard-coloured cover and black writing. On the front, the black outline of a rectangle with rounded corners, the long side stretching from margin to margin. Inside the outline, in block letters, the book's two-word title.

CREATIVE DIVORCE

I understood the words and should have known why one of my parents was reading it. Probably my mom. But I wouldn't let myself make the connection. Convinced myself that divorce was a remote option and not a close possibility, or that maybe the most creative divorce was the one that didn't happen. I viewed the book the same way I did Nat Moore slashing through the Bears' defense on *Monday Night Football*. I saw a fluke, when maybe I should have seen a warning.

As a competition, Super Bowl XX, between the Chicago Bears and the New England Patriots, underwhelmed. Chicago put up forty-six points. New England, just ten. Most of that scoreline as predictable as the winter wind on Chicago's lakefront. The chief plot twists were that New England scored and that Walter Payton hadn't. Sweetness watched from the sideline as Mike Ditka plugged Perry in at running back—a garbage-time touchdown on a novelty play, and a snub to the greatest Chicago Bear in history.

But as a spectacle, and an excuse to throw a family-wide party, it delivered. We piled into Dad's car, and we drove downtown to Uncle Jeff's house. Aunt Peggy flew in from Chicago. My mom's parents even drove out from Mississauga. They didn't often occupy the same room as my dad did. Not on purpose. They would tolerate each other at close range only on holidays, and the Chicago Bears' first Super Bowl appearance qualified. This was bigger than Thanksgiving. Christmas without the gifts.

When the final gun sounded, players flooded the field at the Louisiana Superdome. Photographers from TV networks and wire services followed. Perry and another Bear hoisted Ditka onto their shoulders. Payton, somewhere off camera, fumed. His bitterness with Ditka would ebb, but never fully subside.

Everyone in Uncle Jeff's living room shouted and clapped and traded high-fives as if we had won the game ourselves. Uncle Jeff's phone rang. Aunt Mike, down in Chicago, calling to join the hollering. My dad put on the same proud half-smile he'd wear years later, when Dana would give a recital or I'd score a touchdown. He put an arm around my mom. She squeezed him around the waist.

"Too bad we couldn't shut them out," my mom said. "But I'll take it."

We stayed later than was healthy. Sunday-night functions made for sluggish Mondays, but I'd survive the next day for the Bears' sake. Sometime after 10 p.m., we drifted out of Uncle Jeff's house, across a snow-caked sidewalk, and into the car. Mom clipped her seatbelt into its buckle. Dad released the parking brake, depressed the clutch, put the car in gear, and eased it out onto the street.

Dana sat behind him, grasping the handle above the door. Courtney sat behind my mom, arms folded across her lap, staring out the window. I was the youngest, so I sat in the middle, my legs straddling the hump. A tighter squeeze this time. We were all six weeks bigger than in December, swaddled in winter clothes.

We hadn't sat three abreast like this since the ride to Dr. Yablo's office. And we wouldn't again until the next autumn, when our parents lined us up on the couch to tell us they were separating.

On Becoming

"So, what, class, explains why *The Birth of a Nation* was such a popular film in Canada?"

Mr. Maloney, up at the front of our classroom, southwest corner of the second floor, igniting the kind of discussion that was supposed to separate the enhanced learning program from the civilian curriculum at the Woodlands School. We all studied from the same textbooks, within the same framework, but enhanced learning classes, like this one, Grade 10 History, were populated with the top scorers on the standardized tests we all endured in junior high. On our side of the bottleneck, we had smaller class sizes, more attention from the teacher, and in theory because we learned the basics so quickly, the freedom to dive deeper on stuff like this. Fraught topics. Serious subjects. Material that needed critical thought. Regular kids memorized names and dates. Enhanced learning students could move beyond knowledge to understanding, from recalling facts to interpreting them.

Several confident hands went up. Grade 10 Enhanced History. These kids were used to having answers.

"Technology," said one of the white guys down front.

"Right," Mr. Maloney said. "But let's be more specific. What set this film apart?"

More hands. More confidence.

"Colour tinting and new editing techniques. Movies before this didn't have flashbacks," the white boy behind me said.

I sat at my desk, centre column, two rows from the back, and forced myself to listen. Forced, because in most of my classes, I talked. A lot. Not participation. Just wisecracks and idle chatter until the teacher told me to quiet down. But I had crammed Grade 10 History into the second semester of Grade 9, hoping to open up some space on my timetable the following fall. The enhanced learning program cohort in my grade had a sprinkling of Black kids—me, Ian, Andre, and Kahan. But the crew a year ahead of me had zero. I didn't know the other kids in Grade 10 History, and I preferred it that way. So I kept quiet in class, lest these strangers learn something about me besides my name. But knowing somebody would lure me into this particular discussion, I listened and waited.

"You guys are correct," Mr. Maloney said. "Griffith shot this film with panoramic shots and camera angles people hadn't seen before."

In a normal building, I could have gazed out the window while I awaited a chance to set this conversation straight, but the Windowless Woodlands School, on Erindale Station Road in Central Mississauga, wasn't normal.

Check that. An art class downstairs in the school's east wing had a window. So did a first-floor classroom on the school's northern flank, with views of yellow portables, McBride Public School across the yard, and, if you wrenched your neck hard enough, the patch of concrete between the school and adjoining public library where hardcore slackers would puff cigarettes between classes. Or during them.

But the Woodlands opened in 1969 as an open-concept school, and the second floor was a broad expanse of carpet without walls, hallways, or any other barrier between students and creativity. Teachers set up their classes wherever suited them, and students sat on the floor.

Eventually the school went conventional, and the patchwork conversion of the second floor, from free-range learning space to a series of discrete classrooms, morphed into a permanent solution and gave us the building we inherited. Thin walls that bled sound between rooms. A dust-coloured carpet on the floor. A block of classrooms in the middle of the upper level, and a hallway that ringed them like a moat.

At either end of the corridor, you could look out a bank of windows at the schoolyard between classes on a sunny day and catch some natural light. But inside the classrooms, we just had drab walls and dull carpets, and fluorescent rods embedded in the ceiling behind panels of frosted plastic. Regardless of the weather or time of day, every second-floor classroom looked the same, all the time. Sort of like going to school inside a casino.

At least we had clocks. I glanced up. Class was only half done.

I looked around the class to see if anyone had raised a skeptical eyebrow, or had even a hint of how the conversation would turn if somebody hit on the truth. Weren't these the smartest kids around? Not just in the school, but in the whole city?

I raised my right hand, high, so Mr. Maloney wouldn't miss it.

"Morgan," he said.

"This movie was called *Birth of a Nation*, right?"

"Right."

"Do you guys know what nation was being born?"

Silence. A surprise if you saw these kids as the 98th percentile and a group who always had answers. Less of a shock if you noticed, like I did, that they were every colour but Black.

"This movie is about the Ku Klux Klan."

"I hadn't realized that," Mr. Maloney said.

"Right," I said. "So I'm saying . . . that movie was popular because Canadians were racist."

"It's possible," Mr. Maloney said. "But that doesn't mean people weren't also attracted by the new technology."

"Yeah, but they didn't leave the theatre when the Klan started killing Black people," I said.

"Okay," said the same white boy behind me. "But how can you be sure it was racism, and not the new technology?"

I didn't have time to contemplate white people's willingness to cover for folks who weren't even trying to hide their racism, and how much progress we could make if white folks stopped giving benefits of doubt to people who didn't even want them. Too busy wrestling with the business end of that reality.

"People knew what this movie was about," I said. "The technology doesn't even matter. Would you watch the Blue Jays if you hated baseball?"

"Fair enough," Mr. Maloney said.

To the extent that my classmates knew me, they didn't think of me as a guy who tried hard. And I didn't like school enough to do supplemental reading, so they were probably wondering where I had unearthed all these facts.

But I knew this stuff.

Somewhere between the strikes and layoffs and recalls at De Havilland, but before the hungry years that followed the divorce, my parents found money to buy a VCR. Finally. Among kids I knew, my family was the last to have one. The first winter after we hooked it up, my parents started taping Black History Month programming from WNED, the PBS affiliate from Buffalo. The recordings would live among our fast-growing stacks of VHS cassettes, alongside Courtney's soap operas, my boxing compilations, and the hip-hop video mixtapes that were always under construction.

After midnight on a Friday or Saturday, when everyone else had gone to sleep and I had the living room to myself, I might slide a tape into the VCR and watch Nigel Benn go to war with Iran Barkley for a single frenetic round, or Mike Tyson and Razor Ruddock pummel each other for seven. I might rewatch a week-old episode of *RapCity*, which we recorded every Thursday on MuchMusic, or I might watch a PBS documentary on the racist imagery that bubbled up from the post-bellum South to supply the entire world with a fresh set of anti-Black tropes. The watermelon-eating coon. The broad-boned, big-breasted, bandanna-wearing mammy. The razor-toting jigaboo. All manner of Black folks, who, in the white imagination, were ill-suited to life off the plantation, went from the brains of white creatives to books and popular songs, and from there to the minds of everyday people, where they hardened into stereotypes.

Benign portrayals looked like Uncle Ben and Aunt Jemima: happy, if wistful, former captives who felt the same nostalgia their owners did for the placid years before the war. The sinister images showed up in D.W. Griffith's film adaptation, released in 1915 of the novel *The Clansman*, published in 1905, in which Black folks, without slavery to keep them in line, had gone feral. Without the brave and righteous knights of the Ku Klux Klan restoring the social order with force, who could even imagine what damage these unleashed Negroes would have done to Southern civilization?

When the film hit theatres, it sold out movie houses across the continent. Our textbook laid out that detail without addressing the film's plot, which would have meant explaining how Griffith portrayed the Klan as heroes, which would have meant acknowledging something awful about the white Canadians who packed theatres to watch this movie. Better to focus on the technology than to concede that racism didn't end at the 49th parallel. My first year of high school: an early education in the power of willful omission.

"It's like you're calling all Canadians racist," another white guy said.

"Well, they probably were."

"I THINK WE CAN AGREE," Mr. Maloney said, shouting over us to make us quiet down, "that racism likely contributed to this film's popularity in Canada. But we can't discount the appeal of the new technology."

I shut up and let the class continue. Another early lesson, this one in compromising to keep the peace, even when you know you're right. Which doubled as a lesson in regret.

I had already flipped through the whole textbook, looking for pictures of Black people, and only found one: Ben Johnson, swaddled in a puffy jogging suit, carrying the torch before the 1988 Winter Olympics in Calgary. The textbook was published sometime between the photo and Johnson flunking that drug test at the Olympics in Seoul.

Besides that, no Black person in Canadian history had ever accomplished anything noteworthy. No scientist. No soldier. No politician. Not even the Black predators—white actors in blackface—herded up by the Ku Klux Klan and chased over cliffs to grisly deaths in *Birth of a Nation* rated a mention.

I glanced back at the clock and let the conversation move on, and spent the remainder of class the way I did the rest of the semester: seething and feeling written out of the script.

PART II

For my sister Courtney, Saturday nights meant going out. She had a best friend named Nikki, who had an older sister named Shelly, who had a driver's licence, access to her parents' car, and permission to stay out late. Every weekend they'd head into the city, to the all-ages jams that let you mix with Black kids from across the GTA. If you're Black and grew up in Toronto, and hit adolescence in the late 1980s or early '90s, you made friends and enemies and lifelong memories at places like Spectrum, on Danforth Avenue, in the east end of the city, on the way to Scarborough. Or the Oakwood-Vaughan Ballroom, in the heart of what people now call Little Jamaica.

For me, those places only lived in stories other people told. I didn't have older friends with cars and licences, or the freedom to creep into the house just before dawn, so I had no real social life. Instead, I had a bookcase crammed with issues of *The Ring* and *Sports Illustrated* that dated back to grade school. Saturday nights meant pulling out magazines to form a stack, then reading my way through them, cover to cover, feature by feature.

I probably should have spent that time studying. Other people in my position—C average, without much happening outside of school—might have. After two years in the band at Dolphin Senior Public School, I had quit playing saxophone, and didn't even join any sports teams my first year of high school. I had time.

But other people made schoolwork a priority. I was satisfied with C's if I could make those grades without studying. Homework, for me, was whatever I could squeeze into the single hour I set aside for it every Sunday afternoon. Making time for a study routine would mean scrubbing something else from my weekend schedule.

But what?

Not *Saved by the Bell* or *NBA Inside Stuff*, which aired back-to-back on Saturday mornings on WGRZ. And not noontime wrestling on WUTV, a childhood habit that followed me to high school. It should have abated by Grade 10, but only intensified when Ric Flair came to the WWF and started a feud with Randy Savage. Only college football—a big game with a noon kickoff—could prompt me to leave Macho Man and the Nature Boy alone for a week.

And certainly not *The Power Move Show*, which aired on CKLN, 88.1 FM, every Saturday from 1 p.m. till 4 p.m., but if you grew up near Toronto, listening to hip-hop, you knew that already. And if you knew you'd be busy on Saturday afternoon, you probably popped a cassette into the deck, hit record, and went on with your day, like I used to. You also likely had a library of *Power Move* tapes that, like mine, shrank by attrition. A few tapes eaten by renegade cassette decks, a couple more lost in a move, some lent to friends and never returned.

RapCity tried to cover a wide range of hip-hop music, from east coast backpack rap to the gangsta shit from California, but over on 88.1, DJX's sets leaned toward the east coast incipient rap snob stuff I preferred. Black Sheep and Tribe. UMCs and Gang Starr and the EPMD family tree—Redman, K-Solo, and Das EFX.

So, if you want to know why, as a ninth grader who didn't play in the school band or on any teams, or have a girlfriend or any real hobbies, I put off homework despite having nothing better to do . . . I had plenty better to do, every Saturday afternoon. Why wrestle with abstract concepts from math class, or slog through another stale story from English class, when I could connect my headphones to the record player and cue up "Microphone Fiend"?

> *Any entertainer*
> *I got a torture chamber*
> *One on one, and I'm the remainder*

Sports Illustrated had started showing up in our mailbox late in the summer before fourth grade. My first issue featured Pedro Guerrero on the cover, sprinting out of the batter's box in his white Los Angeles Dodgers uniform, dry Jheri curled hair puffing out from under his helmet, his eyes on a ball he had just launched beyond the infield. I hadn't asked explicitly for a subscription. Maybe I had mentioned to my parents that it would be nice to have one. They found the money and placed the order, probably hoping they could use sports to lure me into a reading habit. And here I came, like a roach to a poison motel.

By prime-time Saturday, Courtney would have vanished for the night, and I'd be in the living room with my mom, the dog, and my stack of magazines. I didn't have a card for the city library, and barely used the one at school, but I knew my *SI* features.

Curry Kirkpatrick on Deion Sanders.

Gary Smith on the simmering tension between Buster Douglas and his father, Bill.

Ralph Wiley on Thomas Hearns.

And Rocket Ismail.

And Grant Fuhr.

Ralph Wiley on anything and anybody, because he wrote about boxing, which I loved, and because he was the first Black sportswriter I could name. That detail meant something to me long before the idea of becoming a journalist flickered into my teenage brain. His back-of-the-magazine feature on Sugar Ray Robinson, and the cost boxing imposes on fighters and the people around them, stuck with me then, and sticks with me now. That story sent me to the dictionary, to learn the meaning of the word *usurped*.

Saturday nights with Gary Smith and Ralph Wiley. I had time to study—just not for schoolwork. If you had asked me for a list of my favourite writers, I could have named a few. I just never saw them in class.

PART III

Mrs. Morgan, petite and tanned with blonde hair, darker at the roots, strolled from desk to desk with graded copies of the previous week's test, placing the stapled pages face down on the table in front of each student. English 2AE only had about sixteen kids, so it didn't take long to hand back our in-class essays on *To Kill a Mockingbird*. I leaned back in my flimsy plastic chair, hands behind my head, fingers laced together, and waited. For once, I had actually read the entire book. I thought I had handled the test well, but one year and half a semester into high school, I had settled into a C average, so I kept my expectations low.

She paused when she placed my test on my desk, face down.

"Great job, Morgan," she said. "You should do this more often."

I flipped the papers right-side up. Line after line of blue scrawl: my handwriting, which people have compared to a doctor's, or a chicken's claw marks in the dirt, or the way humans would write if we didn't have thumbs, so sloppy my fourth-grade teacher referred me to a specialist to check for a motor-control deficit. Mrs. Morgan might have deciphered it and seen some lucid prose, or she might have slogged through until she broke down and gave me a decent grade to honour my penmanship's victory over her patience.

Mrs. Morgan had written a number in black ink in the top right corner of the page and circled the figure so I wouldn't miss it. I peeked at it, then turned the paper face-down again, trying to stifle a smile.

"Guy, what did you get?" asked Vivek, my deskmate and partner in classroom shenanigans.

His heritage was Indian, and no parts Black, but he had hair kinkier than mine and, if we're trafficking in stereotypes, was at least four times the basketball player I was. When the rest of the class discussed *Lord of the Flies* or *Romeo and Juliet*, Vivek and I huddled at the corner table, talking hoops and hip-hop. Except Vivek took school seriously. Graduated a year early to start at U of T, and grew up to become a therapeutic plastic surgeon, helping cancer patients and accident survivors rebuild their bodies and self-esteem. I slacked in class until the last semester of my last year of high school, and matured into a news reporter, then a sportswriter, and then a professional smart-aleck.

"What did *you* get," I asked.

"Eighty-five," Vivek said.

"I got ninety-two," I said, flipping the test paper over and slapping it on the desk like a draw-four in a hot game of UNO.

"YOOOOOOOO!" Vivek said, holding a clenched hand toward me so we could bump fists. "That's amazing!"

"I know!" I said. "I knew I did well. Didn't think I got an A."

Within half a minute, the rest of the class had figured out who scored highest—not just between Vivek and me, but among all of us. They didn't react like he did. Vivek pumped me up like I was Muhammad Ali and he was Bundini Brown. The other kids cut their eyes and whispered. They were friendly most of the time, but competitive always. These kids weren't Black—mostly Asian and white—and had scored above ninety on enough tests to expect it all the time. So if my ninety-two set the curve, they all had to do some quick math on how scoring in the eighties would affect their mid-term report cards.

Because every test was a competition, they didn't expect to lose to me. Ever. Not in math class, where I dozed off while they did extra work for fun. And not even in English, on a test about a novel with Black characters. They knew me as an indifferent student, and the guy who lobbed wisecracks from the back of the classroom.

Except this one, on the first floor, in the east wing of the Woodlands School, had rectangular tables, each with a pair of chairs, but not enough students to fill the space. Mrs. Morgan shepherded us into the cluster of tables near the door. Our classroom didn't have a back, so Vivek and I found a spot in the corner.

Vivek sat with his back to a bookcase, which contained dozens of titles we ignored and a dictionary, which one of us would grab, open, and search. When either of us found a word we liked, we would challenge the other to use it in an assignment.

Ephemeral.

Cornucopia.

Stultify.

Poor Mrs. Morgan, navigating papers from a couple of teenagers larding their writing with words we didn't quite know how to use. Did she laugh at us, the way I did at Oswald Bates, the big-word-spouting prison orator Damon Wayans played on *In Living Color*? Or did she react the way I did the summer after Grade 10, when I read Eldridge Cleaver's *Soul on Ice*, and keep a dictionary next to her whenever I handed in an assignment?

I wouldn't deal with Cleaver for at least another six months. But that semester, *To Kill a Mockingbird* provided one of the few hints our curriculum ever gave us that racism had actually existed anywhere on the continent. Our textbooks were as silent on *Birth of A Nation*'s appeal to Canadians as they were on the federal government's reasons for shipping Japanese Canadians to internment camps during World War II, while people of German and Italian descent mingled with white Anglos and continued living free across Canada. But *To Kill a Mockingbird* made racism simple to address and contain. It happened forty years before we read it, in fictional Maycomb, Alabama, a thousand make-believe miles south of our classroom in suburban Toronto. So, school boards could concede that racism had, in fact, happened. Just not in Canada, and certainly not, according to what our classes served us, anymore.

Thankfully, I knew people who could bridge those gaps. My mom had told me about a train trip she had taken as a grade schooler with her aunt Edith, from their family's home in Chicago to the Family Home in Ruston, Louisiana, and moving from an integrated cabin to a Colored car when the locomotive crossed from Illinois into Kentucky. At one stop somewhere down south, my mom, parched after hours in a dry train car, wandered to the nearest water fountain and pressed the button. Before the water hit her lips, Aunt Edith ran over, snatched my mom, and guided her to the Colored fountain before any white folks could witness the crime.

So I brought some cultural capital to this reading of *To Kill a Mockingbird*. It felt like Grade 10 History again, except this time folks couldn't pretend Black people didn't factor into the story and that racism didn't shape white people's attitudes.

"For real, man," Vivek said. "That's awesome."

"I actually read the book this time."

"You didn't read *Romeo and Juliet*?"

"Most of it," I said. "But I knew we were watching the movie in class."

I was glad Vivek didn't ask me to explain why this essay turned out so well, because I couldn't have done it. The writing felt easy, in a way I would recognize later when I had become a half-decent football player. Time slowed down in my mind. The hour Mrs. Morgan gave us to write the essay felt like a whole day; the gap between thought and action vanished, and I synthesized information on the fly, the way an athlete reacts to a developing play. So, as I addressed race and class and power in the segregated South, I also weaved in a quote from Jesse Jackson and tied it to the lives of the downtrodden Black folks in Maycomb.

"Suffering breeds character, and character breeds faith."

Of course, I didn't get that quote straight from Jackson. I cribbed it from a *Sports Illustrated* profile on Scottie Graham, fullback at Ohio State who prayed as hard as he trained. Another layer of understanding what my classmates lacked, and a rare time my fixation on sports actually enhanced my classroom performance.

As an adult, I would recognize that feeling as the one that bubbles up inside a sportswriter on a tight deadline. No time to search for words, and no need to do it. Writer's block? A luxury for people with spare hours to spend ruminating on the perfect sentence. When an editor needs seven hundred words in thirty minutes, your thoughts crystalize instantly. You start with a full brain and a blank page, and empty the words from your skull. If you're prepared, the writing goes smoothly and the story makes sense. And if you finish a few minutes before deadline, you do a sweep for typos and sentence fragments. Do it daily for five or ten or twenty years and it comes as easily as breathing. You publish some great stories, and you take them, but you learn that great stories aren't a deadline writer's job. Your task is to write good stories, fast, every night.

It all lives at the opposite end of the literary scale from creative writing, which, for me, is a soul-sapping slog on the best days. Writing a column is like cooking a steak. You collect the ingredients, you prep, you cook, and you eat. You might have to think fast and multi-task, but it's safe work with a quick payoff.

Creative writing is more like slaughtering and butchering a steer. Grueling, dirty, bloody labour, shearing skin from muscle, and muscle from bone. You might lose a digit. You might lose your nerve. But if you keep hacking, you'll eat for weeks, not just a day. And you'll feed the whole family, not just yourself. That payoff is supposed to justify the danger and the bone-deep fatigue. They're both ways of putting food on the table. One leaves you full and happy, and the other exhausted and covered in guts.

"So maybe you should read the whole book next time," Vivek said.

I shrugged.

"Maybe."

Mrs. Morgan strode to the front of the room to start the day's lesson. I stared at the top right corner of my test paper, at the grade she had written and circled in black ink. I lingered on the satisfaction of having the highest score in the class. Part of me wanted to experience it more often, but that would have meant developing some study habits. At fourteen, I was more likely to develop liver spots. I should have savoured the feeling longer.

To my right, Vivek had already fetched the dictionary. While Mrs. Morgan talked about Tom Robinson, Vivek leafed through the pages, searching for my next word.

PART IV

My eyes followed my right index finger as I traced it along the spines in my family's living room bookcase. *Poems That Live Forever. The Rise and Fall of the Third Reich. A Concise History of Canada.* I needed something to read. A better student would have started with the stuff my teachers assigned but that I barely touched. Maybe give *The Merchant of Venice* another shot, or one of the Margarets my English teachers loved but I could only use as a cure for insomnia—Laurence, Atwood . . . were there others? Maybe. I couldn't tell. The hip-hop-addled brain of a tenth grader didn't work that way.

A few days previous, I had seen Leaders of the New School perform on *In Living Color* as the closing credits rolled. Three rappers from suburban Long Island, bouncing like pinballs around the stage, dressed in matching denim-on-denim getups, pale blue and baggy, with thick strips of sequin-studded velour across the shoulders and around the shins. Dinco D, Charlie Brown, and Busta Rhymes pumping each other up before launching into the first verse of "Teachers." Above them, on the balcony of a sound stage apartment, their DJ, Cut Monitor Milo, manned twin turntables.

Leaders treated high school hallways like gangster rappers did the drug corner—as the setting for, and a character in, almost every story. They cast structural racism as a potent force shaping public education, and in "Teachers," Leaders of the New School made the case that white-run public schools were the place fertile Black minds went to die. If their first single, "Case of the PTA," hadn't primed you, Dinco D makes it plain in his opening line.

"Don't ring the bell," he says. "I'm not coming to class!"

Busta rapped last. He always did. He rapped the fastest, so he ran anchor. He also rapped the loudest and had a knack for delivering quotable lines, on Leaders' songs or anyone else's. Technically, he was a guest on "Scenario," that legendary posse cut on A Tribe Called Quest's *Low End Theory* album. But the line most people can recite from memory? Busta, on the last lap:

RHAOW RHAOW, LIKE A . . .

. . . if you've heard the song, you can finish the sentence.

But the rhyme in "Teachers" that hooked me came halfway through, from Charlie Brown, who had spent the bulk of his verse laying out the ways public schools brainwashed bright Black kids. In his last stanza, he suggested his own solution.

"I say just educate yourself," he shouted into his cordless mic. "Don't depend on your school for help. Read and write. It's evidence. 'Cause these teachers? Yo! They be teachin' us *nonsense!*"

That line didn't have a right to touch me as deeply as it did. I shouldn't have needed a rap song to jump-start my curiosity.

In the after-school-special version of my life story, the *To Kill a Mockingbird* essay would have triggered a wholesale transformation and prompted me to overhaul my priorities *and* my study habits. Acing that test would have been like the moment in Frederick Douglass's autobiography, preceding the fistfight with his master, where he foreshadows how profoundly his life is about to change: "You have seen how a man was made a slave; you shall see how a slave was made a man."

Except the test wasn't a turning point, just an example of what I could achieve when interest and opportunity aligned. And it did highlight for me just how few Black faces we saw in the pages of our English and history books. There might have been a Black guy in "The Most

Dangerous Game," which we read in Grade 9 English. "Brian, the Still-Hunter" had one for sure; he had a name—Mollineux—and a cow, which he sold to the narrator, but no other details that made him remarkable. We never learn if he had a family or a profession, or an engrossing story about how he landed in Southern Ontario in the 1850s. Was he a one-off or part of a larger Black community? The text didn't tell us, and Mollineux's Blackness didn't advance the plot. He didn't need to be Black. Just happened to be. The narrator mentioned it and moved on, and so did my class.

Grade 10 English felt like a semester at Hillman by contrast. We had a unit on mystery writing, which meant we watched *In the Heat of the Night*, which meant we saw Sidney Poitier play Mr. Tibbs. And, of course, *To Kill a Mockingbird* gave us Tom Robinson and the long-suffering Black people of Maycomb.

But we also had Piggy, the chubby nerd in *Lord of the Flies*, who, watching his marooned classmates divide up into rival tribes, begs them to stop acting like a bunch of "spotted niggers." Other folks in the class didn't have a problem with the N-bomb. I did, and made Mrs. Morgan tell everyone to scratch the word out before we continued. A few pages later the Spotted N*****s roasted Piggy over an open flame like an actual hog.

So, when Leaders of the New School appeared on my TV on a Sunday night in 1991, rhyming about how public schools made Black minds atrophy, I listened more closely than I might have a year earlier, or a year later, when a Black history class first appeared on the Woodlands School's curriculum.

The objective truth is that I attended a very good school. We had dim windowless classrooms, but bright students, small classes, and access to extra-curricular activities—if I were interested, which I wasn't. But by fourteen, I could perceive, even if I couldn't verbalize, that I needed something my school couldn't provide. I was curious, but vulnerable. I wanted answers, but also armour. An anchor. A connection to something wider and deeper and heavier than myself and my immediate experience. If I couldn't have a community the way the Jamaican and Indian and Chinese kids in my school could, I still needed something. Protection. A weapon against anyone who wanted to minimize me— white racists, of course, but also Caribbean Canadian kids telling me Black Americans had no culture, because culture, to a lot of them, was what you brought with you to North America. Their template had no space for people like us, with roots on the continent, so my sisters and I would wind up on the "where are you really from" hamster wheel.

My dad tried to help.

"These niggas wanna know what island you from," he would say. "You tell 'em Stony."

If you didn't know that Stony Island Avenue is a major artery on the South Side of Chicago, maybe *you're* the one with no culture.

Still didn't address a school curriculum, drawn up by white people, that said Black people—Canadian, American, Caribbean, or other— barely existed, and certainly hadn't written anything worth reading.

So, I stood in front of the big bookcase, looking for . . . something. Adam Smith, de Tocqueville and the Federalist Papers, left over from a book club my mom had joined back in Chicago, back in the day. The bulky sci-fi novels that stayed behind after my dad moved out. The *Concise History of Canada* that didn't mention a single Black person; I knew because I had looked—repeatedly, the way you do when you're sleepless and hungry, opening the refrigerator every half hour, hoping if you try enough times, you'll finally find something worth eating.

I could have begun this book search at school, where our library ran the length of the second floor. Or at the public library's Woodlands branch, which wasn't much bigger than a classroom, but was connected to our school, downstairs, facing McBride Avenue, next to the smoking section. That year the city also opened the Central Library, five storeys tall, stocked with titles, at Burnhamthorpe and Confederation, a short ride from my school on the Route 6.

But I didn't need all that choice, just a text or two to get me started.

Spicy enough to hook me, but short enough to suit my attention span. So, I searched for books the way I did for music, by checking out my parents' stash first. When I flipped through their LPs, I would set aside albums whose covers featured the biggest Afros or gaudiest drawings, the most sequins, or the tallest platform shoes. Then I would play the records, listening to each song the way my dad had taught me, from the bass line up.

That's how I discovered War, who, to a man, including the white guys, sported some of the puffiest Afros on the planet. When I heard "Slipping into Darkness," I recognized the bass line right away as the sample that formed the backbone of "Rock Dis Funky Joint" by Poor Righteous Teachers, the hip-hop one-hit wonders from New Jersey.

It's how I found *Togetherness*, the album by LTD whose cover featured a picture of nine winged sphinxes, sitting in a semicircle around a bulbous heart, the whole tableau floating above and in front of a city skyline in the distance. The lead track, "Holding On (When Love Is Gone)," stuck with me. The wet-and-dry hi-hat cymbal, bass drum like heartbeat, and crisp snare, all under the fat, funky bass line that flowed beneath Jeffrey Osborne's brassy tenor.

And it's how I got deeper into the Isley Brothers, whom I heard almost nightly on *The Quiet Storm*. There was Ron Isley on the front cover of *Live It Up*, shirtless in a shiny gold tuxedo with bell-bottom pants and a wide-lapelled jacket. Two spots to his left, his brother, Ernie, in red leather pants and a crop top with baggy sleeves, made of multicoloured leather panels that would open out like a Chinese fan when he raised his arms, which he did on the back cover. The wardrobe made LTD and War look plain as the Penn State football team's white-on-white uniforms.

Back at my parents' bookcase, I zeroed in on a small and slim paperback, bright orange letters on a black background.

THE FIRE NEXT TIME
JAMES BALDWIN

I pulled the book from the stack. It felt heavy in my hands, like the words themselves gave it weight. A paperback, brittle even then, with beige pages browning at the edges. Still, it seemed like an entry-level text for a new reader—140 pages, big print with plenty of air between characters.

"Hey Mom," I called out. "This book . . . *The Fire Next Time* . . . is it yours or dad's?"

"Both of ours, I guess," my mom said from the kitchen. "But I bought it."

"What's it about?"

"It's about being Black in America, and what racism does to us, and how it's all gonna blow up in white people's faces one day."

"Oh," I said, flipping through the pages, the smell of decaying paper wafting into both nostrils.

"That's what the title means," my mom said. "The first time God destroyed the world with a flood. But when Black people rise up, there'll be fire. And look what happened after this book came out: riots everywhere. Newark. Detroit. All over."

"Is it any good?"

"I think so," she said. "But you'll have to read it yourself."

I needed a bookmark, so I grabbed a stray playing card. These pages were dry as winter skin, and I was scared creasing a corner might make the whole thing crumble. Holding the book in my hands, I wasn't sure it would survive daily reading. I would have to bend the spine gently. So, I cradled it like a newborn as I carried it upstairs to my bedroom, where I retrieved my backpack and slid the book into the front pocket. The next day, on the long bus ride to school, I would become a reader.

The first of my many readings of *The Fire Next Time* lasted three days, because of the big type and small pages, and because I refused to put it down. Thirty minutes on the school bus each morning, and another half hour in the afternoon. On page 94, a passage my mom had underlined in blue ink.

Most Negroes cannot risk assuming that the humanity of white people is more real to them than their color. And this leads, imperceptibly, but inevitably, to a state of mind in which, having long ago learned to expect the worst, one finds it very easy to believe the worst. The brutality with which Negroes are treated in this country simply cannot be overstated, however unwilling white men may be to hear it.

My first time reading Baldwin, I hadn't lived long enough, or in the right places, to know any of that like Baldwin did. Like a reaction, learned by rote, or through bruising lessons, the way a boxer learns to slip and counter. It felt deeply experienced, universal and elemental, like a law of science so self-evident you'd never think to question it, like gravity itself.

My mom knew that kind of racism the way Baldwin did. Not as a notion but as a reality, a force that molded decisions and dreams and outcomes. She had grown up in a white neighbourhood in Chicago, attended a mostly white college in Iowa, and heard the stories the old folks told about the South. My mom didn't need James Baldwin or anyone else to tell her whether the average white American placed their colour ahead of their humanity—or hers. But she and a lot of other Black Americans felt vindicated to see somebody put it on paper.

I didn't know that paragraph was true; I accepted it as truth because Baldwin wrote it, and my mom underlined it. I was curious and searching; they were experienced. I was reading about it; they had lived it.

If I had permission to make marks in my mom's book, I'd have underlined one of the passages early in its second section, about turning fourteen, and how, in Baldwin's Harlem, that milestone marked an abrupt transition to adulthood. He and his peers stopped thinking like kids and began bracing for the "long, cold winter of life." White kids could dream of graduation and good jobs and moving to tidy houses in the suburbs. Baldwin, at fourteen, thought about how he would deal with discrimination and disappointment. Education not attained. Promotions earned but never bestowed. Decades in a ghetto never intended as a base from which Black folks could launch fruitful lives. Just a place for us to live, settle, and die, unless we could work an angle.

> *Every Negro boy—in my situation during those years, at least—who reaches this point realizes, at once, profoundly, because he wants to live, that he stands in great peril and must find, with speed, a "thing," a gimmick, to lift him out, to start him on his way. And it does not matter what the gimmick is. It was this last realization that terrified me . . .*

The dilemma felt familiar. I recognized it from the countless profiles I had read in magazines and seen on TV about Black kids from bad neighbourhoods who grew into world-class athletes while friends with less talent or drive or luck bundled up for their version of Baldwin's Long Winter. The motif hadn't yet, for me, calcified into a cliché, but it was headed that way, fast. Some quotes, you could plug in before you even read the story, and just mix-and-match the details, like fridge magnet poetry.

"Without football/boxing/basketball, I'd be dead/in jail/gangbanging," said Williams/Johnson/Jenkins.

None of it described my life.

My parents had moved to Canada to raise children someplace that, unlike Baldwin's Harlem or their Chicago, didn't foreclose on Black kids' possibilities before puberty peaked. My mom's dad saw Canada as an actual Promised Land, where Black folks could flourish just as freely as white people did. My parents figured it was the least racist place Black folks could reasonably expect to live: the best choice among imperfect options. Didn't mean we would never have to navigate racism, but in Mississauga we could, in theory, delay the big decisions Baldwin faced upon turning fourteen. My sisters and I could get diplomas and degrees, and *then* make serious, trajectory-setting choices. Why subject your kids to the pressure of knowing our whole family's chance at something better depended on one of us hitting on a gim-mick before we finished middle school?

I didn't need to superimpose Baldwin's circumstances onto my life, but I did, with gusto, and it spooked me. Two weeks from turning fifteen, I still didn't have a whiff of a gimmick. My birthday would put me a full year behind schedule.

Whatever I thought my gimmick might become, I'd have to find it beyond my immediate family. It wasn't going to be music.

For my mom's folks, it was the family trade; not just a job or a hobby, but a craft and passion, a career and a capital-B Business. Still, it started as the exact kind of gimmick Baldwin described seeking at fourteen. My grandfather was ten when his parents bet the family's future on him, withdrew his older sister from junior college, and fun-neled her tuition money into his piano lessons.

The alternative?

Everyday jobs for everybody, at the library or the lumberyard or the dining car of some passenger train. Stable vocations and realistic goals for Black folks of that generation without college degrees, but those careers had hard ceilings. Music at least offered the possibility of a pay-off, and the kind of windfall that could vault a whole family higher on the social class ladder. That was the hope.

The reality?

My grandpa used to tell a story about being in his mid-twenties and between engagements, living on the top floor of his parents' house, with my grandmother, their three young kids, and kitchen cupboards that were empty except for one can of beans. Then he got a call. For a gig. At a strip club. Playing for go-go dancers. He took it, and got paid, and didn't have to figure out how five people could make one can of beans last until his next booking.

Whether you find playing piano while half-naked women gyrate more or less noble than keeping white people's houses, or pouring molten steel into patterns, depends on how your values run. But recognize that the gimmick is still a gamble. It's not a ticket to riches. Just to the lottery.

My bass-playing uncle Jeff had JUNO Awards on his mantel and gold and platinum records on his wall. So many golds and platinums that he gave some to my grandparents to display at their place. He could see them every day when, in his mid-forties, he moved back in with his parents because gigs had grown so sparse. He drove his mom's car for a couple years. Took a day job. Joined the actors' union and started showing up as an extra in made-for-TV movies filmed in Toronto.

He wasn't some jobber. This was a self-taught prodigy of a bass player, and member of some legendary Canadian rock bands. Ocean. Red Rider. The Infidels. But this was also the music business, about as stable as a first-timer's surfboard.

I could only imagine the vastness of the gap between playing in the middle school band and being good and lucky enough at music to pay the bills and feed a family. As I matured, I stayed happy just imagining. I never wanted to find out first-hand.

But that picture would develop over years. When I first read Baldwin, I was deep into my second year at the Woodlands, the school I chose because of their enhanced learning program, and because after two years playing tenor sax in the junior high school band, and private lessons my family couldn't really afford, I didn't bother auditioning for the arts program at Cawthra Park Secondary. Dana had just graduated from there, and her voice would ring in the hallways for months afterward. Or for years. Might still be ringing today. I could have hired John Coltrane himself to tutor me, and I'd never have played sax as well as Dana sang. Didn't need people reminding me of it every day until I graduated.

As for sports . . .

Still just something I did, in season, without wondering where they would lead me. No serious off-season training, and no fantasies about playing on TV. Ninth grade, I skipped football entirely, still too slow to be that small and hope to get anything out of it except squashed. My school didn't have a team the next year, so I rejoined the city league, got good at a lot of positions but not great at any of them. We played Saturday mornings, and I would return to the house in time for the second quarter of a college game. I would watch and enjoy, and wonder how it felt to run as fast as Terrell Buckley and Desmond Howard, but did I envision myself doing what they did?

Not then.

And what about writing?

What about it?

That was Baldwin's calling, not mine. I didn't even own a spare notebook, and wouldn't have known how to start writing a journal, never mind a novel or a memoir. A career in journalism seemed about as feasible as one in the National Hockey League—something other people did.

But *The Fire Next Time* had me on a timetable. I'd never be fourteen again. I granted myself an extension, but figured I would need a gimmick before I turned sixteen. That or brace for a boring life.

I couldn't make that call yet.

So I kept reading.

CHICAGO, 1992:

Equipment for Living

"**W**e're going to visit your aunt," my dad said, as he turned the key in the ignition, and the small but powerful engine in his black Suzuki Swift growled, then purred.

"Aunt Peggy?" When we visited Chicago with one parent, we didn't usually hang out with the other parent's folks.

"Aunt Julia," my dad said.

"Whose sister is that?"

He released the parking brake and put the car in gear.

"Mine."

We headed south on Lafayette, then turned left on 95th while I did the math.

We didn't have a reason to visit Chicago that summer, but we didn't need one, any more than you needed a reason to hug your spouse, or to stop by your mom's place. They're there and you care, so you do it. Dad had the second half of July off work, so he drove down. Dana and Courtney had summer jobs. I didn't, so I rode with him.

We all knew about Uncle Ernest, my dad's half-brother—older, but not by much. He grew up in Grand Rapids with his mom, which explained why we had a branch of the family there, and he died in a car crash the summer before my parents' wedding. We visited his widow, my aunt Emma, almost every summer, and Granny Mary treated them all like blood relatives. She kept Uncle Ernest's portrait in her living room, next to my dad's. I hadn't heard of Aunt Julia before this instant, so I figured she was another kid from my grandfather's early adulthood, before something compelled him to settle down with Granny Mary.

"Your older sister?"

"Younger," my dad said, eyes on 95th Street.

We rolled east in midday traffic. Outside the passenger side window, Abbott Park, where my dad's family had a reunion a summer or two before the divorce. Avenues ticked past. Michigan. Indiana. Prairie, which my dad and some of his buddies pronounced "Puh-rairie," maybe to distinguish it from Perry Avenue, in the same general section of the South Side, a few blocks west of the stretch of Interstate 94 Chicagoans call the Dan Ryan. We crossed King Drive and could see Chicago State University on the south side of 95th; on the north side, Langley Avenue, where my great-aunt Edith still lived.

A quick left on Cottage Grove, then another quarter mile north and we'd arrive. The whole trip from Granny Mary's took, maybe, six minutes, and my mom would have filled that time telling me every-thing she thought I needed to know before meeting Aunt Julia. Age, kids, where she grew up, who her mom was. My mom didn't tell the abridged version of any story. My dad had, of course, already shared everything he thought I needed to know about his half-sister: existence, name, position in the birth order. The rest, I could fill in myself.

By fifteen, I knew their communication styles. My mom, detailed as sheet music. My dad, sparse as a chord chart. My mom, the Oscar Peterson of storytelling and lecturing: lots of notes and long detours, but always, eventually, playing the song. My dad told stories like Thelonious Monk played solos, music both in the notes and the silence between them.

If this was a song about Aunt Julia, it was also about Prines Campbell Sr. and his life outside his job and his marriage. So what meaning was I supposed to read into the empty spaces?

Until now, my dad mostly conveyed details about his father with sporadic handfuls of heavy words, sharing information in the fewest syllables possible. If you asked where his dad was from, my dad would just say, "Mississippi."

And where did he work?

"Steel mill."

You couldn't prompt my dad to talk, but sometimes, something might trigger him. He might see a rare classic car, say, a 1941 Willys American coupe, like the one the Campbells owned when he was a kid, and he'd give us a little more.

"Your daddy used to drive one of those."

Your daddy meaning *his* daddy, who had forearms like Popeye and a taste for Kentucky bourbon.

Or at a family reunion: "See how that girl looks like Dana? That's from your daddy."

One night when we attended counselling as a family, one of the final attempts my parents made to repair their marriage before the split, my dad did finally release a few more facts about his father. The drinking and staying away overnight. The weekends he would beat on Granny Mary. All new information to me.

In contrast, for my mom, "talking mood" is a factory setting. If I showed her a photo of her father-in-law wearing a fedora, like he did in 90 per cent of the pictures I've seen, she'd fill in some of the gaps, no incentives necessary.

"There goes Pete's dad," she'd say, "in his I Gotta Go Drinkin' hat."

In the pictures, even a stranger could see the son in his father. Same nose, arrow-straight, but round at the tip. Similar skin tone and cheek bones. And if you knew us well enough to look, same ulnar bone pro-truding where the outside of the wrist met the base of the hand—all the Campbells have it. There were exceptions: the father also had shiny, wavy hair that didn't quite curl; skin half a shade lighter than the son's by default, but changed with the seasons, from medium-brown, to sort of light, to "Are you sure that guy's not Puerto Rican?"

Other stuff, you couldn't see in pictures. My mom said he had a smile that could make you melt, and a deep speaking voice, resonant but soft at the edges, oozing charm when he felt like engaging you. Except you couldn't predict those moments, only his drinking. The binges began when the workweek ended and lasted till sometime on Sunday. Mondays meant a return to work as a pattern maker (a detail I learned from Granny Mary) at Inland Steel (info my mom volunteered), then sobriety till Friday night, when the cycle started again.

That Aunt Julia existed told us what happened some of those weekend evenings when he'd vanish till morning. New notes to the song, but still in tune with what we already knew about Prines Campbell Sr. Complicated man. Faithful to his sons and job and drinking schedule, if not to his wife.

My daughter, Nova, at eighteen months, looked exactly like her first cousin, Mica, at the same age. Place a baby picture of my sister Courtney alongside them and you'll think you're looking at triplets. And my big sister, Dana, as a baby looked enough like the other three that, even at a glance, you'd know they were family and wonder which common ancestor had the strong genes.

"That's from your daddy."

Not my dad. His dad. Prines Campbell Sr., whose two sons, half-brothers a couple of years apart, looked like identical twins.

About a month before the cancer diagnosis, walking through Woodland Mall in Grand Rapids, a middle-aged Black dude watched us pass, then wrenched his neck trying to keep his eyes on me and my dad, looking at us like he'd seen a ghost. I don't say this as cliché or even simile: the man really thought he had seen somebody go from Grand Rapids to heaven and back.

"Ernest Brazil!" the man said. "I thought you was dead!"

"Naw, that was my brother," my dad said.

The man looked relieved, like most of us would upon learning we weren't insane or hallucinating. But he also seemed a little disappointed that this reunion with his friend wouldn't happen. Uncle Ernest hadn't just moved to Chicago for thirty years. He really did die in that car crash a few weeks before my parents' wedding.

Uncle Ernest was a standout quarterback in high school and, apparently, a very popular adult. His funeral made the news—for a few reasons. The second was the procession, which stretched for at least a mile, knotting traffic as it snaked through the city.

The first reason?

The fight.

The service took place in a Black church in a changing neighbourhood. That's how my mom described the area, and most other places in the States where Black people lived alongside white ones. *Changing*, because *integrated* implied permanence, or at least stasis. Neighbourhoods in big American cities changed from white to Black after a few African American families would arrive and white incumbents would panic-sell and abandon the city. And they changed from Black to white when they gentrified. Somewhere in those transformations, you could see integration in a snapshot, but only a time-lapse photo could tell the story. Neighbourhoods didn't stay integrated. They just changed over.

Inside the church, it was the kind of funeral my mom always hated—long and hot and sad, with an atmosphere that ranged from mournful to morose. Understandable, since they were burying a beloved man in his twenties, leaving behind a beautiful wife and a cute little daughter, my cousin, Khadijah. But the pastor wasn't there to comfort the grieving family. He prodded until he got what he wanted: mourners collapsing in pews and falling out in aisles. Every person who fainted, the preacher took as a signal to turn up the heat. Longest afternoon of my mom's life.

Outside the church, a white woman and her two grown sons, lounging on the front porch of their home, already presumably pissed about the neighbourhood's gradual blackening, fumed as Black folks flooded in for this funeral. When the service finally ended, as people streamed out of the church and toward their parked cars, the woman and her sons, from the perceived safety of their house and their whiteness, launched the kinds of catcalls you'd expect from people abandoned by white flight, too broke to flee themselves, and bitter about it.

N-word this . . .

Monkey that . . .

Go back to Detroit/Alabama/Africa . . .

My dad and some cousins heard it and, naturally, weren't having it. Uncle Ernest's death had hit them like a punch in the gut, and now came this slap in the face. The mom and her sons should have known to brace for a comeback.

PWT this . . .

Ya mama that . . .

We ain't goin' nowhere till we got damn good 'n' ready . . .

We'd have a different story if the white woman and her sons had been satisfied with insults. Maybe they believed that deeply in their privilege, and the force field they thought whiteness provided. The neighbourhood was turning Black, but they were still white and might have figured things would work out, the way white people do when they climb Everest or run with the bulls in Pamplona.

Either way, the mom shoved her sons off the porch, like a hockey coach sending enforcers over the boards to settle some dumb score. The sons ran out into the street, fists flying. They started the fight. My dad and his cousins stood their ground, fists flying. They finished it. The white woman sent her German Shepherd into the rumble, and the dog caught hands, too. Quickly, the sons and the canine scrambled back to the steps and hobbled onto the porch. The mom kept talking trash, but beyond that couldn't do anything but follow her sons into the house and meditate on the painful lesson they had just learned about staying out of Black folks' business.

The headline on TV: "Family Feud at Funeral."

That's how they sent off the first Campbell man to die young.

My folks didn't have cool stories about Prines Campbell Sr.'s funeral, or many details about how he died at all. We just know it involved a speeding car and Prines Campbell Sr. trying to cross a dark street.

"He was probably drunk," my mom would say whenever she discussed it. "Knowing him."

Before he died, he appeared in candid family photos, like the pictures from a road trip to Denver. They're undated, so we don't know if they happened before or after the brief separation, when Granny Mary moved to an apartment and left her husband in a house her family had owned for two generations. But we know they came fairly late in Prines Sr.'s life because they're in colour, and his taut stomach had softened into middle-aged paunch.

They had stopped in front of Sonny Liston's house, and Prines Sr. posed for a picture there, possibly the first person to drive that many miles to visit Liston's place since Liston was champ and Cassius Clay made a pilgrimage there to taunt him into a title fight. So now we know Prines Campbell Sr. had at least a casual interest in boxing, and a particular affinity for Liston himself. Eventually, I learned that he, like Liston, spent his early life in rural Arkansas, near the Mississippi border. Like Liston, stern and strong and scowling, and protective of his past.

The sign above the plate glass storefront said Julia's Kitchen, but the person behind the counter didn't look like a Julia. He was my height and about twice my weight, with meaty hands at the end of long arms and a belly that stretched every thread of his extra-large navy-blue T-shirt. His face was unwrinkled and deep brown and framed by a pair of greying sideburns. He also wore a close-cropped Afro and, after my dad asked to see Julia, a scowl. Couldn't blame him. If I looked like him, and a guy as handsome as my dad came around asking about my wife, I'd swell up, too.

"Who are you?" he asked, looking at my dad from head to toe and back.

"Tell her Pete's here."

His mean mug melted when he heard the name.

"Her brother?"

"Yup."

"Awwwww shit," he said, breaking into a broad smile and stepping from behind the counter. "Shoulda recognized you, man. That's how I know it's been too long."

He and my dad slapped hands and hugged, and the fat man patted his belly with both hands. "I done put on a little weight since the last time you saw me," he said.

"I wasn't gonna say nothing."

"Aw, man, it's cool," he said. "Workin' in this place don't help."

Brief silence between them. Brothers-in-law, but not really friends.

"Y'all move back to Chicago?"

"Naw," my dad said. "Still in Toronto. Had a couple weeks off so I made a run. Brought my son with me."

The fat man extended his long arm and chubby hand toward me.

"Good to meet you. I'm Tommie," he said.

"Hi," I said. "I'm Morgan."

"Whatchu 'bout fifteen?"

"Yes," I said. "About to start eleventh grade."

"That's great," Tommie said. "I gotta son 'boutcho age, but you really favour my oldest. You might meet him later."

Then back to my dad.

"She know you coming?"

"Yup," my dad said.

"Okay. We don't live but five minutes from here. Lemme call her and let her know you waitin'."

While my dad chatted with Tommie, I gave myself a tour of the bakery. On an otherwise naked white wall were two frames: one held the first dollar the shop ever earned, dated the previous summer, and the other, a black-and-white portrait of Aunt Julia's mother, wearing a black church hat.

I'd tell you that from there I wandered over to the display case holding all the sweet stuff, except I almost ran. I had a sweet tooth and a teenager's metabolism and the curiosity of a future journalist. No way I wouldn't investigate.

I had seen most of this stuff before. Yellow cake with chocolate icing, pound cakes sprinkled with powder or coated in dried liquid sugar. Cake donuts, old-fashioned donuts, donuts filled with jelly, which I hated, and with cream, which I made a mental note to request once Aunt Julia arrived. But I couldn't stop gawking at the red cake with white icing. It looked like it came from another planet.

Even at fifteen, I knew food marketers played games with our brains and taste buds. I had spent enough summers in Chicago to know Canfield's Red Pop, *red* describing both the colour and the flavour. You can't go to a bush or a tree and pick a farm-fresh red, but Canfield's chemists concocted a soft drink that tasted the way you think a red fruit would. The same taste you're imagining right now. Strawberryish.

I liked strawberries, and I liked cake, but hated the idea of strawberry-flavoured cake. If offered, I'd have to sniff before I tasted.

The chime above the front door jingled and I looked over my shoulder to see Aunt Julia, striding toward us in a yellow sundress.

"Pete!" she shouted, then wrapped my dad in a tight hug.

Aunt Julia didn't look exactly like the Prines Campbells, but if you widened the lens, you could tell we were family. She was half a shade darker than my dad, which still made her light. Coffee with two creams instead of three. And she stood about an inch taller than my mom, which still made her short. Her dark brown hair had auburn high-lights, and I wish I could simplify this by telling you she looked like a celebrity, but the best I can do is Ella Joyce. If you remember *Roc*, the Sunday night sitcom from the early 1990s about the sanitation worker from Baltimore, and can picture the actress who played the title char-acter's wife, Eleanor, you can see my aunt Julia.

She walked over and wrapped me in the kind of hug you save for people you know and love and miss. Her embrace felt warm and heavy and reassuring. Then she walked around to the back of the glass display case, grabbed a couple cardboard to-go boxes, and started filling them with one of everything.

Plain pound cake?

Check.

Glazed pound cake?

Check.

Donuts?

Check.

Long Johns, even though they made the donuts redundant?

Of course.

She caught me screwing up my face when she grabbed three pieces of the red cake and put them in a box.

"What, you never seen red velvet cake before?"

"Never," I said. "How does it taste?"

"Well, it don't taste red, if that's what you're worried about," she said. "You're just gonna have to try it and let me know what you think."

Then she looked up and called out to my dad.

"Lemme give y'all a whole cake," she said. "Just in case your mama wants some."

———

One night that summer, my dad and I headed to 49th and Woodlawn to see Minister Louis Farrakhan's urban palace—the mansion reserved for the leader of the Nation of Islam. At the Nation's peak, in the early 1960s, Elijah Muhammad lived there. Inside this house, Malcolm X confronted Muhammad about his mistresses and secret kids, the blowup one more fissure in an ugly split between the Nation's most famous minister and his father figure. I had already read *The Autobiography of Malcolm X* and *The Fire Next Time*, so I also knew this house as the home where Muhammad and James Baldwin broke bread. They disagreed on strategies for Black liberation—Muhammad the staunch

Black Nationalist, and Baldwin, a fierce critic of racism but still an integrationist. This wasn't the venue for Baldwin to change Muhammad's mind, but the writer, the prose showed, felt warmth for the old man.

"He made me think of my father and me," Baldwin wrote. "As we might have been if we had been friends."

We arrived after dark, sat in the car beneath leafy trees, and gazed out at the big house. Black iron gates and a shallow decorative pool spanned by a miniature footbridge. Ground-level lamps illuminating cream-coloured walls. Across the intersection, Fruit of Islam security guards sat in a parked car, casting stony glares at anyone lingering too long near the Minister's mansion.

And when they stared at my dad, he stared right back.

I was certain we would die.

These weren't rent-a-cops. This was the F.O. motherfucking I. Same crew who tossed a Molotov cocktail into Malcolm X's living room. Given half a reason, they'd surely perforate us with bullets.

They stared.

He stared.

I asked what he was doing.

"I ain't doing nothing wrong," he said. "The man's looking at me, so I'm looking back at him."

Eventually we left, but on my dad's time, not theirs.

I was too old then to view my dad as Superman. Not at fifteen. Not after seeing him gutted by divorce. But he never stood taller to me than the night he refused to back down from the F.O.I.—a masterpiece of scene-reading, ground-standing, and bluff-calling. Chicago-raised writer Carlo Rotella might categorize that ability to defuse a situation where violence seemed imminent as equipment for living, a survival skill in a lot of South Side neighbourhoods.

I came to Rotella as a boxing fan. His memoir, *Cut Time*, remains the best book on the sport I've ever read, and I've read almost all of them. Later, he focused those skills on his hometown. In *The World Is Always Coming to an End: Pulling Together and Apart in a Chicago*

Neighborhood, Rotella explores South Shore, where my parents and grandparents lived in the 1960s, where my aunt Peggy and sister Dana still live today, and where Rotella grew up in the 1970s and '80s. It covers normal memoir territory, like Rotella's transitions from grade schooler to teenager to young adult, and his family's upward-bending social class trajectory. But *The World Is Always Coming to an End* is mostly about the neighbourhood itself, and how it wrestles with the same kind of change my mom used to describe—the kind that, for a few years, masquerades as integration.

South Shore was 90 per cent white in the early 1960s, when my mom's family moved into a three-bedroom apartment on Paxton Avenue, corner of 70th Street. A decade later, when the Rotella family settled into a bungalow on Oglesby Avenue, just south of 71st Street, the neighbourhood was already more than half Black. A few years later, the Rotellas moved to a big house on Euclid Avenue, in an enclave called the Jackson Park Highlands, still in South Shore but a few blocks away and several rungs up the class ladder.

At each stop, Rotella picks up "equipment for living," his phrase describing the way institutions like family and neighbourhood shape his personality and influence the adult and writer he becomes. The theme starts early and runs like a nerve through the whole text.

> *By equipment for living I mean the tool kit of ideas, models, and techniques for understanding the world and making your way through it that you pick up from the people around you and from what you see and hear and read . . . South Shore was my first proxy for the world at large, functioning as both filter and laboratory as I stepped from the shelter of home into the street and set about figuring out what to use and how to use it.*

In the next passage, Rotella describes calculating how to stand up to a neighbourhood bully without getting goaded into a fight he knows he'll lose. Except life in South Shore hadn't yet equipped him to thread that needle, so he winds up fighting the bully, who thumps him. Rotella, clearly, escapes without lasting damage. He grows up to write about boxing and the blues and growing up in South Shore.

And what happens to the bully, a big sullen kid named Alfred? He "went to Tuskegee," Rotella writes. "Died young, murdered at the age of 31 while working as a bouncer."

Does the median reader of Rotella's memoir know how the word *Tuskegee* sounds? A hard *G*, and a little extra weight on the middle syllable. TUS-*KEE*-GEE.

That same reader, if they're familiar with the word, probably understands that Alfred is too young to have been a member of the Tuskegee Airmen, the all-Black fighter pilot squadron from World War II. And they'd likely understand the Tuskegee experiment, wherein white doctors gave placebos to unwitting Black syphilis patients, just to see what happened when you left the disease untreated, also unfolded before Alfred's time. But would they automatically know that Tuskegee is a university, historically Black, in an Alabama town of the same name?

Maybe Rotella could have explained it all, the way I just did. Except I'm a Canadian-raised dual citizen with Chicago roots, writing from across the border about my parents' neighbourhood. I'm confident some of my audience will know the name Tuskegee, the places and events to which it might refer, but I'm not sure about the rest.

Rotella? He's a native South Sider, writing about the neighbourhood that produced him—the South Shore of the 1970s, integrated on the way to wholesale racial changeover, and nearly all Black by the time he graduates high school and heads to university. To point out that Rotella came up in a neighbourhood turning Black, fast, is to clarify that he also grew up around a lot of people who didn't need the meaning of *Tuskegee* explained. That kind of cultural capital can transcend race if you let it. Equipment for living.

I had similar tools in my kit, and not just because our parents sat us down to watch *Eyes on the Prize* when it first aired on WNED out of Buffalo, or because I kept my clock radio tuned to WBLK, the way Dad did in his car. We also picked up equipment on those trips to family reunions every summer, where other kids sometimes teased us when we talked, told us we sounded "proper" or "British," when they meant Canadian. At home, speech patterns we learned in suburban Toronto seemed bland and featureless, but in southeast Grand Rapids, they stood out. When you travel, you're the one with the accent. I learned that early.

By July 1992, the summer before I turned sixteen, the month my dad brought me to Chicago to meet Aunt Julia, I had spent enough time around Black Americans to appreciate African American culture as a culture and not, as a lot of folks try to make you believe, just a jumble of stereotypes. My sisters and I learned through deliberate exposure, like when our folks sat us down to watch those PBS documentaries, but also through experience. We had those near annual trips to family reunions, where we could meet close and distant relatives, blood and fictive kin.

And we had food, like the sweet potato pie my mom would bake every holiday. She didn't have a recipe, just guidelines and experience, and techniques she picked up from watching her mom, who first learned from her elders. As a child in Bunn, Arkansas, living with her grandmother, whom everybody called Grandma Oliver. And later, when she moved north to Chicago, to reunite with her aunt, whom we all called Grandma Carrie, and her mom, whom everybody called Grandma Marge. No written recipes. Just knowhow meeting technique and ritual, spanning generations, migrations, borders.

By fifteen, I could hear in Black American English a unique species of a common language, not just slang or a collection of broken grammatical rules. I learned from listening to my dad that "don't say nothing" doesn't mean "say something." It means the opposite. "Don't say a damn thing." A double negative doesn't make a positive. It makes a negative, same in Spanish and French. Standard English gets it wrong.

Speaking to kids my age at family reunions, I learned dropping the verb "to be" from a sentence means the action is happening that instant. "Lisa running" means she's running right now, maybe to catch a bus, or evade a swarm of bees. Add the word "be" back to the sentence, and we're describing a habit. "Melanie be running" means she runs often, as a hobby, or to train for a sport. If you had to handicap a race between Lisa and Melanie, go with Melanie. She gets more practice. She be running.

I picked up from my mom that the word *behind* indicates physical position—"boy, get from behind me!"—but also communicates cause and effect. A synonym for "as a result of."

"If she doesn't smarten up behind *this*," she might say, "then she's a doggone fool."

At fifteen, I probably couldn't have articulated all those details, but I recognized them the way many people growing up between two cultures learn to acknowledge and navigate the divide. If my sisters and I couldn't achieve the fluency with African American culture my parents enjoyed, we could at least know our way around it. Our parents made sure. So, if, at fifteen, I had needed an explainer on something like the meaning of Tuskegee, my parents would have considered me ill-equipped.

A lot of it we learned simply through repeated exposure. But the equipment for living I picked up that summer in Chicago felt deliberate, like my dad wanted to imprint some things I needed to know onto my teenage brain before I grew up.

One morning, we drove the slow way back to Granny Mary's house from downtown, straight down State Street, past the projects. I couldn't tell where Stateway Gardens ended and the Robert Taylor Homes began, but they formed an endless stretch of high-rise, low-income apartment buildings towering over the heart of the South Side, jammed into a thin strip of land between State Street and the Dan Ryan, from 35th Street, across the expressway from Comiskey Park, all the way down to 55th.

Those twenty blocks span two and a half miles, or four kilometres if you're Canadian. Superimpose that layout along Yonge Street in Toronto and you'd have public housing from Queen's Quay to Rosedale Subway Station. If you can't picture it, that's the point. Public housing on that scale is nearly impossible to explain to Canadians, and unheard of almost anywhere outside late-twentieth-century Chicago.

At peak population, those buildings housed more than thirty thousand people—nearly all of them Black, of course, because this was Chicago and segregation ruled. They eventually acquired a reputation for crime and disrepair, and everything else that descends on a neighbourhood that's overpopulated and under-resourced and Black.

My dad called them the Filing Cabinets.

That's what they resembled when viewed from the expressway. Identical rectangles of beige concrete with outdoor balconies running the length of every floor, and a massive chain link fence draped like a veil over the face of each building, from the roof to the ground. And Filing Cabinets because that's how housing projects at that scale functioned: a place to stash poor Black folks the way an office worker stored old papers. Occasionally, somebody with something to gain would open a drawer to retrieve somebody who could sing or rap or dribble through a full-court press, but otherwise those buildings were to a hyper-segregated city what metal cabinets are to an office—somewhere to store stuff deemed no longer useful, to file and forget poor Black folks like old receipts.

My mom's parents would never have rolled past the Robert Taylor Homes with their grandkids in the car. They would rather just tell us to trust them when they said we were lucky to have grown up in Canada.

My dad didn't like telling. He preferred to show me how segregation still worked. We crept south on State Street. Outside the passenger-side window stood the endless column of housing-project towers; through the driver's side, I could see a low-slung concrete building, where a church group was handing out free food to locals who needed it. The line to get in stretched down the block. At least a hundred people in the midday sun, all of them Black.

Another morning, we hit a few spots on 87th Street, looking for sneakers and the warm-weather wardrobe essentials Black folks called short sets—short sleeve shirts paired with shorts of a matching colour pattern. They're the reason the Fresh Prince hustled to the mall in "Summertime."

The last store we visited specialized in sports-team gear that was, like a fifteen-year-old behind the wheel of their parents' car, not officially licensed. Red-white-and-black outfits that said "Chicago" or "Bulls," but not "Chicago Bulls," to dodge a call from a copyright lawyer. But these clothes weren't cheap, like the stuff Granny Mary sourced from her buddy at church. As I flipped through the options hanging on racks, the cotton blends felt thick between my fingers and heavy in my hands. These wouldn't unravel in the washing machine. If—big if—you treated them right, and if—bigger if—the design stayed in style, they could last you a couple of summers.

I copped the Miami set—pine-needle green with clementine orange highlights, and a caricature of a white ibis with fists balled up and cocked. The salesman guided me to the register, where an Asian guy materialized to collect some of my dad's cash. This guy looked in his thirties, less glum than the Asian guy doing the same job at the shoe store farther west on 87th Street, but not quite cheerful, and certainly not friendly.

He took my dad's money and punched some buttons on the register, then handed me back some singles and some coins, along with my Miami short set, folded and placed inside a plastic bag. We made glancing eye contact. He half-nodded but stopped short of thanking me.

Back inside the car, on the way to Granny Mary's, my dad started asking questions, testing my equipment for living.

"Who helped you find what you needed at the shoe store?"

"Uh . . . the salesman?"

"Right," Dad said. "And what he look like?"

"Black."

"Yep. And who handled the money?"

"Not the salesman."

"Exactly. And what that dude look like?"

"I dunno," I said. "Chinese?"

"And who helped you in the other store?"

"Salesman?"

"And what *he* look like?"

"Black."

"But who handled the money?"

"Chinese guy."

"Right," Dad said. "Now what's that tell you?"

Damned if I was answering that question, even though I knew where he was headed. I had listened to Ice Cube rail against Korean convenience store owners charging high prices in the hood. I had seen *Do the Right Thing* and watched Radio Raheem feud with the Korean shopkeeper over his ear-splitting boom box and the twenty muthafuckin D batteries. The previous summer, my dad and I watched *Boyz n the Hood* at the theatre, and right now I felt like Ricky *and* Tre, with my dad as Furious Styles, putting equal weight on every syllable as he explained to the teenagers how Gen-Tri-Fi-Kay-Shun worked. White people and their money come back to retake the neighbourhoods they fled when the first Black person moved in. They buy low and sell high and write you out of the script and the profit.

But I wasn't qualified to speak on it. Maybe I could kick knowledge at a table in the Black section of the cafeteria, to kids who only knew about Black America from what they saw in movies or gleaned from hip-hop songs. But explain it to an actual adult from the actual South Side of Chicago? Not me. I played dumb and let my dad keep talking.

"Which of them dudes looked like they come from 87th Street?"

"Not the manager."

"Right," he said.

Then some more silence.

"These other places ain't no different," he said finally, motioning to the storefronts rolling past outside the car window. "Get a nigga to stand up front and smile when you come in, but the niggas never touch the money. They just hand you over to a Korean or a A-rab and *he* takes the money."

I felt a twinge of guilt over the sneakers in the trunk and the short set in the plastic bag on my lap. We rode for another silent minute.

Grown-up Morgan could have put words to my dad's lesson: beware non-Black business people who view Black neighbourhoods and wallets and bodies as places to extract without investing. The shoe store manager, the dude selling short sets, the owners of the liquor stores dotting the South Side neighbourhoods where we spent most of our time in Chicago. Each of them filling a perceived market need, and all of them about as helpful as a tapeworm.

If my dad liked talking, he might have painted a similar picture with words. But this was my dad, who enjoyed conversation the way most of us enjoy oral surgery. What came next qualified as a long monologue.

"Ask yourself," he said, "if you want to shop someplace they don't let Black folks touch the money."

That was all big-picture equipment for living—my dad trying to outfit me to survive in a country where racism permeated everything from city planning to the purchase of an outfit for the summer barbecue circuit. It governed where you lived, your access to a bank or fresh produce, and the price you paid for almost everything. Life at the business end of racism is stressful, but with the right equipment for living maybe I could navigate the landscape, stay sane, *and* retain some dignity.

But as our visit progressed, the focus narrowed from my place in society to the roles we all occupied in the Campbell family. Meeting Aunt Julia gave us another clear detail in an incomplete picture of

Prines Campbell Sr. My dad could have introduced us any summer, but he chose 1992, maybe because at fifteen, I could figure out for myself that my dad's dad had a kid with his mistress. Maybe turning fifty the previous month triggered something in him. One less detail to have to explain. He could have picked any or all of his kids to meet Aunt Julia first, but he chose me. I'd always be his kid, but I wouldn't always be a kid, and treating me to this privileged information seemed like an acknowledgement.

A family secret. Equipment for living. My dad shared it with me first. I felt loved and trusted and, most of all, grown.

—

"I guess Tommie quit drinking," my dad said, interrupting another silent ride back to Granny Mary's place.

From there, another long soliloquy by my dad's standards, some brief but heavy details on young Tommie—hard-drinking, unreliable, possibly abusive. Wasn't too deep a secret. If my dad found out all the way up in Canada, then his own hard-drinking, wife-beating father clued in, too, and Prines Campbell Sr. wasn't going to let anybody treat his daughter the way he himself treated his wife.

"Your daddy almost took out a contract on that nigga," my dad said.

Your daddy meaning *his* daddy, who owned a chrome-plated .45 and a short temper. He fired that gun at his wife one night, so putting some holes in his trifling son-in-law, or hiring some goon to do it, might not have been a problem.

If we're willing, we can read virtue into this credible threat of deadly violence. If virtue overstates it, then we can credit Prines Campbell Sr. with normal human feelings, like regret and remorse over how he had treated his wife, that we didn't otherwise suspect he felt. And if that's still too much, we can at least acknowledge that by the time his two living kids had married, my dad's dad developed enough self-awareness to want to stop a cycle.

That afternoon I learned Aunt Julia grew up in Yazoo City, Mississippi—"a little bitty town next to a river," she called it—and lived with her grandparents before moving back to Chicago after high school. She quit her job the previous year and opened the bakery because she wanted to work for herself, for once.

I also learned she had four kids, one named Courtney, like my sister. Their oldest, Kendall, shared my stature and my skin tone, but didn't look like a Campbell down the middle of his face. Wider, rounder nose, like Tommie's. His siblings, dark-skinned and doughy, all looked more like their dad than our grandfather.

I couldn't gather much about her personality in the few hours we spent together, but I learned she missed her half-brother even though they didn't grow up together and would never have the kind of relationship Dana, Courtney, and I had. But she was warm and friendly, the way clichés say Southern women are, and considerate enough to make sure we brought Granny Mary some cake.

Dad and I headed inside and through the living room, where Granny Mary displayed pictures of people she loved. A plus-sized studio portrait of her hung on the wall, next to one of my dad, with his beard and glasses and early '80s sheeny, low-cut Afro. His portrait was a few sizes smaller.

Granny Mary also had pictures of Dana at high school graduation, Courtney at her junior high grad, and me in my awkward preteen phase—long thin legs and a short round torso. She had photos of Uncle Ernest in his Air Force uniform, plus pictures of his daughter, and *her* daughters. But she didn't keep any pictures of her dead husband where people could see them.

We headed to the kitchen and placed our haul from Aunt Julia's bakery on the small white table in the middle of Granny Mary's kitchen. Late afternoon daylight filtered through the windows. The small TV on the counter tuned to WGN, like always.

My dad removed the red velvet cake from its box. I pulled the smaller boxes from bags and placed them on the counter. My dad fetched three plates. I found some silverware. My dad took a sharp kitchen knife to the cake and cut three slices from it, one for each plate.

Granny Mary heard us and came in from the back porch.

"Where'd you all get that cake?" she asked.

"Took Morgan to meet Julia and her kids," my dad said.

"Oh?" she said. "They still over at 92nd and Cottage Grove?"

"Yup."

Granny Mary sat at the table and pulled a plate closer to her. One seat over, I was already halfway through my first piece, with an eye on seconds. Dad and Granny Mary chatted some more about the visit. Not idle talk. Just small. He caught her up on the kids, and Tommie's weight gain, and the bakery, about to celebrate its first anniversary.

"I should go over there sometime. I haven't seen Julia in years." Granny Mary said. "I bet she still looks just like her mama."

Then silence as she ate some more red velvet cake.

"Ugly."

The Operation

This fight?

It might have started over cheap shots, like when that clown from the Erindale Raiders hit me after the whistle on a punt return. I was three steps out of bounds and ready to toss the ball back to the referee when he flattened me; that stuff gets people suspended. The referee, feeling generous, only gave him a fifteen-yard penalty. It's a fightable offense, though, especially at the Woodlands School, where the boys' soccer team was still on probation for beating up the Applewood Axemen two years earlier, and where kids fought for all kinds of reasons. To settle problems. To cause new ones. To shatter the monotony of long afternoons.

It might have been proximity. The Erindale Raiders came from across the Credit River, ten minutes west along Dundas Street, our closest rivals in geography and skill. We weren't going to beat Meadowvale or Lorne Park or Clarkson. Those schools had big kids and well-equipped weight rooms, top-end talent *and* depth. But Erindale? They puttered through the schedule just like we did, getting thumped against Meadowvale and Lorne Park, but were convinced they could win *this* game.

We had too much in common to get along. And late in the fourth quarter, with the score knotted at fourteen, on a sunny

Thursday in mid-October of 1993, with the bleachers at the Woodlands School packed for once? Something was going to break. Either the tie or the peace.

Of course, we lost. Erindale had a six-foot-four receiver named Dino, and we had two short cornerbacks: Patrick Dottin, who, at five-foot-eight, was the Tall One, and me, five-foot-seven on a good day. For most of the game, the height disparity hadn't mattered. They threw passes to their big receiver, and our little corners batted the ball away.

On second down, they tried me with Dino, but the quarterback threw the ball long instead of high—made it a foot race, and I didn't lose those. But the next play, they tested Patrick. The quarterback hung the ball up high, so Dino could leap to pluck it from the air above Patrick's outstretched arms. Touchdown, Erindale. They kicked a convert and now had twenty-one points. We still had fourteen, and only a handful of seconds to do something about it.

So, we handed the ball to Granville Mayers, six-foot-one and 205 pounds of fast-twitch muscle, a record-setting long jumper with a deadly right cross. Afterward, he said he did what he did because, after Erindale's players gang-tackled him, one of them started punching him in the ribs. If that happened, I, like the referee, didn't see it. But when the pile of bodies dispersed, Granville had two handfuls of some Erindale guy's facemask, wrenching the kid's head back and forth like a go-kart steering wheel.

From there, the benches cleared, players rushing onto the field to keep the fight going. The bleachers, too. Joining a brawl was the closest most kids at the Woodlands would come to showing school spirit. Erindale had a better football team, but Woodlands had numbers. They won the game, but we ran them off the field, so we won the fight. Typical Woodlands Rams.

I didn't throw any punches. When the fight erupted, I was on the sideline drinking water, having already shed my helmet and shoulder pads, but scrambled to put my gear back on. The team sports code of ethics required me to jump in, but I cared how I looked. One scar, like the mark on the cheekbone beneath my left eye, could give a smooth face some character, the difference between a pretty boy and a handsome man. But more marks are just marks. Dents on an expensive car. I was sixteen and vain and wasn't breaking my nose or chipping a tooth for anybody, or any cause.

By the time I geared up and hit the field, the fight had fizzled, so I sauntered to the west sideline, scowling, sneering, just in case some stray Erindale Raider needed his ass kicked—which none of them did. The fight had ended five minutes ago. I was just showing off.

My team lost nearly every week, but I had played well enough to grandstand. I clung like Lycra to every receiver on every pass play, knocked away balls a cornerback with softer hands would have intercepted, and stuffed every run play that came my way. I launched into my tough-guy strut after opting out of the brawl, but it still felt justified. So I patrolled the edge of the grass, next to the track separating the field from the bleachers, with a swagger that said, "Try me."

Eventually, somebody did.

"Morgan."

My dad, leaning on the fence and staring a hole through me.

Yeah, it was time to leave. I skulked over to him like a naughty dog brought to heel. I felt people gawking. Teammates and opponents. Classmates in the bleachers. Pretty girls from the Mississauga Track Club, who had just showed up for Thursday afternoon practice. The kids who knew me also knew better than to tease me about my dad punking me like that. My friends understood Pete Campbell's intolerance for bullshit.

"Let's *go.*"

And so I went, down the sideline to the gate at the north end of the field, where my dad met me for the walk back to the locker room. Side by side, eyes forward, silent, in the sunlight of one of the last warm days of the year. I didn't dare glance back at the field, lest my dad do me like God did Lot's wife. His future depended on doctors and science and luck, but he could still control whether his only son pissed away a critical football season trying to show off for his friends.

Dad moved slowly, but at least he didn't need a cane. By mid-October 1993, he hadn't mastered his colostomy bag, but he could usually move his bowels without accidentally smearing shit on the bottom of his shirt. The surgeons had to remove a long section of his colon, hoping to head off the cancer festering there, and left a hole in his side so he could empty his large intestine. If he were nude, it would gape like the stoma you see on survivors of throat cancer surgery. But if my dad didn't tell you he had to poop into a plastic bag lashed to his belly, you wouldn't have suspected it. His jeans rode a little higher, but he could still wear them. Sweaters and khakis and Nike Air Monarchs could wait until senior citizenship. Cancer surgery had knocked him off balance, but it hadn't made him an old man.

"You played good," he said as we stepped inside the building.

"Thanks."

Our third straight loss. We would have more.

My dad's second game since the operation. A little cancer still lingered, but, when he felt like talking, he said chemotherapy would handle it before next summer.

———

Pop!

My hands in his chest plate.

Clack!

My facemask under his chin.

I describe it in sequence, but the impacts happened at once. If the kid trying to block me in this two-on-one tackling drill had tucked a white flag into his navy-blue Upper Canada College football uniform, he could have waved it right then, a quarter second after the rep started. He had size, but I had leverage. He had an age advantage—he was actually seventeen, and I just said I was, so I could line up against older, better players at this football camp. But I had him stood up and helpless. I grabbed two handfuls of his jersey and tossed him aside like an empty candy wrapper.

No shade on the practice fields at the University of Guelph. First full week of July 1993, and the humidex hit triple digits Fahrenheit every day. Other kids drank water and watched from the sideline as me and this kid from UCC butted heads in the late morning sun, trying to win this drill and attention from the college coaches scouting talent.

Some coaches came from Canadian schools, like Guelph and Western, and others from smaller American programs. One Division II coach had a deep suntan, a neck-length blonde mane with a hairline that started behind his ears, and exclusively wore sleeveless T-shirts so we could see his guns. Whatever the actual name of his school, we started calling it Hulk Hogan State.

The guy running the camp coached the football team at Morehouse College in Atlanta. He had beige skin, a black mustache, and a catch-phrase: "All on the Same Page," which he said at the end of every speech, before and after every practice, until we all said it along with him.

The Canadian coaches seemed to like me, so I figured this guy would love me. I was one of a handful of Black kids at camp that week, and certainly the only one who knew that Morehouse was Martin Luther King's alma mater, and a place where the Black elite sent their kids. And now I knew they had a football team, and their head coach knew I existed.

For the players, every session was both practice and audition. We wanted to play at the next level. After a week of three-a-days, we would know if we could.

The head-to-head with the UCC kids happened late in a morning practice, midway through the week. I manhandled the lead blocker, but the ball carrier got it worse. I stuck my shoulder in his midsection and he groaned.

Uuunnh . . .

I wrapped my arms around his legs and kept my feet driving. He stiffened, then tipped over like a felled tree.

Oooooooooh!

The guys on the sideline high-fiving and hollering like I had just won the Grey Cup. The two-on-one tackling drill served up a lot of stalemates, blocker and defender locking up, and a ball carrier trying to sneak past before the tackler could disengage. But I had just delivered the cleanest hit of the week, and as I jogged back to the sideline, the other campers let me know they appreciated it.

"Way to go, Campbell!"

"Put his ass in the dirt, bro!"

"He's seeing stars right now!"

And the university coaches watching the drill? I noticed them, too. Looking my way. Nodding. Taking notes.

I took to the routine that week. A twelve-minute run before breakfast every day, then practice every morning, afternoon, and early evening. I had just finished my first season running track—led off the relay team that made the regional final even though we barely practiced as a unit—and arrived at football camp feeling fast. The stopwatch said something different.

Four-point-eight seconds for my first forty-yard dash.

And my second.

And my third, no matter how hard I pushed or how high I lifted my knees.

Forty-yard dash times were football's equivalent of the credit score—a metric powerful people used to measure your potential, character, and worth. I was years away from applying for a mortgage but already learning that a single number could make or break my dreams. Playing corner in college with 4.8 speed is like trying to finance a home purchase with 400 credit: not impossible, but risky for everybody involved. Before I left high school, college coaches would want to see a 4.4. I had some time, and a new project for the rest of the summer.

But on the field that week, I made progress every session. In the Mississauga Football League, we practiced three times a week and played on Saturdays. Here, I could cram a week's worth of practice into a single day, except with better coaches and stiffer competition. Guys around me would earn scholarships and graduate to the CFL. It felt like the enhanced learning classes back at my high school, except this time, I was the curve-setting straight-A student.

After the end-of-the-week scrimmage came the awards ceremony. The head coach from Morehouse shook my hand and patted my shoulder and handed me my trophy. Not an everybody-gets-one participation trinket: the coaches had voted and named me the best defensive player in my age group. I smiled and held the award up high so my folks could see it from where they stood, on the grassy embankment beyond the sideline.

After the ceremony came the walk with my parents, along a paved path back to the dorm. They had made the thirty-five-minute drive from Mississauga and functioned like two people in a peaceful limbo. Not a married couple anymore, but closer than a pair of co-parenting exes. Dad walked to my right, holding my trophy. Mom, on my left, with her purse. I lugged my helmet and shoulder pads in my left hand, using my right to greet the people who stopped to congratulate me. High fives for the white kids, dap for the Black ones, and firm handshakes for the coaches.

Up ahead, on a patch of grass off the path, a big bald-headed Black dude with a goatee chatted with a cluster of teenage campers. His calf muscles bulged like small pumpkins. So did his biceps and shoulders, under mahogany skin that shimmered in the midday sun. When I envisioned myself as an adult in the NFL, after a solid decade of hard weight training, the Morgan I pictured was still only half as jacked as this guy.

"Good *God*," my mom said. "You didn't have to play against *him*, did you?"

"Naw, Jeanie," dad said. "He's probably a coach."

Wrong. That was Orlando Bowen. Eighteen years old and already built like an All-Pro linebacker. A future Northern Illinois Husky and

Toronto Argo and, that week, a football camper, just like me, prepping for another season in high school. I grew up playing in leagues with age and weight limits, but was heading toward open-class football, where welterweights like me shared the field with heavyweights like Orlando. Every level I ascended had more Orlandos and fewer Morgans. I stayed quiet and kept walking. If I told my mom that football now involved collisions with Orlando-sized guys, she might never sign another consent form.

We saw the coach from Morehouse. He fixed his eyes on the horizon as he walked past us. Not that he didn't see me. More that he saw me and didn't want to look, ignoring me with a focus that showed I had his attention. Only a handful of Black folks on campus that week, and every Black person on the continent knew the rules in settings like those. Eye contact, upward nod, and, if you speak the same language, a quick verbal greeting. Coach knew the code—and broke it.

"What's that nigga's problem?"

My dad, wrenching his neck to double take.

"He stopped talking to me," I said. "After I asked if it was true that people at Morehouse were stuck up."

"Well . . ." my mom said.

"Uh huh," my dad said. "So what's that tell you?"

I shrugged and nodded and kept walking, eyes on the path and my mind on the short-term future. Coaches told me I would need to get stronger. With no access to a real gym, it would mean even more time in my room, with my boom box blasting Onyx and my department-store York barbell set with the cement-filled plastic plates on the floor next to my bed. More push-ups, more bicep curls, more calf raises. Weight training on the slimmest possible budget. And speed training would mean daily sprints up the toboggan hill across the street, which, by mid-August, had my footprints beaten into the green grass. The path to a faster forty time.

I felt focused and motivated. For the first time in my life, I had visible abdominal muscles and clear goals. Purpose, time, and momentum, all working for me.

A white coach from a Canadian school stopped to congratulate me. "Great job this week, Campbell," he said, shaking my free hand.

"Thanks, Coach."

"Get that forty time down," he said, "and we'll be in touch."

———

A week into the new school year, Dad had started complaining about constipation. That he even opened his mouth should have told everyone how serious this might become. Dad didn't pause for health problems, and he certainly didn't talk about them. He just muscled through. One time a fleck of debris from a machine at work dodged his goggles and landed in the white meat of his right eyeball. The doctor cleaned his eye, then patched it with a gauzy bandage, and Dad returned to work with bulkier eye wear. He might have missed a day. Definitely not two.

Same with his cranky back. When it acted up, he'd visit his chiropractor, who would wrench his vertebrae into something close to alignment. When Dad felt better, he'd be back on the factory floor. Usually took about thirty-six hours.

But this time, his bowels hadn't moved in a week, and it hurt him as much to stand up as it did to fold himself into a chair. Our family doctor examined him and told him the muscles in his sphincter were ten times tighter than they should be, which backed up traffic in his intestine. She prescribed him a muscle relaxer, and for a few days, it helped.

Then came the pain. After midnight. Sharp and sudden and burning, like someone had stabbed him in the side with a rusty knife. He rolled out of bed and shambled into blue jeans and a black T-shirt, then shuffled out of his apartment and down the long hallway to the elevator, with one hand on his stomach, as if trying to cover a leak. A few minutes later, he nosed his black Suzuki Swift out of the parking garage and onto Mississauga Valley Boulevard. Fifteen minutes after that, he parked at Credit Valley Hospital and hobbled into Emergency.

To find him, I had to descend a set of stairs from the hospital lobby, then walk down a long hallway with rooms on my right. On my left, a bank of windows opened out onto a sunny courtyard where people could eat lunch, or patients with enough mobility could absorb some natural light and fresh air. Mom headed straight there. I stopped at the bathroom. When I arrived, Dad was dressed in a green hospital gown, with his bed tilted so he could sit upright. Mom slid a thin pillow between his spine and the mattress, extra support for his temperamental back.

"You need anything else, Pete?" she said. "Water? A snack?"

"Naw, just hand me the remote," he said. "I been watching CNN three days straight."

He looked haggard. Grey stubble over sunken cheeks. A small Afro sprouting on his head because he was at least three weeks overdue for a haircut. But he sounded bright and alert and cheerful. Emergency surgery had cost a big piece of his colon, but, suddenly unburdened of a month's worth of shit, and pain-free for the first time since August, he felt lighter. Any of us would.

"Not much on this time of day," Mom said. "Unless you like soap operas."

"*Another World* comes on at two," Dad said. When he worked the day shift, he taped it every afternoon.

Tight sphincter, we knew now, wasn't a diagnosis. Just a ripple on the surface of colon cancer. Mom had explained some of it before we left the house, but the full weight of the information wouldn't land on me for months. Throat cancer? Lung cancer? I recognized those as killers. But as far as anyone in my family knew, doctors could treat colon cancer, and an otherwise healthy person could beat it. The news didn't feel like a death sentence. Just a detour.

My mom's dad had it when I was in grade school. Midway through a six-week booking in Germany he felt . . . unwell. He came home with two weeks left on his engagement, which said a lot to people old enough to understand. For all the ways he and my dad differed, neither of them ever missed work.

Back at home, Grandpa figured he would recover for a few days, then leap back into his regular schedule—six nights a week, nearly every week, nearly all year. But his energy never rebounded, and my grandmother noticed a blue tint beneath his fingernails.

That got Grandpa's attention. He doted on his hands because they made his money. I would say he acted as though his hands themselves were instruments, but if an accident wrecked his grand Steinway, he could buy a new piano. There was no replacing his hands, so he always did as little drilling, hammering, and sawing as a married man of his generation could get away with.

"You guys don't understand," he would say. "I *need* my hands."

So did a bus driver or a secretary, my mom would point out, later, when he wasn't around to argue about it. But we understood.

Grandpa visited his family doctor, who sent him to Mississauga Hospital for some tests, which revealed colon cancer. The surgeon snipped out the diseased section of intestine, then spliced the ends back together. Grandpa spent a few weeks recovering at home, then went back to playing piano at night.

Before the operation, among family, close friends, and even his grown kids, he went by his nickname: Beeed. Afterward, he issued a decree. His kids could call him Dad or Daddy, and to everyone else, he was Mr. Jones. He said he deserved a title, and not a nickname. He had just survived cancer.

Most of those details came to me years later. In real time, as a second grader, I just knew Grandpa was sick, and then he felt better. A few years later, he retired—because he wanted to, and not because his health forced him to stop working. He could have played into his seventies, but he quit at sixty-three. As an adult, I can line up those details and see that they all point toward early intervention, second only to prevention as a strategy to keep cancer from killing you.

"How you feeling, Pete?" my mom asked.

"Better," he said, running his palm across his jaw. "My beard starting to itch, though."

"And what did the doctor say about the colostomy bag?"

"Imma have to wear it for a while," he said. "We'll see after a couple months."

This was grown folks' talk. I sat in a chair next to the bed and stayed quiet while I learned new words.

Colostomy: the plastic bag they attach to your stomach to catch your shit after they re-route your colon out the side door.

Metastasize: a fancy word for spread.

Prognosis: outlook, which I knew already.

The cancer that surgeons cut from my dad's body had been growing unchecked for at least two years. If it had sent him signals before the achy gut and the chronic constipation, Dad ignored them. The night he woke up feeling like somebody had slid a knife blade into his belly, a few inches above his hip bone? That, doctors said, was the moment his tumour burst.

The operation cleaned up the main site, but the rupture sent debris floating through Dad's midsection. A few malignant cells settled on his liver. If he didn't treat them, they would land like seeds, sprouting roots and then blooming. But with chemotherapy, they might fall more like snowflakes—staying a while, then melting away.

"When do you start chemo?"

"Few weeks," Dad said. "After I get out of here and get my strength back."

He made it sound simple and minimally disruptive, like a person with mild diabetes tracking their blood sugar.

"I ain't gonna live forever, but I figure I got another ten years," he said. "Maybe fifteen."

Some people, Dad said, even had a small IV rigged to a tiny backpack containing their medicine, so they could get a steady dose of the drug and still live their lives. If he could score one of those, he might not even have to miss any work.

The Prayer

I crept out of bed just before midnight on the first Wednesday in September 1994 regretting writing that essay in English class the previous spring, the one about Christianity in James Baldwin's novels, and how churches used ideas like salvation and deliverance to keep Black people poor and powerless. At seventeen, I believed it. I hadn't stepped inside a church in the eight years since my sister Dana's confirmation, I didn't listen to Sunday morning gospel on WBLK, and I didn't think much about how God affected my life.

But that night I needed a miracle and could only think of one place to seek it.

My dad's liver cancer had overtaken him in the eleven months since doctors discovered it, and as I gathered my notebook and pen, he lay in a hospital bed four miles away, eyes yellowed, legs swelling, full of drugs to numb the pain. I had never seen anyone die, or even known anyone who had, besides my two great-grandmothers, each deep into old age. My dad was just fifty-two, but when I saw the jaundice and the hollow cheeks, I recognized death even if I couldn't accept it.

If the oncologists at Credit Valley Hospital couldn't stop cancer from killing my dad, maybe prayer would. I was too proud to kneel, and too self-conscious to talk to God out loud, so I sat at my desk, found a clean page, and hunched over it.

Dear God, I wrote. *If you're listening, please let him live.*

"Pete," my mom said, seated near the head of his hospital bed, her hand on his shoulder, her lips near his ear. "Pete, it's Jeanie. I just talked to Jimmy, and he said he'll be here Monday. You want to see Jimmy, don't you? Just hold on. Pete. You'll see Jimmy next week. Earl's coming, too, so just hang in there, Pete."

Sssssssss . . .

Jimmy grew up on Lafayette Avenue, a few houses down from my dad. They became best friends in grade school, and at St. James AME, and stayed that way through graduation from Fenger High. They had planned to room together at the University of Illinois in Champaign, but the summer before, something happened that nobody ever fully explained to our generation. A fight between my dad and his mom that ended with him deciding that no place in the state was far enough from home.

So, when Jimmy went ahead and enrolled in school, my dad joined the Navy. By the end of freshman year, Jimmy had made friends with Earl. Those two pledged Kappa, flunked out and re-enrolled—Jimmy in Champaign and Earl at SIU in Carbondale—and, eventually, graduated. My dad went from basic training at Naval Station Great Lakes in Gurnee to training as an aircraft mechanic during hitches in Jacksonville and Memphis and, finally, to San Diego, where he worked on a carrier and hurt his back trying to help pull an engine from a fighter jet. By twenty-two, all three of them had moved back to Chicago, driving buses for the Transit Authority and working toward something bigger. For Jimmy and Earl, grad school. For my dad, a metallurgy program at the Illinois Institute of Technology. They were grown, with girlfriends and fiancées, but they stayed tight. My dad and Jimmy stood as the best man at each other's weddings. Jimmy was Earl's best man, too, and warned him in the limo on the way to the church that he could still change his mind. He got married anyway. Later, after my parents divorced, and after they realized Earl and his wife should have, and they were in a mood to joke about their bad marriages, they blamed Jimmy.

In 1976, seven years after my parents left Chicago, my mom gave birth to me, and my parents named Jimmy's mom, Lula McGee, my godmother. But by then, time and distance and career arcs had separated my dad and his best friend. Jimmy piled up degrees, moved on to Washington, D.C., secured a series of progressively higher-paying jobs, got married, had a daughter. Same with Earl—a wife and one daughter, whom they enrolled in Jack and Jill, the social club for children of the Black elite, with chapters in most big American cities. They lived the kind of class trajectory my mom's parents envisioned but none of us could quite achieve, from working class to Black bourgeoisie in a generation.

My dad left metallurgy behind for reasons he never completely laid out to my mom. She could only ever tell us that something in my dad feared failure and made him back away from challenges. Back then, I thought it was just a quirk of his personality—I didn't know that living in fear of failure eventually made you scared to succeed.

Dad stayed in blue-collar jobs the rest of his life. The Transit Authority in Chicago. McDonnell-Douglas on the Mississauga-Brampton border, near the airport. De Havilland and Boeing in Downsview. Union jobs, with dental plans and paid vacation, but also tethered to the strikes and layoffs and lockouts endemic to collectively bargained work. Before the divorce, my folks would sometimes talk about moving to a detached home, like the big brick houses going up on the other side of Meadow Green Park. If we finally got our money right, Dana and Courtney could each have their own bedrooms, and we'd have a backyard big enough to fit something besides my mom's blackberry bush. Maybe a pool or a trampoline. But the next set of layoffs at De Havilland kept us in our little townhouse, and later, divorce made sure we never left.

I had heard about Jimmy my whole life, and he visited us in Chicago in the summer of 1991. When I went there with family, we mostly travelled between the same set of South Side spots. From Aunt Peggy's condo to Aunt Edith's house to Granny Mary's. From somebody's place to Abbott Park for the family reunion, or Lem's BBQ at 75th and King Drive, or Comiskey Park to watch the White Sox play the Blue Jays. If we left the South Side, we left the city, usually for a day at Six Flags in Gurnee, near the Wisconsin border. I never saw downtown Chicago up close until Jimmy took me that summer. He also brought my mom and me to Hyde Park to tour Robie House, the Frank Lloyd Wright masterpiece on the University of Chicago's campus.

But I had never seen him and my dad in the same room. As adults, they had so many drains on their time—jobs and families and, in my dad's case, divorce. Real life had dragged them into habits that wouldn't let them prioritize the living, so they carried on like most grown-ups do: talking themselves out of spending precious vacation days to visit healthy relatives and loved ones because something else always seemed more urgent. But now they had to make time, because my dad was dying.

After football practice, I would take the bus to the hospital and walk into these vigils. Mom on one side of the bed and maybe Courtney or Uncle Ken on the other. I fit in where I could. Granny Mary flew in from Chicago midweek, and if she wasn't at our dad's apartment, she'd station herself near his feet.

My dad lay on a metal-framed hospital bed, dressed in a green gown, a half-drawn blind shading him from the late-day sunlight filtering in through the window. His eyes, when they opened, only went halfway, so I couldn't, on entering the room, figure out if he was still living. But the humming machines and the beeping monitors and the rhythmic hiss of his breathing told me he wasn't dead.

Sssssssss . . .

I watched his chest rise and fall, and as long as the tempo held steady, I told myself I wouldn't panic. A tube jammed into one arm kept him fed, and another one drained piss from his bladder. Through a third tube, a painkiller trickled straight into his veins. No other drugs could help him now. Earlier in the week, he could control the dosage with a button. But now he wasn't conscious enough to notice, or strong enough to work the control. He just stayed in the bed while the narcotic dripped.

Sssssssss . . .

I still couldn't process how fast this all happened. Three weeks earlier, Dad and Uncle Ken and Courtney and I had driven together to the SkyDome to watch Team USA in the gold medal game at the Basketball World Cup. No Jordan or Bird or Magic—this was the first big post–Dream Team tournament, so the second-tier superstars took over. But they were still Hall-of-Famers—Shaquille O'Neal, Joe Dumars, Dominique Wilkins—dunking all over the Russians and winning by forty-six.

The last Sunday of summer, Dad showed up at the house while I was home alone. We ordered pizza and watched the 49ers play the Chargers. He came in that night skinny and unshaven, using a cane to stay upright, but coherent and conversant, asking when my mom would return from Chicago.

By Wednesday, I was praying for him to live, and by Thursday my dad's eyes couldn't open past halfway. Sometimes his lips would move, but without sound. Just a silent monologue. What was he trying to say? Who did he imagine he was talking to? I watched him and wondered if this was how your life passed in front of your eyes before you died. Not in a flash, but in a reel that unspooled over days.

"Pete, Morgan's here," my mom said. "Did you want to talk to Morgan?"

Sssssssss . . .

She turned to me.

"The doctor says he can hear, even when he can't respond," she said. "So if you want to talk to him, you can."

I wondered how anyone could know that.

And even if he could hear me, what would I say?

That I wished I had prayed harder, and sooner?

That I would try not to unravel after he died, but couldn't promise it?

That if I had known he was that close to needing a hospital bed, I'd have skipped the football game and called an ambulance? That I wished he had taught me to drive so I could have hauled him to the hospital myself?

All true, but I couldn't find the words.

I grabbed my dad's hand, still warm and big, but limp.

I squeezed.

"I love you, Dad."

Ssssssss . . .

—

One year, Granny Mary came with us to my mom's parents' annual Thanksgiving dinner. As usual, our parents loaded Dana and Courtney and me into our dad's blue Oldsmobile and drove across Mississauga to the high-rise where my grandparents lived. From there, we'd head down to the party room in the building's basement. I hated it. Pale tiled floors and drab yellow walls bathed in low-wattage light. The smell of cheap cleanser, and plastic cloths draped over long tables. For a family gathering, it always felt antiseptic.

But that one year, Granny Mary drove up from Chicago in her own Oldsmobile—candy-apple red with a white vinyl top. A few years later, she would upgrade to a red Cadillac and gift the Olds to Cousin Khadijah in Grand Rapids.

Of the dozens of people who attended most years, only a few of us were actual family. Me and my parents and my two sisters. My grandparents. Uncle Jeff would come when his schedule let him, but he was a musician like his dad, and on the road a lot. Aunt Cheeky came, and when she married Uncle Ken, he started coming, too.

But everyone else? They were friends. Grandpa's friends, mostly. People he met after moving to Canada. Neighbours who grew close.

Jazz fans who hung out at the places he played. Some of them had aged out of their nightclub years, so now they visited him where he and my grandma lived. They grew up in places like Hamilton and Denmark and small-town Quebec. And besides a kinship with my grandparents, they all had something else in common. Something Granny Mary found as unsettling as I found the plastic tablecloths.

"For a family gathering," she said, loud enough for anyone near her to hear, "there sure are a lot of *Hhwyte* people here."

And then, almost under her breath.

"Claude Jones always was a *Hhwyte* folks' nigga."

My grandpa's relationship with race was like his relationship with his family: tangled, and tense in ways it didn't need to be. He grew up in a white neighbourhood, but he didn't choose it. His parents moved from Bronzeville to West Pullman when a lumberyard down there hired his dad. The Joneses weren't chasing whiteness when they relocated. They barely spoke to their neighbours, and all sides preferred it that way. And they stayed because the city spent money where white people lived, which meant small class sizes at school and streets without potholes.

But as an adult, I noticed the distance my grandfather kept from the Black people he met in Canada. Our extended-family gatherings could have looked like Uncle Ken's summertime cookouts, with our family and Black folks who fit in with us: the Chase brothers from Windsor; Randy Padmore, a downtown guy with Nova Scotian roots; Uncle Ken's buddy Richard, a cabinet-maker whose folks were Underground Railroad descendants from Owen Sound. Grandpa could have made friends like that on the job or in day-to-day life, but the white folks he invited to Thanksgiving were the associates he chose.

There was the time he and my grandma were shopping at The Bay, and she tried to buy him a red-and-black checkered shirt.

"Put that back, Mag," he said.

"Why, Claude?"

"Because I don't wear plaid."

"You don't? Why not?"

"I don't like how it makes me look. Like a workie."

So even if Granny Mary wasn't right, was she completely wrong?

If my grandpa didn't view himself as too refined to socialize with Black folks, he did place himself above a certain class of manual labourer. Not musicians, obviously. As a pianist, he made his living, literally, with his hands, and maybe the tuxedo he wore on stage made him a white-collar craftsman. But common workies weren't his peers. Any level-headed ranking of career prestige would rate Claude Jones, pianist, far ahead of people who used their hands on factory floors or assembly lines. Claude came home smelling like cigarette smoke, but with stories about hanging out with Aretha Franklin, or Billie Holiday, or Bill Lee, Spike Lee's dad. Workies just came home smelling like soot. Like Prines Campbell Sr., a pattern maker who shaped hot metal with big tools at Inland Steel in Chicago. Or Pete Campbell, bus driver turned aircraft mechanic, the father of Claude's first three grandkids.

By late high school, I had also noted how eagerly my grandpa elevated my uncle Jeff's girlfriends, and their folks, all of them white, to family status. Grandpa would use that word when describing how they functioned among us, or how he treasured them. He regarded them as relatives, even though, technically, they weren't even in-laws; he and Granny Mary, meanwhile, acted colder than strangers, even though they were family by marriage. She would say Grandpa embraced those new de facto in-laws because they were white, and that's possible. But maybe he was just happy they weren't Campbells.

Picture the person you liked least in high school, the one who made you grateful for graduation, so you could leave that phase behind you. Now imagine that person re-entering your life as an in-law. They're standing opposite you as your first-born marries theirs, each of you working to maintain distance lest something erupt between you. How would you feel, seeing that person's sneer at milestone events like weddings and funerals, and finding their features in the faces of your grandkids? You could learn to live with it, but it might still make you bitter. Granny Mary and Grandpa both knew how it felt. One more thing they had in common.

———

When my grandparents arrived for Christmas dinner, I relocated from the loveseat to the dining room table. I preferred the spot on the two-seater closest to the TV, but so did my grandpa, who always claimed eminent domain. They showed up late because my grandpa liked to keep people waiting, just like he enjoyed making them watch him enter the room.

By then, my dad had already settled into his seat, with his food on a big paper plate on his lap. He always showed up on time. If he told you 6 p.m., you could expect him at 5:58. At our house, you'd usually find him in his preferred spot, in the corner of the big couch, where he had leaned so heavily, so often, for so long that the cushions curved to fit his torso.

Before my grandpa hung up his jacket, he helped my grandma remove her black beret, and the shiny floor-length black fur coat she saved for special occasions. Christmas dinner, 1993, qualified. My dad's first Christmas after cancer surgery, and none of us knew how many more he would get to celebrate. Before my grandma greeted the rest of us, she walked toward him.

Seven years earlier, during the first De Havilland strike after the divorce, she used to tell my mom to stop feeding him. He was still covering his lawyer, and his rent, and our mortgage on strike pay, a fixed income that didn't fix much. Three daily meals weren't an option, so he would eat half a TV dinner before driving to Downsview to picket, then return to his rented room to eat the second half. By late spring, he had dropped two weight classes.

Still . . .

"Stop cooking for him, Jeanie."

"But Deeer, I can't look at him like that," my mom said. "He's a skeleton."

"Not your problem," my grandma said. "If he'd been a better husband, he wouldn't be starving."

Now she stopped in front of my dad and bent forward and hugged him, then said something in his ear the rest of us couldn't hear. When she straightened up, she took his right hand in both of hers.

"I mean it, Pete," she said.

"Thank you, Mrs. Jones," he said.

"I really mean it."

"Appreciate that."

My grandpa didn't glance their way. Just headed to the seat I had vacated, sat with his hands folded in his lap, and waited for my grandma to fix him a plate. Eventually, he greeted the rest of the family—my mom, my sisters, and me; Uncle Ken and Aunt Cheeky; our dog, a border collie-beagle mix named Bandit. Everyone except my dad. We all watched. Grandpa had chances. This wasn't an oversight. Given my dad's condition, we all figured Grandpa would, like most mature people with a sense of empathy, initiate a truce. Man to man. Father to Father. Cancer survivor to cancer patient.

Except my grandpa wasn't just a survivor. He was, as far as the public knew, an advocate and a fighter on behalf of everyone with cancer. At some point during treatment and recovery, Grandpa connected with the Canadian Cancer Society, which featured him in a campaign. Soon after, you started seeing a portrait of Claude Jones, white hair and a black turtleneck, staring soberly into the camera, on Cancer Society ads that appeared in bus shelters and on billboards and on TV, urging people to stay vigilant for signs of cancer and act on them quickly. My grandfather. Claude Jones. Not famous, but adjacent to it, and well-known among certain folks. Maybe they saw him play piano at Café des Copains or Inn on the Park. People with sharp eyes and fine memories might have recognized him from a General Motors commercial in the early '80s, or a Mott's Clamato ad a few years later. And now he was the face of the fight against a deadly disease.

My dad, in contrast, was a rank-and-file cancer patient, without a publicity apparatus behind him, or the good outcomes that follow early detection. He would also have to learn to live with quarterly rounds of chemotherapy. When he went on drugs, the poison ran black in his veins, killing cancerous and healthy cells alike. His wavy black hair would straighten, then fall out like needles off an old pine tree. The hair would grow back when chemo ended, but he still had the colostomy bag. By Christmas, he had finally mastered keeping it sealed to the hole in his stomach and sneaking away to the bathroom to change it without leaving a mess behind.

Grandpa dodged those problems, but we figured he could imagine how easily he might have landed in my dad's position. Nobody expected a new friendship to bloom, but everybody at Christmas dinner kept an eye on my grandpa, thinking he'd see my dad as a fellow cancer patient and father, terrified of dying before his kids could grow up. We all saw an opportunity.

Not my grandpa, though.

For him, this was all competition, and he didn't intend to lose. This grudge between his family and my dad's dated back to the 1930s. Nobody could pinpoint how it started; we all just knew it existed like a chronic condition—always there, never convenient, subject to ugly flare-ups. Walk across the room to shake my dad's hand? Wish him good luck and good health? Why not surrender instead? Why not just admit that this whole intrafamily conflict, which, as far as we could tell, rested on the perception that the blue-collar Joneses and the blue-collar Gibbses came from different social classes, was a useless drain on everyone's time and energy?

My grandpa didn't admit stuff like that. Too much like acknowledging he was wrong, which he never was, or that he had lost, which he never did.

Still, we all watched for the Hallmark movie ending, two enemies and an olive branch, sealing a truce as holiday snow fell softly outside. Everything but the crackling fireplace. Our little townhouse didn't have the space, or any place to vent the smoke.

In the movie version, Grandpa would try to keep a hard heart, but it was Christmas, and he knew what the Bible said about loving your enemies. He would stop fighting the feeling, find my dad, and place a reassuring hand on his shoulder.

"I guess we're on the same side now, Pete."

"Yup."

"I have connections at the Cancer Society. I'll send them your way and make sure we beat this."

"Thanks, Mr. Jones. Means a lot."

Or . . .

"I really admire how you still put your kids first."

"Yup. They still my babies."

Or at least . . .

"I just wanted to wish you good luck and good health and a Merry Christmas."

"Thanks, Mr. Jones."

In real life, he took the long way to the bathroom to avoid passing his former son-in-law. Wouldn't even let his eyes drift, even if working that hard to ignore somebody betrays that you're doing the opposite.

I watched it all, trying to imagine how bad you had to hate somebody to disrespect him like this. On Christmas. In front of his kids. In a house where he still paid the mortgage. While he's terminally ill with the same disease that nearly took you out. It's a level of trifling I still can't fathom. I didn't know how my grandpa reached that point, and even though I didn't have the words for it, I knew this: if we can distill character to choices you make under pressure, nothing besides my grandpa's character pressed him to make those decisions. He chose vengeance all night. I watched him, sitting on the couch my dad bought, food piled high on his paper plate, acting like the man who subsidized that meal didn't exist.

My grandpa loved how his name sounded in French—not "Clod" but "*Clode*"—and fronted like he knew something about the language. I'm not sure he realized that English borrowed the adjective *petty* from the French *petit*, but he lived it that night. Smiling at my mom, trying to make conversation with Aunt Cheeky, freezing my dad out, and looking smaller than I had ever seen him.

—

Sometime after Christmas, my mom found a story in the *Toronto Star* about treating liver cancer with cryogenic therapy. Surgeons would use some super-cold substance, maybe liquid nitrogen, to freeze the tumour, then scrape it off with a scalpel and leave the patient with a healthy, functioning organ. She clipped the article and gave it to my dad, who showed it to his oncologist, who told him the new procedure wouldn't work on him. The cancer had already eaten too deeply into healthy flesh. My dad's best chance to beat the disease leaned on chemotherapy, good luck, and a great attitude.

My dad told my sisters and me he'd keep his cancer in check and live until at least sixty-five. Didn't seem like a compromise to me; more like a promise. At seventeen, another decade felt like forever. Later, I learned he told my mom the truth.

They grew closer that year than they had seemed even before the divorce. They started sharing things. Conversations. Secrets. Hugs. For short moments, at scattered intervals, we felt like a family again.

That summer unfolded as normally as the previous one had. Football camp in June, twice-daily workouts in July and August. College coaches still sent me letters, but mostly from programs in Canada, or third-tier American schools. I wanted a higher calibre of attention. In May, the University of Michigan had sent me a recruiting letter, and I spent the spring and summer chasing that first high. I wanted big stadiums and games on TV. One more season of high school football left, and I planned to make it count.

The whole time, cancer gnawed at my dad's liver. In the eleven months following surgery, you couldn't tell most days if the disease had made him sore or worn him down. He figured out how to disguise the damage.

Or maybe I evolved ways to ignore it. I certainly learned to rationalize. In late August, when I noticed my dad's gait stiffen, I blamed his achy back. It hadn't acted right since his Navy days. He dropped a few pounds fast, but who didn't lose weight in the muggy summer heat? When I spent the night at his apartment one weekend late in August and saw the swelling in his legs, I couldn't explain it, so I didn't try. I just hoped my dad would snap back to normal somehow. The next morning, he shuffled out of bed and sunk into his new recliner, with the soft cushions wrapped in blood-red leather, and drifted back into something like sleep. When I asked if he was okay, he said he was just gathering strength to get up for real.

"Is it your back?" I asked. "Or . . ."

He cut me off.

"Morgan," he said. "It's the cancer."

Those three words froze me. I groped for words of my own but found none. Couldn't even clear my throat. Just stood there with my mouth half-fixed to say something.

"It's cool," my dad said, cluing in to how stunned I was. "I'm starting chemo again in two weeks."

By the first Friday of the school year, I had established a new afternoon routine. After football practice, I would change clothes fast, then hurry out of the locker room and out on to Erindale Station Road, and jog south to Dundas Street. From there, I would board the northbound Route 44, like I was headed home. But instead of riding through Streetsville and all the way to Falconer Drive, I'd hop off halfway, at the corner of Mississauga Road and Eglinton Avenue. Along Eglinton,

I would walk twenty minutes west to Credit Valley Hospital, where my dad still lay in that metal-framed bed, in the room with the big window and the dull beige paint.

I saw my mom there every day, usually parked near the head of my dad's bed, talking in his ear. Granny Mary showed up midweek, stationed at the other end of the bed, praying or rubbing my dad's feet. Sometimes Uncle Ken made it. My mom's parents never did. She succeeded in keeping them away, but she would pay for that. Grandpa never conceded for free.

I walked west, down Eglinton's gentle slope, toward the traffic light at the corner of the Chase, where the street flattened out. Four days into the school year, I tried to focus on bigger goals despite all the drama. The next morning, Saturday, I was scheduled to head to Waterloo for a one-day football camp, a showcase staged by a recruiting agency, who, if they thought you could play, would spread the word to college and university coaches across the continent. I had put it on my calendar in mid-August, when my dad still felt strong enough to think weeks ahead. Back then, I didn't question whether he'd adjust his schedule to get me there. I just knew he would, and so did he.

By Labour Day, we knew better. Even the best-case scenario, a steady levelling-out of his condition in place of the steep daily decline, would still have him in the hospital when I needed to be in Waterloo. Early that week, when he could still talk and listen, he told me not to miss that camp for anything. Not even for him. Just find a way to get there, then do what I had trained for all summer. So, every night after my hospital visit, I'd return home and start phoning friends who played football and try to find a ride.

I passed the traffic lights at the Chase and followed Eglinton back uphill, trying to keep my mind on the rest of the school year, like I didn't know what came next. Earlier that week, I arrived at my dad's hospital room to find him chatting with a bookish white man who looked in his mid-fifties. Dark hair, wire-rimmed glasses, and a thick

Bible in his small hands. I didn't recognize him, but my mom intro-duced him as Dr. Sheppard, the pastor from Streetsville United Church. I shook his hand and nodded at him, trying to figure out what his pres-ence meant. A year ago, when my dad had cancer surgery, nobody summoned a pastor. Twelve months later, another year weaker, he landed back in the hospital, and now here came the preacher.

My dad never went to church.

That's when I knew, even if I didn't want to believe.

Believing would mean preparing to navigate the most important year of my life without him. So many milestones. So many big decisions. Football games and track meets. Creating and then narrowing a list of post–high school options. I could have tried to accept that my dad was about to die so I could brace myself to deal with all that I'd have to confront without him. But preparation didn't matter. I had already thought about it. I'd never be ready.

I walked past the hospital's sliding doors and through the lobby, then bore right into a hallway toward my dad's room. They had him on the main floor, where local folklore said the hospital placed people near death to simplify removal. Late-day sun slanted through the window on the wall outside the room where Dad lay in his green gown, in that metal-framed bed, looking even smaller and more exhausted than he had the night before. His cheeks looked so hollow I thought he was sucking them in. I couldn't see if his jaundice had deepened because his eyes stayed closed. The machines helping keep him alive still beeped and whirred. Granny Mary, seated near his feet, eyes closed and hands clasped, didn't notice me enter. My mom, in her usual spot, next to my dad's bed, stroked what remained of his hair.

"Hi, boy," she said.

Granny Mary didn't look up.

My dad didn't even twitch.

"Hi, Mom," I said.

I walked in and bent to wrap an arm around Granny Mary's shoulder.

"Hey, Morgan," she said. "Sorry I didn't notice you. I was just here praying for your father."

Dad's chest rose and fell in a slow and steady rhythm.

Sssssssss . . .

"Did you find a ride to football camp?" my mom asked.

"Yeah," I said. "My friend Austin is driving down with some guys from Toronto. He said they can take me."

She kept stroking my dad's hair. If he felt it, I couldn't tell, but the motion and repetition seemed to soothe her.

Sssssssss . . .

"They coming by the house?"

"Naw," I said. "I'm gonna meet them at South Common."

"Good," my mom said. "Your dad wants you to go. Don't worry about him. He'll be fine here with us."

I nodded at my mom, then found a chair in a corner of the room and sat. Granny Mary said another silent prayer, and my mom doted on my dad with a tenderness I never saw them share as a couple. People in peaceful marriages didn't even treat each other like that. She pampered him like a newborn.

Machines droned and chirped. Granny Mary's lips moved. My mom said nothing. I wanted to tell Dad I'd be fine the next day, but it was Friday night and we had all stopped pretending he could hear. He lay there, hollow-cheeked and still except for his chest, which rose and fell with his breath.

Granny Mary leaned forward and peeled back the bed sheets from my dad's right foot. She kneaded the sole with her thumbs, as if trying to work the tension out of tight muscles. She ran her right hand across the top of it, still swollen. Still swelling. After a few moments, she covered the right foot, took his left, and started over. After that, she tucked both feet beneath the sheet, then closed her eyes and pressed her palms together.

Years later, the hands Granny Mary used to comfort my dad would write one of his daughters out of her will. Decades earlier, she had used them to flog her only son, with switches cut from trees, or with one of her husband's leather belts. Back then, people treated kids that way. Mary Jane Campbell loved her Bible, and knew what the book warned would happen to kids whose parents spared the rod. If she didn't have a literal rod, she could substitute an extension cord across her young son's bare back.

The Bible is silent on what becomes of children when their parent smashes them across the cheek with the broad side of the blade of a kitchen knife, but that happened, too. To my dad. By Granny Mary's hand. As for the hand that prevented that assault from causing visible damage? Had to be God's. Even Granny Mary would agree.

"You'll be okay, Pete," my mom said, smoothing my dad's hair with her palms, and soothing him with hopeful words. "Jimmy and Earl are on their way. They'll be here Monday. You just hang on."

My mom's hands: strong, fast, accurate, and firm. She only ever swung them because she loved my sisters and me, and because we had done something to deserve it. She almost never missed.

For years, when we were kids, her purse held a wooden spoon. If our parents brought us to Square One, and one of us acted up, Mom would haul us into a corner or a stairwell, open her purse, and say, "*Look* in *here*." We'd peer inside, see the spoon, process what it meant, and calm down. My mom didn't need to use violence if she could imply it.

Well, usually. She did break that spoon on the hard plastic seat of Courtney's tricycle as my sister, having just committed some little kid caper, tried to flee on three wheels. Mom still had a lightweight wooden paddle, too, a novelty with caricatures depicting parents spanking their kids. It didn't travel with us, but in her right hand it would move fast from the tabletop to somebody's backside—usually mine. It, too, broke during a spanking one day, and exposed the flaw in the African American maxim that a Hard Head Makes a Soft Behind. Grade-school-aged Morgan, concrete at both ends.

But my mom didn't spank us often, and never beat our butts if we didn't deserve it. She never did anything that hurt us long-term, and never touched our faces.

If she had, she could have done real damage. She had short fingers and blunt hands like her dad's, and bulbous knuckles like mine. No jewelry, though. Not even a wedding ring. Neither of my parents wore one. I'd asked why, before the divorce, and they each told me their fingers had fattened over the years, and their rings no longer fit. I understood, numb to the built-in metaphor about two people outgrowing a marriage.

That can happen after twenty-three years, with normal marriage stress, plus my dad's jagged edges, and two sets of in-laws rooting against you. My folks had been apart eight years by the time we all landed in that hospital room, but my mom never shed the Campbell name. Twenty-three years and three kids aren't a sunk cost. They're an investment, even if the relationship crumbles like my parents' marriage did.

The divorce cost my dad so much. Time with his kids. Dollars diverted to lawyers and child support, his rent on top of our mortgage. His pride, too. He liked nice things. Before kids, he drove shiny, loud, overpowered Corvettes. He traded in his second 'Vette for a Lotus Elan. After the divorce, he had to borrow his mom's car, and spent three years renting bedrooms and basements before he could finally afford that apartment in the high-rise on Mississauga Valley Boulevard.

A big part of him still had to see divorce as the best way to spend his time and money. Why do it otherwise? If the mental cost of staying married feels that steep, you write the cheques to liberate yourself, and write some more once you're free. Twenty-three years is enough time to decide you no longer want a relationship, and to calculate a fair price for leaving it.

But after the diagnosis, my dad started spending more time at the house, and not just with Courtney and me. Talking to my mom. Co-operating with her. Functioning like a friend, which was brand new for us. That first week of September, with cancer hacking at him, my dad showed up at our place, looking for my mom, because he knew. She was in Chicago that weekend, but rushed back to help. She knew, too.

The person you called when you thought you were dying—that's your partner. Whatever years-long conflicts you were nursing, they dissolved in a crisis like this. If you survived, the two of you could promise to do better by each other in the future. And if not, at least you would go out knowing peace with the person you loved most.

My dad's eyes stayed closed. The machines helping keep him alive still beeped and droned. My mom stroked his hair and told him to hold on so he could see Jimmy and Earl. Twenty-three years and three kids outweighed whatever bitterness lingered after the divorce, and even had my mom ready for a truce with Granny Mary.

"You'll see Jimmy on Monday," she said. "You just relax and hang in."

Granny Mary stayed quiet, down there at the foot of the bed, eyes closed, hands together.

Sssssssss . . .

September 10

Saturday morning, September 10, 1994, I packed my black and white Nike football cleats and my red-and-white, foam-insulated water bottle in my blue adidas gym bag.

My mom zipped open her red leather purse and dug around until she found her lipstick. She applied a layer, then moved through the rest of her morning routine. Eventually, her friend Marilyn would arrive to drive her to the hospital and check on my dad.

I pulled on a pair of track pants over my red shorts and grabbed my yellow plastic Sony Walkman and the tapes I'd need: Nas's *Illmatic* and Onyx's *BacDaFucUp*. The Nas album was uncut hip-hop, full of samples and curse words and raw, violent stories about life in the projects. But it was still cerebral enough for a rap snob like me, perfect for late-night meditation and long rides to school on the Route 44, or to Waterloo in the back of some teenager's car. And the Onyx tape was nearly two years old, but it still got me hyped. Well, not the whole tape. One track. "Shifty." I'd play it late in warmup. It hit me like a stimulant. I slung the gym bag over my shoulder, kissed my mom on the cheek, grabbed my bus pass, and headed outside to wait for the northbound Route 44 to Meadowvale Town Centre.

My mom didn't say goodbye. She almost never did.

"Be careful," she said, like usual.

From Meadowvale Town Centre, I'd catch the 48 and ride back south to South Common Mall, then connect with Austin and the Toronto guys, whom I had never met, for the forty-minute drive to Waterloo. I knew my preparation wasn't perfect. Ideally, I'd have spent the week resting and stretching, visualizing at home after school. Instead, I attended a bedside vigil every night, and wrestled with the idea of death, and girded for the family drama about to erupt.

But it's not like I had a choice. When Dad could still talk, he told me to attend the camp and play well, no matter what happened with him. And I didn't know when I'd have another chance to play in front of talent scouts, who could tell college coaches that I was worth recruiting. The new school year brought more mail from college coaches in Canada, but I wanted attention from teams I saw on TV, Notre Dame or Florida State or Michigan. That showcase wouldn't wait for me just because my dad was dying and my grandparents were set to melt down. I found a seat near the back of the bus and sat and popped in *Illmatic*. Then I closed my eyes and tried to envision a successful afternoon.

Forty minutes and one transfer later, I hopped off the 48 and arrived at the meeting place, in the parking lot next to No Frills, facing the community centre. Austin said to meet him at 10 a.m. I arrived at 9:55.

10 a.m., no Austin. Fine. For me, on time meant five minutes early. In that way, I mirrored my dad, who could never unlearn that habit after he picked it up in the Navy.

At 10:05, I didn't sweat. For most other people, on time meant five minutes late. Austin's time wasn't my dad's. I paced the parking lot while I waited.

At 10:15, I started wondering whether I had arrived early. Maybe he meant 10:30. If they came much later, we wouldn't reach Waterloo on time. But I almost welcomed this stress. A chance to worry about something besides my dad and the hospital and the brewing family feud. I walked to the pay phone inside the bus terminal lobby and called Austin. No answer. Maybe he was on his way.

At 10:25, I could see my football future evaporating. If I showed out at camp, maybe college coaches would have a reason to come to the Woodlands School to see about me, possibly on a side trip while in town checking on players from better programs. But if I couldn't grab their attention today, they wouldn't have much incentive to scout talent on a team that averaged one victory a year. I dropped another quarter in the slot and called Austin again. No answer.

By 10:35, I had moved past panicking, straight to resignation. Over the next few years, I would learn a lot about accepting imperfect situations, and that morning I understood that the uphill battle to keep big-time college coaches from forgetting about me just became a little steeper. If I wanted to improve the situation, I would have to accept it first. If I couldn't perform at the showcase, I wouldn't waste the day. I told myself that once I arrived home, and if my dad was still stable, I'd run sprints up the hill in the park across the street. At least ten. To burn off the pent-up tension. To stay ready, just in case.

At 10:45, I walked back to the pay phone, pulled my last quarter from my pocket, dropped it in the slot, and called my mom. One ring. Two. Three. In the early days of call display, I hoped she knew enough to answer a number she didn't recognize, and had to calculate how much longer to stay on the line. I couldn't risk losing my coin if the call went to voicemail.

"Hello?"

"Hi, Mom."

"Hey, boy," she said. "Why aren't you in Waterloo?"

"My ride never showed up," I said. "I've been here almost an hour."

"Well," she said. "I have to tell you. Your father passed away this morning. Right around ten o'clock."

"Okay," I said, unsure what I could even add. "How's Granny Mary?"

"She's holding up," Mom said. "So far."

"Okay."

"But your father wasn't in any pain, so don't worry about that," Mom said. "He was just . . . tired. He was tired, Morgan. It was time."

"I know, Mom."

"Oh, and a heads-up: your grandfather's not happy."

"What happened?"

"When I called the Folks to tell them Pete had died, he asked if he should go to the hospital," Mom said. "I told him there was no need. Nothing anybody can do now. Pete's already dead. Just stay put. Well . . . he didn't like me saying that. Got all quiet and huffy. But I don't need him over there fighting with Mary."

Mom knew she made sense, but Grandpa felt slighted and minimized and, worst of all, upstaged. We would all learn how personally he took it.

"Anyway, you might as well come on home," Mom said. "We'll be here."

We said our goodbyes, and I hung up the phone and walked outside to check the schedule. Northbound Route 48 was fifteen minutes away. If I made my connection, I could be home in an hour.

The Homegoing Heist

Granny Mary wanted a funeral for her son that matched both her imagination and every Black church stereotype: something long and loud and flashy and sad. A big, hollering crowd and an S-Curled, gold-chained preacher delivering a grief-stoking, fire-and-brimstone eulogy. The kind of service that ends with relatives threatening to leap into the grave alongside the coffin.

My mom wanted something more like the good side of my dad's personality: loving and kind of funny, but concise. He would never have taken a thousand words to say what he could have covered in eight, so it didn't make sense to celebrate him with a service as long as a workday. Maybe a lunch break.

He also told my mom he wanted to be cremated, but this wasn't his party. Funerals serve the people you leave behind, and Granny Mary wanted a dark shiny coffin propped open to reveal her son inside, dressed like his wedding day. A tuxedo and a clean shave, a fresh haircut and polished black dress shoes. If you've heard the term "casket sharp," you'll understand Granny Mary's vision for her son at his homegoing. And if you didn't know casket sharp before, you do now. Granny Mary wanted him to look like the Pete Campbell she remembered, not the one who withered after liver cancer tore him down from the inside.

Plus, Granny Mary claimed to have caravans of cousins ready to roll out from Detroit and Chicago and Grand Rapids to send Pete home, but none of them were driving to Canada for a memorial. They wanted a body and a long procession, and to gather around an open grave so they could grieve some more.

Another in a long list of demands Granny Mary hadn't fully thought out. Burying my dad in Canada would put him a long way from her, and turn periodic flower-laying from a day trip to a pilgrimage. Whatever Granny Mary thought she wanted from a big funeral and a graveside vigil, it wouldn't have justified the time and money she'd have to spend driving to Toronto twice a year. Plus, Granny Mary always resented that my dad lived in Canada, so far from her and so close to the Joneses; in death, she would want him nearby. Burying him in Chicago would mean hauling the corpse and casket back home, a feat neither simple nor cheap. Granny Mary wasn't paying, but she didn't doubt she'd get what she wanted. And regardless of cost, what kind of person would veto the earnest wishes of a woman forced to entomb her only child?

My mom, who wouldn't budge from the plan or the budget, not even for Granny Mary. Especially not for Granny Mary.

The day my parents married, in my mom's folks' big apartment on Paxton Avenue in South Shore, Granny Mary kept hounding the newlyweds to mash cake in each other's faces so she could take a picture of the mess. She thought a photo of them with icing smeared like war paint on their cheeks would look cute. My mom thought it inconvenient. Why ruin a makeup job that took half an hour for a photo op that would last ten seconds? Dad didn't want to do it, but had grown used to his mom's demands and, if my mom had agreed, he would have done the cake smash just to shut Granny Mary up. My mom refused, because why establish that pattern? If you give her the messy cake photo now, she'll want more later. My mom believed you teach people how to treat you, so Granny Mary learned something on their wedding day.

If she thought my mom would buckle before the funeral, she thought wrong. So, they compromised. Granny Mary could pick the urn and keep the ashes, but there was no debating cremation.

———

My tweenage years lined up with some of the ugliest moments I witnessed of my parents' breakup. Emphasis here on what I witnessed, because I can only imagine what my parents said to each other with nobody around. My two older sisters had jobs and activities and social lives to draw them out of the house. I spent more time at home, so I saw and heard a lot.

Like that warm and overcast afternoon sometime after Christmas of my sixth-grade year, when my dad stopped by to discuss some grown folks' stuff with my mom. I heard voices and temperatures rising, but I just sat on the couch and focused on the TV and pretended not to notice. Didn't turn my head when the loud talking turned to shouting. Didn't actively listen, even when it got personal. But I heard.

Mom: Pete, you do this, this, and that.
Dad: Well, you do that, that, and *this*.
Mom: Okay, but at least I never A, B, and C.
Dad: Yeah, but you damn sure X, Y, and Zee.
Mom: Blah, blah, blah. Yap, yap, yap. You don't even listen.
Dad: Blah, blah, blah, blah . . . Jeanie, you a *bitch*!

And then:

"Waaaaaaaah . . ."

Me, on the couch, halfway through sixth grade and crying like a three-month-old. Dad rushed over and cupped my cheek in his huge hands and used his thumbs to wipe my tears. Then Mom hunched over me, too. And then a fresh fight started over which one of them had made me cry. Dad did, technically, but I knew it was my fault, really. I had a brand-new skateboard and snow-free streets on a warm winter day. I could have taken my toy for a ride. Instead, I sat and heard adults fight like adults, and I paid for it.

Other times, while my sisters were out being real teenagers, I'd be at home with my mom, and if something divorce-related had left her fuming, she might vent to me about how my dad torpedoed their marriage. The stonewalling. The thoughtlessness. The cheating, which, in fairness, couldn't keep pace with *his* dad's cheating. One mistress beats a series of them, right?

Or I'd be with my dad in the furnished basement where he lived, a five-minute walk from our place, and a big step up from the room he rented elsewhere in that same townhouse complex after he first moved out. We'd be watching football or boxing or a kung-fu movie we had rented from Queen Video, and he might unload about the heavy cost of divorce. One day he added up everything he'd paid the lawyer, divided by the actual time they had spent together, then showed me the per-hour cost on his calculator screen—144 dollars and some change, or as much as he made in an entire shift at De Havilland.

The lesson I absorbed back then: grown-ups make 144 dollars a day, though I'd need a while to figure out whether that was a lot of money.

The wisdom I take from it now: try to be a good husband, because it's what you signed up for, and because you don't have Bad Husband Money. If you don't invest in your marriage, you'll pay for a divorce. Only one of those options is affordable.

By seventeen, I had already sat in on adult conversations, and witnessed big decisions and the bare-knuckle brawls that often precede them. So maybe that's how I wound up in a showroom at Lee Funeral Home on Queen Street in Streetsville, watching Mom and Granny Mary haggle over a container for my dad's ashes.

Granny Mary was there because it was her son; my mom, because it was her money. Aunt Emma had come up from Grand Rapids. She

was my dad's half-brother's widow and still close to both Mom and
Granny Mary, which is why we needed her there, too. Few other people
had enough capital with each of them to act as a referee, and to keep
them both focused on choosing from among the dozens of urns lining
the walls like sneakers on display at Foot Locker.

"How about that one?" Aunt Emma asked, pointing to a pot-
bellied, copper-coloured urn like the one the Undertaker brandished
on Saturday afternoon wrestling shows.

Granny Mary sat with her hands folded in her lap, head down. She
raised her eyes to peek at the urn, then shook her head. My mom
sighed. The funeral director waited. Aunt Emma kept browsing.

The shiny brass one?

Granny Mary shook her head.

The plain wooden one?

Granny Mary shook her head.

The silver one shaped like a lava lamp?

Granny Mary didn't want that one either.

"How about that one," Aunt Emma said, pointing to the polished
wood urn perched high on the wall. "With the praying hands."

Granny Mary glanced up at it, then stayed silent. But she didn't say
no, and that felt like progress. She stared at her hands, still in her lap,
clasped tighter. She tilted forward an inch, then rocked back, as though
this process tormented her. And it might have. Burials feel final, but
you can exhume corpses. Once they slide you into the furnace to burn
your flesh, and then grind your bones to dust, it's final-final. Maybe
Granny Mary wasn't ready.

The funeral director waited. Aunt Emma patted Granny Mary's
forearm. My mom sighed and rolled her eyes. Nobody else saw, but
I noticed and felt a flicker of shame. In the moment it seemed so cal-
lous and out-of-character. We all hurt that week, but Dad's death
wounded Granny Mary most deeply, and my mom mocked her.
Years later, as a grown-up, I'd realize my mom was the only person in

the room who knew Granny Mary well enough to distinguish her mourning from pure performance.

"Mary?" Aunt Emma asked. "Do you like this one?"

Granny Mary bit her bottom lip and stared at her hands. My mom sighed again. I cut my eyes back and forth between them.

Granny Mary raised her head. She locked eyes with the funeral director and nodded. The polished wooden box with the tiny gold praying hands stamped on the corner, a lifelong reminder she had lost both a son and a power struggle.

—

Dad died two days after Dana turned twenty-three, a week into her final year studying vocal music performance at Wilfrid Laurier University. I used to joke that she and her friends were music jocks, but I also meant it. They dug music like I did football, studied and built future plans around it. Music was plan A and plan B for her.

Dana was a natural singer, but don't misunderstand: she worked at it. She went to high school at Cawthra Park, a forty-five-minute school bus ride away, in the opposite corner of Mississauga from where we lived, because they had an arts program and accepted her into it. She took all the classes and sang in all the choirs, and worked with a private coach to polish her vocals to an even brighter shine. At Cawthra, they gave her a nickname: "Tiger Pipes," because her vocals were so fierce. But—and this is crucial for aspiring stage and sport parents—talent is a gift. You can refine and develop it, but you can't buy or learn it. You can only choose your parents well.

Except neither of our parents sang, so that left the Jones and Campbell grandparents to issue competing claims about the source of Dana's glass-shattering soprano. Claude Jones thought Dana's talent came from him, because he had a five-decade career as a pianist, and because he thought he was the centre of everything. Plus, his youngest son, my uncle Jeff, had JUNO Awards and platinum records on his wall, if you're wondering which side of the family possesses the Music Gene. It expressed itself at full strength in Dana.

But Grandpa wasn't a great singer, or even a good one, if you asked my dad.

He was a pianist who also sang. If you're good at sifting through family archives, you'll find a few recordings of Claude Jones performing, and you'll hear him hit all the notes. But you won't hear the range or dynamics or ad-libs you'd expect of somebody who sang as a vocation. He sang to supplement his piano playing. Find the right sequence of the right solo, and you might mistake him for Erroll Garner, but he'd never trick you into thinking he was Joe Williams or Johnny Hartman or Billy Eckstine. Those guys were all-star vocalists. Grandpa could carry a tune.

Put another way, if some calamity had robbed Claude Jones of his singing voice, he probably still would have paid the bills and raised four kids playing piano. But if some injury had crippled his left hand, which played low notes and strummed chords like a rhythm guitarist, or his right, which handled melodies and the top end of improvised solos, and Claude Jones had to sing for a living, they all might have starved. Those Canadian talent agents didn't recruit him for his vocals. If he hadn't mastered the piano, my sisters and I might never have been born.

Grandpa knew he wasn't a singer. For years, he drove a big white Oldsmobile Delta 88, with a vanity plate that read CRJ 88—homages to the instrument he used to fashion a career, and raise a family, and transport his whole clan to a new beginning in Canada.

When Dana hit sixteen-ish and had done enough singing and learned enough theory to begin thinking of herself as a musician, Grandpa issued a ridiculous proclamation. Real musicians, he said, played instruments, and so instrumentalists were the only true musicians.

That decree excluded a lot of people from the fraternity, most notably Dana. And it triggered a recurring debate we'd endure every time we visited my grandparents at their apartment. Grandpa would restate his resolution, and Dana would issue the logical and self-evident rebuttal that anybody who studied and practiced and made music intensively, as a matter of craft and not just a hobby, was a musician.

"Yes," Grandpa would say, pausing and raising the stubby index finger of his left hand to indicate he had some mind-blowing new detail to reveal. "But with an *instrument*."

"My voice is my instrument," Dana would argue. It's a bald-faced, inscrutable truth to most people, because most of us recognize that a voice trained to make music is as much an instrument as Uncle Jeff's bass guitar, or the concert-sized Steinway in my grandparents' living room. But to my grandpa, that argument was Achilles, and he'd raise that stubby finger once more to tell you he'd found the heel.

"But a voice isn't an *instrument*," he'd say.

"Then what is it?"

"It's a voice."

This stuff would consume entire afternoons.

"But if I use it to make music, it's an instrument," Dana would say.

"No, a piano is an instrument. A voice is a voice."

"So you're saying Ella Fitzgerald isn't a musician?"

"Ella's a *singer*."

Right here is where the sheer pointlessness of these debates would become clear to one of the people entangled in it. Usually, the person making the more rational argument. So, almost never my grandpa.

But let's follow Grandpa's logic where it leads, because if Dana wasn't a musician, neither were any of the vocalists whose names he liked to drop on days he felt like talking to us about music. Billie Holiday? He played piano for her on stage one night in Chicago, not long before liver disease overtook her. Not a musician, apparently. Neither was Joe Williams, a friend of Grandpa's from Chicago who succeeded Jimmy Rushing as the featured singer in Count Basie's big band.

Grandpa liked to tell a story about being on the stand one night in some ritzy lounge in downtown Chicago, when Dinah Washington strutted into the club and called across the room.

"Claude Jones! You piano-playin' *son of a gun*!"

Now imagine Grandpa, strumming those rhythmic chords with his left hand, riffing on the melody with his right, and shouting back, "Thanks, baby! But you're not a musician!"

You can't imagine that, and neither could he, because on this particular point, Grandpa was full of shit. If he didn't know it, he sensed it, because he would never have said, "You're not a musician" to Ella Fitzgerald's face. Grandpa introduced Dana to Joe Williams once, when Williams played the Bermuda Onion in downtown Toronto, back when Du Maurier cigarettes still sponsored the jazz festival every June. Grandpa didn't ask Williams to sit Dana down and explain why neither of them was a real musician; he just caught up with his old friend and let Dana be a fan.

But within our family, he knew he could start real fights, like the one brewing the week we cremated my dad, or fake ones like the Singers Aren't Musicians debate, on the flimsiest premises. Then he'd refuse to give up and declare himself the winner simply because he resolved to keep fighting when a normal person would drop the conflict and move on.

Granny Mary had a piano in her living room, too—an old upright slotted into a corner near the window. It was the opposite of Grandpa's Steinway. Carolina blue paint, chipped along the ridges. White keys yellowing like old newsprint. Where Grandpa treated his Steinway like the heirloom it was, Granny Mary treated her off-brand upright like a useful tool.

When Grandpa retired from the music business, he also stopped playing piano. Cold turkey. He would pay a professional tuner to come to his apartment and tighten the Steinway's strings, and he'd play for a few minutes to make sure it sounded right. Then he wouldn't touch that piano again until the tuner returned six months later. Meanwhile, Granny Mary's battered upright piano was always a touch out of tune, but she never hired anyone to fix it. She just kept playing and lived with the sour notes.

As pianists, they weren't in the same class. Granny Mary was like your uncle who played a mean right field in his Sunday afternoon softball league. Grandpa was like your uncle who pitched for the Blue Jays.

But Granny Mary sought whatever spotlight she could find. She sang alto in more than one church choir, and was a self-accompanied hymn singer in her living room. And she loved Saturday night banquets at family reunions in Grand Rapids and Chicago, where the evening's programming began with the Negro National Anthem. We would Lift Every Voice and Sing, but Granny Mary would raise hers higher and louder and with more vibrato than anybody else in the room, just so folks would look. Just so they'd know she could do it.

She couldn't sing as well as Dana, but unless you're Kathleen Battle or Lalah Hathaway, neither can you. Granny Mary was enough of a singer, though, that if she told you Dana got her Tiger Pipes from her dad's side of the family, you could believe her.

Either way, Dana had this big, bright, clear, resonant singing voice, and she knew how to use it.

The previous summer, maybe six weeks before my dad's cancer diagnosis, Dana and two opera-singing friends performed the anthems before the Blue Jays played the White Sox at Comiskey Park, and we travelled as a fragmented family to listen in person. Dana rode to Chicago with my mom and her parents, then stayed with Aunt Peggy in South Shore. Courtney and I travelled with my dad in a rented minivan, first to Grand Rapids for a family reunion, and then to Chicago. From there, Courtney and I defected to the Jones camp. Nobody wanted to fiddle with the rabbit ears on the old TV on Granny Mary's back porch, or suffer the stifling heat the South Side served up every July. Aunt Peggy's place was crowded, but she was young and fun and cool, and had cable TV and an air conditioner.

The Joneses drove to the ballpark and sat in premium seats—lower bowl, behind third base. When Dana and her friends sang, my grandpa moved in behind home plate, right to the edge of the field with his handheld video camera, and recorded through the holes in the mesh that protected people in the expensive seats from foul balls. Dad and Granny Mary, meanwhile, took the Red Line to 35th Street and bought tickets in a discount section of the upper deck, high above the first-base line.

We all heard Dana and her two friends, Sandie and Jackie, smash "O Canada" and then "The Star-Spangled Banner." If they were more famous and this were a bigger game, we might remember this performance the way we do Marvin Gaye's funked-up anthem from the 1983 NBA All-Star Game, or Whitney Houston hitting those big notes before a fighter-jet flyover at the Super Bowl in 1991. Three sopranos in the summer of 1993, three-part harmony, 31,000 spectators in a standing ovation. Maybe I'm overstating it there; they sang an anthem, so the fans were already standing. But we know Dana and her friends blew minds. One of the umpires even wiped a tear from his cheek before he thanked them.

"You ladies . . . you are truly blessed," he said, sniffing back another tear.

If Dana and her Tiger Pipes could squeeze tears from a dour and stone-faced Major League Baseball umpire, imagine what she could do to mourners at her own father's funeral, primed to cry after spending all week stewing in their grief. Imagine the catharsis. Imagine the wailing. Imagine the waterworks if Dana stood up in front of the church and hit the right note at the right volume.

Granny Mary had played it all out in her mind. She wouldn't get the long and lachrymose funeral she wanted, but Dana could wring some tears from people if she sang. Dana had come home from school in Waterloo expecting to attend a memorial service, and walked straight into Granny Mary, who wanted to stage a show.

"Dana, are you going to sing at your father's funeral?"

No.

"Your *father* would really *appreciate* it if you *sang* at his funeral."

You don't know that.

"Seems to *me*, a *good* daughter, who *loved* her *father*, would *want* to *sing* at his *funeral.*"

I guess I'm not a good daughter.

Granny Mary had a million techniques to pry what she wanted from people, but none of them worked this week. My mom wouldn't agree to a big funeral with a lavish casket, and now my sister Dana wouldn't sing at the service. All this stubbornness frustrated Granny Mary, but it shouldn't have puzzled her. Dana, after all, was her grand-daughter, and Claude Jones's too.

Ever watch some seven-foot-tall phenom in an NBA game, then learn during the broadcast that his mom is six-foot-four, his dad is six-foot-nine, and they both played college ball? My family's like that, except with stubbornness. Both ends of the gene pool equally deep. We come from people who bend about as easily as your grandpa's fused ankle.

James Baldwin used to talk about his own father, and the price of pride. The old man wasn't built to swallow insults; he did it because he had to stay employed and out of jail so he could feed his nine kids. He absorbed as much as he could, for as long as he could, but he was too proud to function forever in a society bent on demeaning Black people. Racism eventually drove him insane, Baldwin explained, because he could no longer accommodate it.

"There was something in him which you could not bend," Baldwin told an interviewer once. "He could only be broken."

We each had to negotiate terms with racism in the broader world, but within our family we just had to make space for each other, so we had options beyond bending and breaking. If you were Claude Jones or Mary Campbell, you could also just stake out your position and refuse to move or apologize, then watch the relationships around you disintegrate. You'll let anything break, as long as it's not your pride.

—

Besides Granny Mary and Aunt Emma, nobody else drove up from Chicago or Detroit or Grand Rapids. My mom's parents didn't even drive twenty minutes across Mississauga. Grandpa had wanted to see a dead body, too, just for different reasons. But my mom had already kept him away from the hospital and Grandpa was more than miffed, so he and my grandma boycotted the funeral, while a few dozen of my dad's friends dotted the pews at Streetsville United Church.

His co-workers sat near the back, quiet and mournful. Some of them had come directly from the morning shift at De Havilland. Others would head straight from the church to the factory in Downsview for the afternoon shift.

Granny Mary sat in the front row, moaning and leaning on Aunt Emma, whose own cheeks glistened with tears. My mom sat across the aisle, sobbing. My sisters and I flanked her. Dana cried. Courtney and I didn't.

Afterward, Granny Mary wanted pictures, so she gathered Dana, Courtney, and me by the sign in front of the church. We didn't want to linger, but we posed and let her snap, just to keep the afternoon moving. She took frame after frame, then paused to pop a new roll of film into her Nikon, then started clicking again. So many photos. As if she were scared she'd forget how we looked. As if she didn't expect to see us again for a while.

—

The superintendent came because nobody else could unlock my dad's apartment. Granny Mary had driven back to Chicago that morning without calling to say goodbye or stopping to drop off his keys. My mom came because she had been in charge of everything all week.

Her friend Marilyn came because we needed somebody to drive. Normally, one of my mom's parents would have volunteered, but my dad's death had us feuding again, and landed my mom back on my grandparents' no-call list. My grandpa needed the spotlight, and my dad wouldn't let him have it. Claude Jones doesn't cede centre stage to anybody, not even to cancer patients at the end of their lives, or deceased people the week of their funeral. He had to punish somebody for overshadowing him, and my dad was dead. That left my mother and my sisters and me.

And I came because I spent more time in that apartment than anybody besides my dad himself, and I knew where to find stuff. My dad died without a will and bequeathed us a ton of work. Granny Mary could have saved us time with a heads-up that she was leaving, but instead let us burn the six hours it took to figure out she was gone.

The super sprung the lock and turned the knob, leaned into the door with his shoulder, then stepped into the apartment and turned on the light.

Dad's place looked ready for a new tenant.

No black leather couch, no blood-red leather recliner he had just bought on credit from The Bay. No TV, no stereo, and no music collection.

"That bitch," my mom said.

Two words. So much fury.

Unlike my dad and Uncle Ken, who, when they got to talking shit, could N-word this and MF that as deftly as any rapper from the generation that claimed to reinvent those words, my mom only swore on special occasions. She could curb-stomp you with language, but most times swearing could only dilute her power. Instead, she practiced the principle of creative limitation, avoiding curses and squeezing impact from the safe-for-network-TV words still in her tool kit. Anybody could ask, rhetorically, if you were "fucking crazy," but only my mom would inquire whether you had "*lost* your *ever* lovin' buh-*lack* and *fuzzy mind.*"

That's a real thing she said, by the way. Spontaneously, and not pulled from a satchel of one-liners, like when she said an ugly person looked like "fifty miles of bad road," or "death warmed over." Ever Lovin' Buh-lack and Fuzzy Mind was an original, formulated in the moment. Not a print, but one of one from an artist. Catch her in the right moment, and you might hear another once-in-a-lifetime insult, but she reserved curse words for people who really deserved them, like Black Republicans—usually but not always men—who stooped to lick trickle-down privilege from the shoe tops of racist white conservatives.

"Look at this bitch Ben Carson with his shit-eatin' grin, cozying up to Donald Trump. Black people don't want you anymore, and these white people will never respect you. Go on somewhere and take Koonye West with you."

Other members of the short list of people at whom my mom has hurled R-rated barbs:

Herman Cain.

Candace Owens.

Diamond, Silk, Tim Scott, and Clarence Thomas.

Also, Granny Mary, who, as far as we knew, voted Democrat.

"That trifling, conniving, back-stabbing bitch," she said. "Morgan, what else is missing?"

The glass-top coffee table and the dining room set.

The books and the photo albums.

The dark-blue pea coat my dad had owned since his Navy days and had told my mom he wanted me to have.

If you're wondering how a seventy-year-old woman who, two days earlier, was too weak and grief-addled to lift her index finger to point at the urn she wanted, could load the entire contents of a grown man's apartment into her car, the superintendent told us she had reserved the freight elevator the previous afternoon. And if she'd booked the elevator, she must have rented a truck, because all that stuff wouldn't fit into her big red Cadillac. And if she had a truck, she must have hired dudes to move the merchandise. No other way to make so much stuff disappear so quickly. Over time, the detail and strategy Granny Mary invested in this caper would become clear, slowly but unmistakably, like a picture developing from a negative.

Mississauga wasn't Granny Mary's city, but she figured out where to find a truck and some reliable movers. And you can't bring that much stuff into the U.S. without handing officers at the border a manifest. Otherwise, you'd spend thousands of dollars and countless hours clearing all those belongings through customs. Trucks don't get packed by magic and manifests don't write themselves. It all required planning.

Not a month before all this happened, Granny Mary drove up from Chicago with my aunt Julia and her husband and their four kids. Granny Mary stayed at my dad's place; the Aunt Julias stayed down the street at the Novotel. The Canadian National Exhibition had just started, and Granny Mary insisted my dad take his half-sister and her family. They had never visited Toronto before, and she said they deserved an immersion in a cherished local custom.

The CNE tells Torontonians that summer's about to end. You have your fun and ride the rides and eat all the Tiny Tom Donuts you can, because after a couple weeks it'll be Labour Day. After that, it's back to school and work and real life. If you want to know what kind of shape my dad was in when CNE 1994 opened, consider that the day after it closed he was in palliative care at Credit Valley Hospital, painkiller dripping straight into his veins, his cheeks hollowing out because he couldn't eat, legs swelling with fluid because apparently that's what happens when you're set to collapse after battling cancer for three years.

Dad had learned how to disguise the extent to which his body had broken down. Sometimes he'd mention a sore back, then let you assume it was an old chronic pain instead of a new one that deepened as cancer advanced. So, he took Aunt Julia and the crew to the CNE and he didn't complain. He spent one of the last afternoons of his life strolling the midway with his tourist relatives.

Granny Mary?

She stayed back at Dad's place, talking about she was tired.

That move was either strange or sinister. She either wanted to spend time with her cancer patient son, or she didn't. Either she drove eight-and-a-half hours just to sit in my dad's apartment, or she made a road trip from Chicago to case it.

She got almost everything she could have wanted, but left behind Dad's black Suzuki Swift. We found it sitting untouched in the parking garage—but we didn't know for how long. Granny Mary had the key to the car, and a long list of people she could send up from Chicago to retrieve it.

"I've got half a mind to call that evil bitch right now," my mom said as we walked back into our house.

But she knew it was too early. We all had an internal clock that calculated driving time from Mississauga to the South Side of Chicago, and could adjust for driver, vehicle, route, and delays at the border. Before cell phones, the mental hourglass let you know when to expect a relative on your doorstep, or a phone call from someone who had left that morning. If my dad drove, just call it seven hours. With anyone else, you set your mind's timer for eight, assuming they exited I-94 in northern Indiana and took the Chicago Skyway into the city. My mom's parents preferred that route. Easier access to people who lived east, like Aunt Edith and Aunt Peggy.

You'd add thirty minutes if they took I-94 around the bottom of Chicago and exited at 87th Street, near Granny Mary's house. I liked going that way because it brought you within sniffing distance of the Jays Potato Chips factory at 99th and Cottage Grove. The smell of grease and salt signalled you were ten minutes from the finish line.

But Granny Mary clearing customs in a packed moving van would need at least eleven hours, maybe fourteen if she detoured to Grand Rapids to drop off Aunt Emma.

The math meant Granny Mary was likely still driving, but that Aunt Emma might already be home.

Mom dialled.

And waited.

"Hello?"

"You have fun driving that moving van?"

"Jeanie?"

"Yes, this is Jeanie. Did you drive the truck or did that evil bitch Mary drive it? And Emma, don't you *dare* lie to me."

My mom adored Aunt Emma and resented Cousin Khadijah, who wasn't even in grade school when that car crash killed her dad, my dad's half-brother Ernest. Aunt Emma held both their lives together, moved to Detroit and raised Cousin Khadijah solo while working long hours at Michigan Bell. She saved money and sent Cousin Khadijah to a Catholic high school, which was supposed to propel her to college and a good job and a comfortable life.

Aunt Emma returned to Grand Rapids and married Uncle Larry. Cousin Khadijah stayed in Detroit and got pregnant, then landed back in Grand Rapids and handed off her daughter for Aunt Emma and Uncle Larry to raise. Natasha grew into a straight-A student. Cousin Khadijah drifted back and forth between Grand Rapids and Chicago, in and out of jobs.

Sometimes my mom talked about Cousin Khadijah, usually in the context of what she could have achieved if she had worked as hard for herself as Aunt Emma had worked for her. Or she'd mention Cousin Khadijah in the light of the quiet and child-free married life Aunt Emma and Uncle Larry would have lived if Cousin Khadijah hadn't dragged them back into raising kids.

My mom revered Aunt Emma, the way aspiring writers do Toni Morrison for writing *The Bluest Eye* while working forty-plus hours a week and rearing two teenagers on her own in New York City. People who spin such big results from so few resources earn a special kind of respect from folks engaged in the same struggle, so Aunt Emma always seemed to my mom a super-parent. Working at Michigan Bell was one full-time job. Getting a high school diploma into Cousin Khadijah's hand without a scandal or a detour or a meltdown was another. But there's no Nobel Prize for people who accomplish what Aunt Emma did.

That all-star parenting job didn't even pay cash. As far as my mom was concerned, Cousin Khadijah should have compensated Aunt Emma by earning a degree and starting a career, and letting Aunt Emma and Uncle Larry spend their free time doing whatever they chose.

Mom dialled Aunt Emma's number feeling heated and betrayed, ready to browbeat her sister-in-law like a bad cop. But then Aunt Emma started talking. Mom's temperature dropped. She could hear Aunt Emma crying.

She told my mom about the moving van and the freight elevator, and the cross-border drive with all my dad's stuff. But she also told my mom how much she loved her brother-in-law Pete, and how Granny Mary rounded up my dad's belongings as if she had permission to do it. Aunt Emma said she'd have acted better if she had known better. She also confirmed that if either she or Granny Mary could drive a stick shift, that black Suzuki Swift would be in Chicago.

———

First Commandment of the Street: Thou Shalt Not Snitch.

But my mom's not from the street. So, when The Bay's credit department called, asking when Pete Campbell might get around to paying for the red leather recliner he had just bought on his store credit card, my mom told them everything. Pete was dead and the chair was in Chicago, along with the rest of his possessions, against his dying desire if not his written will, which didn't exist. When the rep asked about recovering the chair, my mom said it was possible. My dad hadn't had many chances to rest in it; it might be so gently used that they could resell it. Best thing to do, she said, was to call Mary Campbell and have her arrange to send it back. Here's her number. Tell her you got it from Jeanie.

She also called the Canadian Cancer Society to tell them what happened to the donation they'd been expecting from the guys at De Havilland. Granny Mary had that, too, even though she couldn't use all of it. U.S. banks don't process Canadian coins, and Americans sometimes confuse those colourful Canadian bills for food stamps, except food stamps have purchasing power. But if the Cancer Society wanted to repatriate that cash, Mom told them they could find it at Mary Campbell's house, Lafayette Avenue, south of 92nd Street, South Side of Chicago.

Then came the letters.

First one went to the pastor at St. James AME, a few doors south of Granny Mary on Lafayette, letting him know his parishioner, Mary Campbell, had violated the eighth commandment. She didn't just steal from her kids, but from their future kids. And not just from them, but from Canadian cancer patients who had better use for a few hundred Canadian dollars than Mary Campbell did.

She had also broken the flipside of the fifth commandment, because Honouring Thy Father and Mother implies at least a little reciprocity. It certainly doesn't empower parents to loot their grown children's estates. That's the opposite of honour.

So, if the pastor asked Mary Campbell where she got all that new furniture and electronics, and she said anything different, that's commandment nine up in smoke.

Then Mom ripped off a copy of that same letter to the pastor at Lillydale Baptist, Granny Mary's other church. She didn't expect either man to read her words and haul Granny Mary into the principal's office for a scolding, or to banish her from the church for her egregious sins. She just thought they'd want to know what Pious Mary Campbell was capable of.

If they thought they knew her, they'd have been shocked.

If they knew her like my mom did, maybe not.

The Next Season

The Bramalea Broncos' centre snapped the ball, then squashed the defender across from him. To his right, Bramalea's guard erased our defensive tackle. From my position at middle linebacker, I watched the Woodlands Rams' defensive line part like double doors to reveal Bramalea's fullback, bearing down on me with his white jersey, blue pants, big biceps, and bad intentions. I stepped forward to meet force with force.

Every football team had a play like this one. They called it Power, or Fullback Lead, or Iso— short for isolation, because it pits one team's fullback against the other team's middle linebacker, and sets them up for a head-on collision. On this day, on this play, my job was to dispatch the fullback and tackle the guy with the ball. And the fullback's job was to bulldoze me and pave a path for the ball carrier.

This play was basic, fundamental, foundational football, and you'd see versions of it in games from little league all the way to the NFL. It tested strength, will, manhood, and skill. The best middle linebackers made their reputations crumpling fullbacks on Iso, then grinding ball carriers into the turf. Dick Butkus. Mike Singletary. Ray Lewis. They didn't lose these showdowns.

I bit down on my mouthguard and readied for contact. He scowled and leaned forward. I stepped up. He accelerated. We both heard a loud crack as our heavy plastic helmets crashed together. If he was human like me, he also saw a split-second flash of black, and maybe felt the same warm buzzing inside his skull.

But he had a weight advantage and a running start. I stood five-foot-seven and weighed 150 pounds, and had never played middle linebacker before that afternoon. He finished moving forward. I stumbled to keep from landing on my back. Somehow, I delayed their tailback long enough to keep him from scampering all the way through our defense, which, on its strongest days, leaked like a warped O-ring. Otherwise, we were more of a burst pipe. But he still gained a first down, and Bramalea kept advancing.

This all happened deep in the second half of my final high school season. Football wasn't a simple after-school activity; it was career plans A and B. My choices went NFL first, CFL second, and writing as option 2.5, because if I wanted to live in Toronto on a CFL salary, I'd need an off-season job. To make any of that happen, I would need to play in college. Every day, I came home from school and looked for recruiting letters. Most days I found one.

And to play in college, I needed to keep standing out in high school. So, where other guys on our team considered football something in which to dabble, I went all out. I trained for it, watched it, read and thought and dreamed about it. Some guys saw a hobby, but I looked at football like a class. More correctly, I regarded it like other kids, with better study habits, did *their* classes—the key to my future. Each game was an exam. The move to middle linebacker, then, was a trick question.

When Bramalea ran laterally, I made plays. I could cut through traffic and tackle running backs before they barrelled through our whole defense. But when they came straight at me behind a lead blocker, I got trampled, and highlighted why good teams don't put little fast guys at middle linebacker.

But the 1994 Woodlands Rams were not a good football team.

We had some first-class athletes, guys who would have stood out on any squad. Our best players could make an average team strong, and a strong team unbeatable.

Kevin Gregory was a unicorn. He stood six-foot-five, played centre on the basketball team, and ran the 110 hurdles. Later, he would play junior college ball in Montreal, and score a scholarship offer from the University of Kentucky, but our coaches didn't know what to do with him. He played a little tight end and a little linebacker, but never in a scheme that showcased his gifts.

Patrick Dottin played cornerback, and intercepted passes as if they had always been intended for him. He tackled bigger guys, though, at just 140 pounds, he rarely saw anyone smaller than he was. But he made enough plays to land on the all-district team.

And if you could turn a fighter jet into a human being, you'd have Rayon Henry, who played tailback for us. Six feet, 170, long-limbed and quick. He had elite speed—faster than I was . . . maybe—and could change directions without braking. That mix of skills didn't exist in our league. We'd see a Black prime minister before we saw another athlete like Rayon Henry in Tier II football.

For us, losing wasn't a function of bad luck, or small faults we could fine-tune between games. We had dropped five straight games before Bramalea. The Woodlands Rams lost as a matter of habit and conditioning, and a losing culture that simultaneously trickled down from the top of the program and seeped up from the bottom.

Good teams prescribed weight-training and running over the summer, and would convene for workouts in late August so they could start the school year with chemistry and continuity. At the Woodlands School, football season ended in November, and coaches lost track of you until the next September. Whether you spent your summer in the weight room or at Dairy Queen, they didn't know or appear to care. First day of school, they'd put out the call, and the next few afternoons, kids would wander down to the coach's office, fill out forms, and receive their equipment. By Friday, in a good year, we'd have enough people in pads to run a full practice.

As chronic late starters, the Woodlands Rams never developed elaborate hand signals to communicate plays from the bench to the field. My junior year, our head coach would just shout to the quarterback from the sideline, loud enough for both teams to hear.

"Give the ball to Granville! Sweep right to Granville!"

When the other team decoded that message, he'd switch it up.

"Sweep left! Sweep left to Granville!"

Granville Mayers had more natural talent than any athlete I knew back then, and still ranks in my top five, including the Olympians and NFLers I know in real life. He ran forty yards in 4.3 seconds and rose eyebrow-high to the rim when he would slam dunk a basketball.

In Timberland boots.

He set long jump records that still stand, and could outrun our coach broadcasting our plays to the other team, but only for so long. When the other team knows who's getting the ball, *and* where he's going, playing defense becomes easy, even when you're trying to stop a human bullet train like Granville Mayers. So if you want to know how we started losing, even with the local equivalent of Bo Jackson in our backfield, that's how.

The next year, my final high school season, we added an assistant coach on defense who threatened to cut me from the team. Mr. Aubrey was a bull-necked, broad-shouldered, cinder block of a man, who taught gym and coached wrestling. He spoke with a lateral lisp and considered grieving a form of weakness. I missed all four practices the second week of school, and when I returned, he met me on the sideline and said I should have stayed away.

"But Coach, I wasn't at school at all," I said. "My dad died last week."

"Doesn't *matter*! You come to *practice*!" he said. "If it were *my* team, you wouldn't *be* here!"

A coach in a less dysfunctional program might not have burrowed in on a kid still mourning his dad's death. Or if he needed an example of a kid not committed to winning, he wouldn't have chosen the guy who attended football camp every summer, and worked out twice a day, every day, until fall. But coaches at the Woodlands School excelled at missing the point, and our win-loss record reflected it.

At Bramalea, we hit halftime trailing by two touchdowns, with no way to close that gap. Their offense was simple as vanilla ice cream. They ran the ball and bled the clock, and only passed when they had to. But against the Woodlands Rams, they never needed to. They held possession and piled up points by leaning on our weaknesses.

Like size.

Bramalea and other teams were built around eighteen- and nineteen-year-olds who spent summers running and lifting weights. We filled our roster with guys from every grade, and of every stature, from sort of big to way too small. Our team even added guys, assigned by the school board, from other schools that didn't have football programs.

We picked up a pudgy Black kid from Applewood whose parents named him Ralston but whom we called Arthur Ashe. He didn't like lotion; he didn't own lotion; he wouldn't let us talk him into using lotion; and it showed. Skin dry as autumn leaves. From a distance, I thought he wore grey leggings under his football pants. Up close, I saw the leg hair and the scales, and the white trails his fingernails left every time he scratched an itch.

We also had a guy we nicknamed Daddy—not for wisdom or worldliness, but because he looked old. Not mature. Just aged. Daddy had a thick brown mustache and a fuzzy shoulder-length mullet and dressed like an extra in a Def Leppard video. Tight jeans and white hi-top sneakersw and T-shirts with sleeves that reached just past the elbow. Daddy said he came from T.L. Kennedy, the high school ten minutes east of us. Daddy lied. Daddy came from 1982.

With adult size and strength, Daddy could have helped. But he had regular-guy dimensions and sapling arms, and wasn't much stronger than the little tenth graders who got more playing time than was healthy. Small and slow is a crappy combination, and our roster had plenty of both.

If player size was our first big obstacle, our tiny roster was the second.

Our team might have totalled thirty players. We rode to away games in a single school bus, and nobody shared seats. Other schools had a platoon of players for each phase of the game—offense, defense, special teams—and shuttled them on and off the field to keep guys fresh. We had a handful of standouts and irrational hope that guys like Daddy wouldn't hurt us too badly. Entering the season, we knew we faced slim odds of winning, so Kevin, Patrick, a few others, and I would have to play offense and defense *and* special teams. If we wanted water, we'd need to run to the bench and hydrate between quarters. Otherwise, we were on the field, trying to save our team from the rest of our team.

I played wherever my coaches needed me, and wherever college scouts wanted to see me. Cornerback because I could run, and safety because I could tackle. That overcast afternoon in Bramalea, I also played running back, because I had good balance and vision and change of direction, and because Rayon didn't show up. Stuff like that happened with the Woodlands Rams. Whether symptom or cause, high turnover and underperforming workplaces tended to stick together.

Rayon would reappear a few years later as an R&B singer named Ray Robinson, with a single called "Missed Your Chance," that made a small wave on the local scene. I can't blame him for abandoning the Woodlands Rams mid-season. Music is an unforgiving grind—I knew that from my grandpa and Uncle Jeff—but Rayon had a better chance of going platinum than he did of winning a football game with us, especially against Bramalea's defense. They didn't dazzle you with fancy schemes, but their front seven were fairly big kids who knew their assignments, which gave them two huge advantages over the Woodlands Rams.

I took a handoff and ran right, and an avalanche of Bramalea defenders buried me. Ran left and saw a wall of white jerseys, snowed under again. Any run up the middle became a frantic scramble for daylight. One guy dove at me, and I put my palm on his helmet and guided him to the ground face-first. Another guy bear-hugged me and I spun out of his arms. I zig-zagged past a third guy, then burst forward before the rest of their defense collapsed on me. All that action in a span of five seconds. All that work to gain one yard. That afternoon, it qualified as a success. Two plays later, we punted the ball back to Bramalea and I lined up for another series at middle linebacker.

Our first-stringer was a brown-haired senior named Doug, who carried most of his 225 pounds around his waist and his cankles and his mouth, which ran out of all proportion to his skill. He didn't tackle many Bramalea Broncos, but he did kick a guy late in the second quarter, which got him ejected. We replaced Doug with our starting free safety, skinny kid named Roman who had transferred in from Applewood, and who embodied the stereotypes that gave white coaches and sports writers wet dreams.

White?

The whitest. Looked like Axl Rose with a haircut.

A vocal leader?

Yep. Never stopped talking. Shouting orders. Berating other kids after their mistakes. Ignoring his own.

Slow?

Slower than an early '90s modem. But it didn't matter to our coaches because he was also an Aggressive High-Motor Guy. Gritty. A Tone-Setter with a Hard Hat, a Lunch Pail, and a Blue-Collar Work Ethic. Roman would hit you on the whistle, or a half-second after if the refs let him. He leapt into collisions with his forehead, and with the crown of his helmet if the refs didn't see it.

Our coaches loved Roman and trusted him in ways we didn't know adults could believe in teenagers. Not just that they kept him in the starting lineup despite other teams' slowest receivers outrunning him every week; we didn't have replacements, so we didn't have a choice. But they let him call plays on defense, like a coach on the field, even as he racked up bad decisions.

Against Streetsville, Roman called a blitz—for himself—and we watched a receiver stroll through the territory he had vacated, catch a pass, and run untouched into the end zone. Touchdown, Tigers. Another loss for the Woodlands Rams.

And at Bramalea, the referee flagged Roman for hitting a player after the whistle. Most players would eat the penalty. Roman raised his middle finger at the official, who tossed him from the game. Next week, Roman was back at free safety, calling plays as if he had earned the right. If you're tracking the factors that made our team the league's biggest losers, watch the way we paired a lack of depth with a dearth of discipline, and note which players our coaches favoured and why.

I spent the second half outrunning blockers to chase down ball carriers and butting heads with Bramalea's fullback as I tried to clog running lanes. I saw stars between plays and sipped water between quarters. Tried to keep Bramalea's margin of victory under thirty points, but I was miscast at middle linebacker. A Corvette hauling bricks around a construction site.

After the final whistle, I stood near midfield and peeled off my jersey and shoulder pads. Bramalea had beaten us by thirty-one. The bruises would appear over the next few hours: a small circle on my right bicep, and a splotch on my left thigh, the shape of the island of St. Lucia and nearly as big. Soreness would set in the following morning, when my whole body would feel like an assortment of rickety joints and rusty gears.

I walked toward the team bus, trying not to scan the sidelines for my dad. Tough reflex to override. At home games, I'd always see him leaning on the fence between the track and the bleachers. At other schools, he would watch from lane one of the track that ringed the field.

Always as close as possible to the action. Never said much, but projected pride with his posture: chin up, shoulders back, chest forward, spine straight, half-smile on his face. When I tackled somebody near the sideline, I could almost feel him beaming.

He missed one game the previous season, but only because we kicked off the same time he was being discharged from Credit Valley Hospital after cancer surgery. If we had played a day later, my dad would have found his way to lane one, even if he had to lean on a cane or my uncle Ken.

Over in the bleachers, the big fullback who had battered me all afternoon sat next to a brown-haired girl with white and blue paint smeared on her cheeks. He looped his left arm around her shoulders and pulled her close. She roped both her arms around his waist and squeezed. Their running back sat nearby, in the centre of a circle of friends, rehashing the way his team had thrashed us. A few grown-ups dotted the stands, but none bearing clipboards and hats with team logos, or anything else that would mark them as recruiters.

I caught myself and turned my head. I was searching the crowd for college scouts, but I was also scanning for my dad. Six games into the season I wanted to stop, and still couldn't.

Eyes forward, I followed my teammates, walking with my head high as they trudged toward the bus. Bramalea had trounced my team, but they hadn't beaten me, so I wouldn't mope off the field like some loser. I strode with purpose. I felt a palm, broad and coarse and warm, on the skin of my left shoulder.

I turned around and saw the referee.

"Number two, I just wanted to tell you that's the best game I've seen a kid play all season," he said, extending his right hand.

One more compliment than I had received from our coaches that fall. Kevin and Patrick and I pumped each other up before games and after big plays, but our coaches operated like they had just read a manual on demotivating a team—or were writing one. As an adult, I would recognize anchor habits in malfunctioning newsrooms, but I saw them first in high school football: elevate the mediocre when they don't deserve it; work your best people to exhaustion, and never tell them you appreciate it. Wasn't the only reason we didn't win that day, but it helped explain why we always lost.

I shook the man's hand.

"Thanks, ref," I said. "Just wish we could have won."

"Who you got next week?"

"Erindale."

"Keep playing like that," he said. "You'll get 'em."

"I hope."

"Well, good luck the rest of the season," he said, then trotted off to join the other officials. I turned again to face the parking lot, and the toughest moment of every week.

On the field that season, I had learned to channel my anger so it burned like a furnace instead of a wildfire. Inspired, I made plays. Angry, I made errors. I had a handful of games to pry a scholarship from a college team. I couldn't afford mistakes. From warmups through the final whistle, I existed in a bubble that sealed out everything unsettled about my life. I could blot out distractions and just play.

But the end of every game meant seeing other players with their parents; the bubble burst and current circumstances flooded back in. Not just trying to continue without my dad. My anchor. My armour. But the burden his death dumped on my mom, and the way all three of my living grandparents vanished. The problem wasn't just my dad's absence, but the presence of tension between my family's factions. Grief and conflict occupied space in my brain. Competed for it. I didn't feel empty in the moments after games, when I'd look for my dad on the sidelines. I felt heavy. That autumn, I grew used to losing, but I never adjusted to loss.

I walked faster toward the school bus. Chin up, shoulders back, chest proud. One last glance at the bleachers. Nobody there I recognized.

—

Before high school football, back in the city league days, my dad would back his car into our driveway with precise timing—thirty-five minutes before practice and ninety minutes before games. The vehicles changed, from his off-white Hyundai Stellar to Granny Mary's big red Cadillac to the fast little black Suzuki Swift. But they all carved the same curved path: hard right until the front bumper nearly touched the lamp post across from our house, then backward into the driveway.

My dad always parked hemline-straight, parallel to the border between lawn and asphalt. He always walked in without knocking, and our dog, Bandit, always welcomed him in a tail-wagging, shin-sniffing frenzy—the leader of the pack returned. And by the time Dad finished petting Bandit, saying hi to my mom, and hugging whichever of my sisters was home, I had better be geared up and ready to leave. I knew it, and never tested him.

Football wasn't just a string of wins and losses and blocks and tackles and touchdowns, but also a series of car rides with my dad. To Guelph in July of 1993, eight weeks before the cancer diagnosis. I won an MVP award there. The first recruiting letters from Canadian universities came the next month.

To London, in October of 1993, a month after surgery. Coaches at the University of Western Ontario had summoned a cohort of high school football stars to campus on homecoming weekend to watch them play the University of Toronto. They didn't know my dad was coming, but they found him a ticket to the game, and he sat in the rain, in the parents' section of J.W. Little Stadium, and watched Western throttle the eventual national champs from U of T. Then he met me in the parking lot and we drove ninety soggy minutes back to Mississauga.

The following May, four months before my dad died, a letter arrived from the University of Michigan, inviting me to their football camp in

June. First mail from a U.S. school, and not even some Division II backwater sniffing for a bigger program's castoffs. Michigan was a college football titan, a launching pad for NFL careers. They produced superstars like Desmond Howard and Ty Law and Tyrone Wheatley. Imagine singing at local talent shows and earning local attention, and then getting a phone call to schedule a meeting with Clive Davis. That's how the letter from Michigan felt. Like a chance to change my life.

Except the camp cost more than either parent could spare. I prepared for a let-Morgan-down-easy speech from my mom, and tried to figure out how to keep Michigan interested. But then my mom's tax refund arrived—one-thousand-four-hundred well-timed dollars—and my parents engaged in a seamless kind of teamwork I rarely saw during their marriage. My mom flipped me four hundred dollars to register for the camp, and my dad pledged to get me there.

If he could have done it without busting his budget, my dad would have driven me to Ann Arbor himself, maybe rented a hotel room near campus and spent mornings walking the football fields, hoping to catch me in a scrimmage or running drills. But he didn't have the money and he didn't have the time. He had taken the first week of June off work and driven to Chicago to spend his birthday with Granny Mary. Dad told us he had at least a decade to live, but he still had that tumour on his liver. He knew better.

The Saturday before camp started, my dad drove me to the bus terminal on Bay Street in downtown Toronto. He gave me Canadian money to buy a Greyhound ticket to Ann Arbor, and one hundred dollars U.S. to sustain me during the week. He hugged me and wished me good luck. I climbed onto the bus and found a window seat and rode for the whole afternoon, reading a college football magazine and imagining what they'd write about me in a couple of years.

Another flashback from the city league days:

My dad holding the door open as I lugged my muddy football gear across the threshold of the small brown townhouse. Dirt-caked cleats in a plastic bag in my left hand. In my right, I clutched my helmet's facemask, pushed upward through the collar of my shoulder pads so I could carry them together like a briefcase. It all came downstairs into the basement my dad rented.

He had lived there at least a year, still a five-minute walk from our house but a big step up from the room he used to rent in another townhouse in the same complex. He still shared a kitchen—this time with the divorced mom who owned the place, and not the dudes who drifted through the rooming house where he spent the first eighteen months after the divorce. But now he had his own bathroom and shower. He had a hallway, and a door that locked, and a main room big enough for some space between his bed and his TV.

He even had a little two-seater couch, where I tried to flop that afternoon after a long morning spent getting shoved into the mud by bigger kids at my football game.

"Get off my couch with them dirty pants," he said in his room-shaking baritone.

Two types of players finished every youth league football game with filthy uniforms. First: the kid so athletic that coaches couldn't justify ever taking them off the field. They carried the ball on offense, made tackles from sideline to sideline on defense, and if their team needed them to punt or to return kicks, they did that, too. By late high school, I had grown into a version of that player, and I'd wake up the morning after games feeling like I had fallen down a flight of stairs.

But my sixth-grade growth spurt mostly just hit my waistline, and a year later my physique hadn't tightened up or lengthened out. Short guys without strength or speed to compensate became the other type of player guaranteed to leave every game covered in mud and grass stains: the small kid at the bottom of the pile. That was eleven-year-old Morgan. Still deep in my chubby phase and a few years away from peak adolescence, when I sprouted to a towering five-foot-seven, outclassed in every way against kids in the opening throes of puberty.

If my dad ever grew tired of watching eighth graders ragdoll me, he disguised it. He still scheduled his shifts at De Havilland to keep himself free to drive me to as many practices as possible, and attended almost every game, same as he would years later, when I shed my tweenage blubber and became the kind of player to whom college football coaches mailed Christmas cards.

And if he ever pondered where else he could have spent the cash he'd dropped to enrol me in football, he never guilt-tripped me for squandering his money. He just treated the fee like a down payment on my well-being, even though, in late 1988, he didn't have seventy extra dollars. I had two sisters, each with needs of their own that cost money. I also played tenor sax in the Grade 7 band, which meant 110 dollars to rent my instrument for the year—one more drain on family finances. Another seventy dollars for me to get stampeded on the football field four times a week wasn't just a luxury for two divorced parents. It was an extravagance.

Word of the predicament drifted back to Alexandre and Cathy Tremblay, a well-off white couple, close friends of my mom's parents. Alexandre wouldn't struggle to find seventy dollars. He could probably locate that much between the cushions of the couch at their cottage. Alexandre decided *he* would pay for me to play football. He told my mom, who told me, who told my dad, who, within thirty-six hours, found the seventy dollars, because he wasn't going to let this white man pay for *his* son to play football.

And I repaid my dad's sacrifice by serving as a human speed bump, and then trailing my mud-stained uniform into his small but militarily neat apartment.

I changed quickly into the ill-fitting corduroys my mom sent with me. No disrespect to the pants. All my clothes fit poorly because nobody sized anything for short kids with round bellies, skinny legs, and little boy boobs. I sat back on the couch and started removing the pads from my football pants so I could air everything out before tossing the pants in the laundry.

I slid the thigh pads out of their pouches. They were light but solid, hard plastic sheathed in foam and curved to hug your upper leg. This small but sturdy piece of armour stood between your thigh muscles and a hematoma.

Jimmying the flimsy knee pads took a little more work. Same size and shape as a slice of white bread, except the bread might have offered more protection. Just foam, with no stiff plastic to give it shape. If you squeezed them between your thumb and finger, you could feel your digits touch. And if your knee met a helmet or a goalpost or a hard patch of playing field? Thoughts and prayers to your patella.

"Lemme see that," my dad said from his seat on the edge of his bed.

I gave him the knee pad and he took it in his hands, then ran his fingers around its edges. He pinched it like you would a baby's cheeks, then he frowned.

"This all they give you?"

"Yeah."

"Hmph."

He turned it over and over in his hands and figured out what my knees already knew. I had no protection besides hope and flimsy foam, and hope shouldered most of the load.

"When's your next practice?"

"Monday."

He got up off the bed and walked down the hall with the knee pad in his hand, then stuffed it into the pocket of a jacket hanging in the closet.

"I'm going to need that on Monday," I said.

"Then you'll have it Monday."

Monday night, 5:50 p.m., I came downstairs to wait. I kept my cleats near the front door, next to my helmet and shoulder pads, and wore my pants with two thigh pads and one knee pad. At 5.55 my dad backed into the driveway. When he moved farther away from us, or was coming from work, he'd leave earlier or drive faster, but he never made people wait.

He strolled through the front door with his man purse in his left hand. Yes, a man purse. Didn't matter whether they were in style in the late 1980s. My dad carried a man purse because *he* was cool, not because man purses were.

His other hand carried what looked like four duct-tape-covered discs. Same size and shape as the knee pad he had borrowed, but made from a much stiffer foam. They still bent enough to slide into the pouches in my pants, but now my kneecaps had more than a ghost of a chance of surviving the kind of hard fall I suffered a dozen times every practice and every game.

"Where did you get these?" I asked.

"Made 'em."

"Where?"

"At work."

"Thanks."

My dad couldn't, in half a weekend, make me big and strong enough to compete against the eighth graders who steamrolled me every Saturday. And he couldn't, in one workday, transform me into a fearless blocker and tackler with technique so immaculate that my size didn't matter. But he could take my paper-thin, team-issued knee pad to the De Havilland plant and find a higher grade of foam, then sneak off to a workshop during his break and make me two new pairs, duct-taped to seal out the water from the mud puddles in which I landed face-first damn near every weekend. It must feel helpless, watching your only son live the week-in, week-out ego-and-body-bruising reality of life as a short and chubby football player on the wrong side of puberty, but at least he could help keep my kneecaps from cracking like nutshells.

———

Second quarter of the first game after my dad died, I took a handoff from Don Ballantyne, our quarterback, and time slowed down in my mind. Our offensive tackle steered his guy to the right. Our guard pinned his man to the left. Kevin slid into position to block their inside linebacker. It happened in a second that felt like half a minute. The Woodlands Rams never executed plays this flawlessly, and I wouldn't see another running lane this clean for weeks. If I burst through the line and hit a quick jump cut to the right, Kevin would flatten Number 44 and I'd have the entire sideline to run. From there, it was a foot race to the end zone, and I wasn't about to lose to any of the Chinguacousy Chiefs. Once I hit that jump cut, I'd shift gears. After that, you could put six points on the board.

Except I didn't hit that jump cut.

I ran straight into Number 44—willfully, like he was a condemned building and I was a wrecking ball. Like he didn't outweigh me by twenty-five pounds. Like I played my best seeking out collisions instead of running room. He groaned when my shoulder hit his chest. I kept driving my legs. He tipped over backward and grabbed my ankle, then his teammates swarmed me and dragged me to the ground.

Didn't matter. I had made my point. He made the tackle, but I won the collision.

"I'm 150 pounds," I shouted to Number 44. "And I just *ran you over*."

Kevin grabbed my collar and hauled me away.

"Dude, why didn't you bounce that outside?" he said. "I had that guy blocked. With your speed, that's a touchdown. Easy."

I had an answer but couldn't put words to it. If you wanted to catalogue the costs of my dad's death, you could start with me shrugging at Kevin and jogging back to the huddle to hear Don Ballantyne call the next play, instead of celebrating my team's first touchdown of the season.

We played the Thursday of my first week back at school after the funeral, and I took the field angry. I wanted to play my game—speedy and cerebral and versatile—but I needed to vent some of my pent-up heat. I didn't own a punching bag, and I couldn't come back to school and pound on some weakling to make myself feel better. In real life, fighting got you suspended, but in football coaches begged us to knock people senseless. So when that hole opened up, and I spied the alley along the right sideline, I also saw Number 44, standing there, looking like a chance to make somebody else feel the same pain I'd been dragging around.

My teenage brain didn't grasp the opportunity cost of running that kid over. I figured I could score later, and I did: turned a short pass into a long touchdown, heard the crowd cheer from across the field, and watched jaws drop as I sprinted past Chinguacousy's bench. They didn't expect to see speed like that from a bottom-of-the-table team in Peel Region Tier II football. I wouldn't have, either.

But I traded another touchdown for the adrenaline boost that came with smashing Number 44. If I had scored twice, maybe my name would have hit the newspaper in bold print. Maybe Michigan would have written to me again. Maybe the Woodlands Rams could have actually won a game. Probably not, but I would have shortened the odds against us if I hadn't sacrificed six points for the chance to knock the taste out of that kid's mouth.

Old-time Michigan football coach Fielding H. Yost meditated on the true connection between sport and sacrifice. The team painted his thoughts on the weight room wall in Ann Arbor, and drummed the words into our skulls that summer at football camp.

> *To me, no coach in America asks a man to make any sacrifice. He asks that he do the opposite: live clean, come clean, think clean. That he stop doing all the things that destroy him physically, mentally, and morally. And that he do the things that make him keener, finer, and more competent.*

Everything else we normally categorized as sacrifice was, according to Yost, actually an investment—in yourself and in your team's success. Real sacrifice, he argued, meant giving up meaningful, long-term gains for short-lived, short-term fun. For Yost, sacrifice was the easy, tempting option, so he urged us to do the opposite. On that play against Chinguacousy, I sacrificed in the Fielding H. Yost sense. We needed a touchdown, but I wanted to hurt somebody. I traded the greater good for a quick thrill.

Neither meaning of the word *sacrifice* quite fit the other process ongoing that fall, as playing college football changed from a dream to an intention to a strong possibility. I knew gaining an opportunity meant giving up something else I treasured. Each time I reached a new level, something I wished I could bring along would have to stay behind.

———

By the time I finished playing football for good, I had felt the rush that comes with running from the tunnel onto the field at a sold-out Rose Bowl Stadium on New Year's Day. Underfoot, a lush field of grass so firm and fresh and uniformly short it almost felt fake. Overhead, a stunning Pasadena sunset. Beyond the stadium, the San Gabriel Mountains.

From the sideline, I witnessed Keyshawn Johnson's effortless dominance. Early on, he ran a flawless corner route and plucked the ball from the air in front of our bench, keeping his feet in bounds and earning a first down. Late in the game, he caught a pass at midfield and sprinted through our secondary for a back-breaking touchdown, and finished with more receptions and yards than any other player in Rose Bowl history.

The next year, in Orlando for the Citrus Bowl against Tennessee, I marvelled at how Peyton Manning could decode our defense in a split-second, then sling pinpoint passes to Peerless Price and Joey Kent. A few days before the game, we all attended a charity event, with players from both teams, dressed in sweatpants and jerseys, playing carnival games with grade schoolers and making small talk about the game. I glanced over at Al Wilson, Tennessee's middle linebacker, and Ray Austin, who played cornerback, and wondered why they had already put on their shoulder pads. A second look, and I realized those weren't pads but actual shoulders, round and dense, looking heavy as cannonballs.

We were a very good team. Tennessee beat us by twenty.

College football brought me face to face with people and events I had only ever seen on TV, and into contact with enough NFL players to know I'd never become one. It gave me stories and anecdotes other sports fans love hearing, and some shaky assertions, like my bad-faith claim that I was a better college player than Charles Woodson. He won a Super Bowl and a spot in the NFL's Hall of Fame, but my team beat his in college. Twice. I rode the bench and he won the Heisman, but a win is a win. Campbell 2, Woodson 0.

As a young adult, I missed college football's weekly routine, every afternoon building toward Saturday's game. And I missed the daily schedule. No guessing where to find me between 2 p.m. and 7 p.m. on weekdays. I'd only be in one of three places: film room, weight room, practice field. I cherished the shared suffering and achievement, surviving the three-practice-a-day slog of August training camp with my teammates, then celebrating a conference title with them in November. I missed the idle talk in the locker room as much as I did proximity to the big time, like playing Wisconsin at homecoming, or Penn State in a showcase game on ABC.

But you know what I already missed when I *started* college ball?

City league Saturdays. Crisp October mornings in the sun, on the field at, say, John Fraser Secondary School, with my dad watching from the edge of the track. Sometimes my uncle Ken showed up, with his bald head and goatee and shades, and a toothpick dangling like an unlit Kool from the corner of his mouth. In big-time football, you didn't hear the play-by-play commentary. With Uncle Ken, you had real-time analysis, in a West Side of Chicago blaccent that cut through the chatter.

When I crushed some running back:

"Maybe next time, padna!"

When they'd send another runner my way, and I'd squash him, too:

"Gone 'head and try the other side. Ain't nothin' happenin' for you over here, brother."

When I took on some oversized fullback and dumped him on his butt:

"My nephew wearin' *yo'* big ass *out!*"

And my dad, silent but present. Projecting his pride with his posture and that half-smile.

By seventeen, I knew that if I played well enough, long enough, I'd outgrow those moments. I might land at a school far from home, or at some place that sold tens of thousands of tickets every Saturday. The grumble and roar of a full stadium would replace the intimacy of a personal cheering section. Both sounds moved me, for different reasons. Graduating to college ball meant playing without my dad watching from within shouting distance, and I had prepared myself for the transition. Just wasn't ready at seventeen.

———

Don Ballantyne took the snap and tossed me the ball, and for maybe the second time all season, the Woodlands Rams executed a play precisely as designed. A wall of red jerseys formed along the offensive line, without a single green-shirted Erindale Raider knifing into the backfield to disrupt me. No missed blocks by the little guys on the perimeter, where a good cornerback would have closed in from the sideline to steer me toward his pursuing teammates. Kevin manhandled Erindale's outside linebacker to give me a clean running lane, and this time I had to take it.

Final quarter of the second-last game of the season, facing the only beatable team left on our schedule. Trailing by just four points, instead of our usual ten or twenty, with only a handful of minutes remaining, I couldn't afford to seek out a big collision here. A touchdown would give us a late-game lead. Our defense remained about as airtight as a screen door, but if the offense could pull off this one perfect play, maybe our defense could figure it out, just for a series.

I turned upfield and hit the afterburners. The faster I ran, the slower time seemed to unfold. I could already picture this touchdown run on the highlight tape I planned to send to college coaches after the season. Only question, as I sped past Erindale's bench, was whether to lead or to close with it.

This run felt like vindication after a summer spent training instead of doing fun but pointless teenage stuff, for investing instead of sacrificing. The week after my dad died, as the two sides of my family found new and familiar ways to feud, I would still sneak out of the house, to the hill in the park across the street, and run sprints. I needed a break from the bickering, but I also wanted to sharpen myself for moments like this, when I'd hit top speed with the Erindale Raiders flailing in my wake, looking at the back of my jersey and the soles of my feet.

When I returned to school after the funeral, I took a black marker to my white Nike football cleats. On the heel of the left shoe I wrote, "P.C." On the right, "T.R.O.Y."

Pete Campbell, They Reminisce Over You.

I didn't cross myself after first downs, or say a silent prayer every time I flattened a ball carrier. But my dad flashed across my mind as I sped down the sideline, past Erindale's bench, where players and coaches groaned because their four-point lead only had seconds to live.

Ten strides from the end zone, I thrust my left hand overhead, then pointed my index finger to the sky. It cost me a little speed, but nobody on the field had a top gear faster than mine. I could have moonwalked to the end zone. The Erindale Raiders weren't chasing me down.

The number one symbolized nothing for the Woodlands Rams, who dwelled as far as possible from top spot in the standings. No wins. Fewest points scored. Most points allowed. But if we played mistake-free defense after this touchdown, it could represent our win total that season. I didn't consider it in the moment. I just felt like a winner as I dashed past Erindale's bench, so I gave them the index finger.

When I crossed the goal line, I expected elation but felt relief. Satisfaction at the payoff for hard work. I paused in the end zone, my back to the field, spread my arms, and bathed in the sensation. I tilted my head back and gazed at the sky and raised my finger once more.

P.C.

T.R.O.Y.

Six points for you, Dad. A win, too. Finally.

I pivoted to face the field and the setting sun, which turned the blue sky orange in the distance. In a few minutes, it would duck behind the hulking police station that stood on the other side of Erin Mills Parkway, at the corner of Dundas, but seemed to loom over the whole neighbourhood.

And I saw the bright yellow penalty flag lying crumpled in the grass near midfield. Knew what it meant even before I saw Kevin and Don begging the referee to change his mind, or the guys on Erindale's sideline smiling and high-fiving.

Holding.

Offense.

Ten-yard penalty from the spot of the foul.

The referee stood fifty yards upfield and signalled for another official to bring him the ball.

Woodlands Rams. Losing habits.

I sighed and shook my head and started a slow jog back to the huddle.

Morgan vs. Virginity

Two days after my eighteenth birthday, Kelly Charles found me in the cafeteria and told me to come to the basketball game after school so she could give me a present. I had planned to go anyway, just to see if my friends could beat the Erindale Raiders in *something* before I graduated. But now Kelly Charles had a birthday gift? I'd show up early and stay late for that.

A lot of guys would. Kelly was fine—short and sturdy and curvy, but soft in the right spots. She had light brown skin, smooth with red undertones, and chestnut-coloured eyes, close-set and intense. Her voice had a slight, sultry Kathleen Turner rasp, and her smile was toothy and bright. She didn't show it off much, but when we passed each other in the hallway, she always let me see it.

A few minutes before tipoff, I walked into the gym and sat alone in the last row of bleachers. Kelly entered and parked near the front. The discretion was necessary. Whatever Kelly and I had, nobody else knew we had it. Shoot, I had no clue what we were doing, or what we even were to each other. I just knew I was sprung on Kelly Charles. She knew it, too.

Early in my final year of high school, I learned the limits of petitionary prayer. I had begged God to give my dad a few more years; Dad died three days later. So I didn't pray for good things to happen. I just set goals, then I worked and I hoped. And I knew what I wanted out of my senior year.

I wanted to win a football game. Just one. For the Woodlands Rams, it would have felt like a world championship. And I worked to make it happen—attended every practice, did hundreds of push-ups nearly every night, just to make myself stronger and faster. And we still lost—in Mississauga and Brampton, in close games and blowouts, to good teams and bad ones. The Woodlands Rams weren't big or skilled or well-schooled, but we were consistent.

And I still wanted a football scholarship to one of those name-brand American schools on TV every weekend—Notre Dame or Florida State or USC. The recruiting letters in my mailbox tended to come from lower-profile places—Edinboro and Slippery Rock in Pennsylvania, Mount Allison and Manitoba in Canada—but it was still autumn, technically, and I could still hope a major program would gamble on a five-foot-seven defensive back from Canada.

Either way, I planned to be in some team's training camp the following August, and before I left for college, I planned to get laid. The right way, though, with somebody I loved and who loved me back. Having sex sounded fun, but frivolous. But making love? That seemed intense and intimate and fulfilling. I had zero experience with either one, but in my brain the distinction was critical.

Blame the music.

Most weeknights, I stayed up past what should have been my bedtime, listening to *The Quiet Storm* on WBLK. I heard all kinds of slow jams, but I identified with the age-appropriate ballads about tuning into a girl's feelings and waiting patiently for sex. "Comforter" by Shai. "Sensitivity" by Ralph Tresvant. "Whenever You Say" by Hi-Five. Build a friendship first. Console her when some other dude dumps her. Nurture deeper feelings over the long haul. Eventually, she'll gift you with something more precious than sex, like trust . . . but also, sex.

It's a solid plan if you can invest two years in a teenage relationship. Fully clothed and horizontal at sixteen, half naked at seventeen, and by the time you're old enough to vote, you'll be ready for the main event. But you won't just have sex. You waited for the Right Moment. You'll make love.

I didn't have two years, though. By November 1994, I was set to turn eighteen. Seven months later, I would finish high school, and by August I would start football training camp. I had a compressed schedule. This was me versus virginity versus the calendar.

Then here came Kelly Charles.

Didn't know when any of this happened. We had talked on the phone a few times over the summer, aimless teenage conversations about music or school or *The Simpsons*, watching the same TV show from opposite ends of the line and commenting on the action. When Homer scammed the company drug plan for a prescription hair tonic, she recited lines from memory. That impressed me.

But early in the new school year, she grew on me, and I had a hunch it was reciprocal. More than a hunch, actually. One day in the cafeteria, she handed me a condom. Her gym class had visited a sexual health clinic that morning and the kids grabbed rubbers as souvenirs; she gave hers to me.

A month later came the basketball game.

The buzzer sounded at halftime and Kelly shot a half-glance toward me as she walked toward the exit. She didn't need to drop that hint. I'd spent the entire first half with one eye on the game and the other on Kelly in that tight black turtleneck. When she moved, I moved, out the door and into the lobby outside the gym.

I caught her at the opening of the hallway leading to the heart of the school. The kids milling around the atrium disappeared in the distance behind us. We walked.

"So what's this gift?"

"I can't tell you that, Morgan."

"Okay, so can you give me a hint?"

"Nope."

"C'mon, girl! Don't make me walk all this way just to disappoint me."

"Oh, I won't disappoint you."

I breathed deep and braced myself. We walked and I watched her body. Her green tartan kilt stopped closer to her hip than to her knee, and her thighs stretched her black pantyhose thin.

When I met Kelly, she was sexy in that tomboyish TLC kind of way, like the women LL Cool J rapped about in "Around the Way Girl." Baggy overalls and basketball shoes, and billowy airbrushed T-shirts that forced you to imagine what was underneath.

But that fall, even TLC was wearing silk pajamas, strategically unbuttoned. I recorded the video for "Creep," watched and rewound it a dozen times that first weekend, and paused it when T-Boz's shirt fluttered open and I thought I saw the underside of her boob. And now here came Kelly in that tight turtleneck and hiked-up kilt, beckoning me to follow her down the hallway.

Kelly wasn't my girlfriend, though. Not then, not ever.

The week after my dad died, his friend Jimmy McGee, in town for the funeral, took me to a pharmacy to buy condoms because Angela Broussard had stopped by the house to check on me. He thought we were in a relationship, and he wanted me to stay protected during all the sex he imagined I was having with her. And she was stunning— hair down to her waist, petite with more body than her small frame could contain. I had imagined having sex with her, too—several times a week over the three years I had known her. Didn't mean it was ever going to happen.

I didn't have girlfriends. I had girls I liked and girls who liked me, and they weren't necessarily the same girls. Most times they weren't. On a Venn diagram, the circles would barely touch.

I also had girls I kissed sometimes—like Marie, who would walk with me to Blockbuster and rent the videos we watched in her mom's basement, then accompany me to the bus stop to catch the last Route 38 home, and kiss me on the lips before I boarded. Made me happy, but it never went further. She said we were better as friends.

And there were girls I made out with occasionally. LaTasha was my parents' friends' daughter from Chicago, and over Christmas break she brought me to a Jack and Jill party at the South Shore Cultural Center. Afterward, I slept on the couch in her family's living room, and she snuck downstairs, and some things happened. Not many things, though, so relax. I didn't experience anything in high school that you couldn't have seen on *Beverly Hills 90210*, and my romantic life was actually far tamer than that. At least Brandon Walsh and his friends had implied sex.

But mostly I had girls I dreamed would take my virginity, and girls I thought would actually do it. In that Venn diagram, the circles overlapped at Kelly Charles.

She grabbed my left hand with her right and led me farther down the hallway, toward the classroom where I took chemistry. I followed, because why wouldn't I?

That semester, we shared the same spare period, which flipped between early morning and late afternoon. I spent those mornings in the cafeteria. I could have slept in and arrived later, but that would mean paying to take public transit. So, I rode the school bus for free and showed up early, then spent the extra seventy minutes catching up on homework I'd been putting off, unless Kelly or Patrick was in the cafeteria. Then work wasn't getting done till lunch.

Last period, if Kelly wasn't at school, I'd wander to the library and look for books by Black authors. I read Gloria Naylor novels the way our team lost football games—one after another after another. *Bailey's Café. The Women of Brewster Place. Linden Hills.* But if Kelly was around, I'd skip the library and we'd hang out in the lobby and flirt until football practice started.

Kelly revealed to me a home life that didn't seem like fun. Her older brother pressured her to behave less like a kid and more like a grown woman. Her father hadn't acted right since that neck adjustment during a visit to the chiropractor. Both men had tempers. Her dad's was volcanic. When she wasn't dealing with them, or at school, she had a job at a hair salon. She didn't have much time to socialize.

I loved that even though work and family drama burdened her, she spared some time and energy for us. Just me and her. Kelly was one of a few kids at school who knew about my dad, and she knew how bad I was hurting. I loved that she listened, and always stopped in the hallway to hug me.

It started to feel like a tune I knew when I played tenor sax in the eighth-grade band, and spent afternoons in my bedroom, working out melodies to pop songs. I taught myself to play Terence Trent D'Arby's "Sign Your Name."

> We started out as friends
> But the thought of you just caves me in

That was me the first semester of my senior year. Kelly caved me in, and suddenly everything about her enthralled me.

Her bow-legged, tomboyish walk?

Adorable.

Her wet chestnut-brown eyes?

Mesmerizing.

The murals she painted in art class?

Straight-up sexy.

One Monday, she showed up at school with a miniature mural on a stiff piece of white paper, bubble letters in splashy bright colours spelling out "Don't Disturb This Groove." If you listened to *The Quiet Storm*, you knew it was the title of a classic slow jam by The System. I hung it outside my bedroom door because that's what the song says to do.

I wouldn't groove like that in anybody's bedroom for a while. Like, a seriously long time. But I still needed privacy late night, when I would close the bedroom door, cut off every light except the small lamp on my desk, grab a pen, and crouch over a notebook.

When I had time, I wrote poetry so bad I should have been ashamed to show it to anyone. Too many words that didn't advance the story, flourishes about "uninterrupted passion" and "the healing power of my love," on and on, down the page. It was like somebody put Johnny Gill's vocal gymnastics into words. But I shared it with Kelly because I assumed she would like it, and hoped that kind of romance would nudge her closer to sleeping with me. I couldn't afford to give her flowers or jewelry, but bad poems only cost time and some effort.

I also wrote short stories for English class—sports-inspired fiction with roots in real life. One piece focused on a football star named Marcel Carter who passed up a chance to make millions in the NFL, deciding instead to play one more season of college ball. His favourite assistant coach, youngish and Black with a Malcolm X poster in his office, told Marcel to Take the Money and Run—the story's title, naturally. But the smarmy white good ol' boy head coach leaned on Marcel with appeals to loyalty and accountability and all the other clichés college football coaches pretend to value, and Carter caved.

Of course, he blew out his knee in his next game, and his life unraveled from there. He flunked out of school, returned to his hometown, and took a job at the local bowling alley, the only place that would employ a washed-up ex-jock with a half-completed degree in communications. Eight hours a day, he would fetch stray pins from gutters and spray fungus killer into bowling shoes. Occasionally, he'd make eye contact with a customer, and he wanted to disappear every time someone recognized him as the dude who used to be Marcel Carter.

I wrote another story about a different football star, this one a high school senior named Eric Ellard. He was handsome and smart and popular, and concealing his virginity from everyone but his girlfriend. One night, she invited him over—her mom worked overnights as a nurse—and Eric snuck out of his bedroom window with his parents' spare car key and drove to see her. A few minutes later, nobody was a virgin anymore.

She wanted him to spend the night, but he needed to return his folks' car before they woke up and noticed it missing. On Eric's way home, a white cop pulled him over on some bullshit, yanked him from the car, and forced him to the ground. The cop drew his pistol, then shot Eric to death when he said he saw Eric reach for a gun. Of course, Eric didn't have a weapon—only a wallet and those car keys. The cop knew it just like the reader did. He just wanted an excuse to shoot.

The cop got a few weeks' desk duty. Eric got a fancy open casket and a sad funeral. A few weeks later, his girlfriend missed her period, and we all knew why.

No, my stories weren't subtle, but when I wrote them, they felt fresh and creative and brave. I gave my fictional high school football star an alliterative name and two parents in a happy marriage, and set his story in Grand Rapids, but anyone who couldn't tell the Real Secret Virgin was Morgan Campbell didn't read closely enough.

Two months after my dad's death, I knew none of us was bullet-proof. But I was still an eighteen-year-old athlete working hard to look confident despite the uncertainty that had nagged at me since the day they diagnosed my dad with cancer. Feeling vulnerable was a default setting; showing vulnerability terrified me, even if I knew it would help.

At school, in the hallway, I could hide insecurity behind football star swagger. I had recruiting letters from half the university football teams in Canada, and a few in the U.S. I had a future. I had a reason to strut.

At football practice, I could smash people during tackling drills, and in games I could hit even harder because I wasn't flattening my teammates. If you were there, you couldn't tell if I torpedoed people out of anger, or to mask a nagging inadequacy. To somebody watching from the sidelines, or next to me on the field, it all looked like intensity.

But football only consumed a couple of hours every day, and I hurt nearly all the time. Writing stories about guys who made bad choices in good faith, or who managed not to get laid while their friends collected sexual conquests, felt like a start.

I shared those stories with Kelly, too. She read them even before the teacher did, and I hoped that made her feel special. Also, she had options, and I wanted to stand out from all the other dudes pursuing her. Lots of guys at lots of schools played ball, but none of them took Writer's Craft—except me. A sensitive jock was a rare creature, and I thought all this writing made me seem deep, and that a gripping story with a tragic ending might get me closer to Kelly's bedroom.

When I pictured all the ways I might give my virginity to her, most often I saw something like the scene in *Boyz n the Hood* where Tre finally gets some tail. We'd be alone at night, somehow, even though we both lived with siblings and parents in little townhouses. After some seismic personal event—maybe I saved someone's life, or almost lost my own—I'd drop my guard and a few tears. She'd reward me by leading me to her bed, or to mine.

But another part of me really did just need to shed my armour. I hadn't even cried at my dad's funeral because I thought sitting stone-faced conveyed strength, and that staying strong would have made him proud. Really, I just felt like an orphan; when I talked to Kelly, I felt connected. And it felt even better to hug someone who wasn't a blood relative, who whispered in my ear that she was glad to see me, who would cuff the back of my head and pull me closer when I snaked my arm around her waist.

"So you're really not gonna give me a hint?"

"No hints, Morgan."

"Is it money?"

"No, it's not money."

"Is it—"

"*No hints.* Just wait."

She led me toward the drama wing, which at 5 p.m. on a Friday was even more deserted than the rest of the school. Teachers had left an hour ago, and kids heading home didn't exit that way. She might as well have taken me to a hotel room.

Forget the rest of the basketball game. I loved my friends, but this was bigger than them. This was a mystery gift from the girl I had been trying to corner all semester. If we stayed away longer, the other kids would figure out something was up between Kelly and me, and neither of us needed that drama. Our relationship didn't have a label, or formal boundaries, but it was our business. Our pleasure. Our secret. Which made the prospect even sweeter.

But here I was, the closest I had ever been to alone with Kelly. Whatever was coming justified blowing our cover. I never starred in school rumours, but would happily endure months of innuendo if this ended the way I hoped it would.

We walked slower, which I loved. I wanted to prolong the whole process, remember every detail. Burnt-orange lockers. Dull yellow paint on hallway walls. Her hair pulled back into a bun, the elastic bauble holding it in place. Everything.

She walked me to her locker, then stopped. She backed me up until my spine pressed against the metal door, then parked in front of me. You could barely fit a textbook between us. I couldn't wriggle out from in front of her even if I'd wanted to, but why would I want to? I wanted a football scholarship and a functional family, and a chance to escape the weight of my father's absence. Everything else I wanted was staring me in the face.

We linked pinky fingers. She placed her free hand over my heart and pushed, as if to pin me in place. I breathed deep again.

"Morgan, you know you're special to me."

"Nice to hear you admit it finally."

"Look . . . I wish I could say more. It's just . . . my life is complicated."

"I know it is."

"But I just wanted to let you know you're special, and . . ."

"And?"

"And . . . Just . . . Just close your eyes."

I'd spent the whole semester playing out this moment in my mind, and knowing I'd have to stop imagining it seemed a little strange. I closed my eyes and pictured Kelly on her tiptoes. I tried to concentrate on sensations. She waited a beat. Then another.

She slid her hand from my heart to my hip, and hooked her thumb in my belt loop. Her fingertips gripped my right forearm and she pulled herself toward me.

I sensed her warmth as she drew closer.

I smelled her breath.

Then I felt her lips.

For a second.

Two.

Then three.

Not just the thought of kissing her.

Reality caved me in.

In the Coloured Section

"I could never play for the Packers," I declared to Kevin and Patrick on the last Monday of first semester, during our weekly de-brief on the previous day's NFL games. "It's too damn cold up there. I'd be afraid to make the playoffs. Did you see those guys shivering on the field yesterday? If they drafted me, I just wouldn't report to training camp. I'd hold out till they traded me to Miami."

"I'd just keep thinking about the money," Patrick said, blowing his hands like he really was standing in the secondary between plays at Lambeau Field. "I know I'm freezing, but I'd just think about the ducats."

A bunch of us had gathered in the Black kids' section of the cafeteria at the Woodlands School—east end, hard against the wall, next to the Coke machine, socializing when we should have been studying. Patrick and Kevin and I occupied one table, talking football. Leighton sat in a stray chair nearby. His buddy Leon leaned against the wall, gazing toward the bank of windows at the far end of the room.

Patrick and Kevin and I were still trying to decide where we might play in college. I had a shoebox full of recruiting letters at home. They had been trickling in from Canadian schools for a year and a half, but the previous week Harvard had called, and so had Lehigh, and so had

Williams College in Massachusetts. Kevin got letters from big-time schools, like Cal and Kentucky, because he was rare—tall enough to play centre in basketball, but fast enough to anchor the relay team. College coaches discovered Patrick just before Christmas, when I dragged him with me to a recruiting showcase because somebody outside our circle needed to know he was one of the best players in the city.

None of us knew how hard it really was to make the NFL, but we talked like the league needed us.

"Man . . . I don't know how Terrell Buckley plays in Green Bay," I said. "That's too cold for me. Even if we go to college in Manitoba or New Hampshire, at least the season's over in November. We'll still freeze, but not as bad."

"Yo, *shut up,* Star!"

Leon, butting in. We didn't even know he was listening. He had strong opinions on college football recruiting, though.

"Pure bench you a grab nex year, star!" he said, nodding toward Patrick. "Boat you!"

Patrick and I had played two years of high school football together; we'd made all-star teams and landed on college coaches' recruiting radars. When we discussed playing college ball, we weren't just talking, even though we didn't see many guys like us in the NFL.

I stood five-foot-seven in running shoes and weighed 150 after a big dinner. Patrick was five-foot-eight in stocking feet and scaled 145 in full equipment. I ran like I was turbocharged, and could play cornerback, free safety, or tailback. Patrick could catch any ball he could touch, and some you didn't think he could reach. We had both grown used to tackling guys who outweighed us by fifty pounds.

In the broader world of big-time football, you'd find running backs who weighed 200 pounds or more, but who also moved fast, and rippled with muscles. If they ran full speed into a clump of defenders, bodies would scatter like bowling pins.

Our high school opponents were mostly just big, and sometimes fast, but hardly ever both. Technique and timing could trump size or speed, so Patrick and I handled the running backs in our league.

But based on height and weight, we didn't profile as major players at the next level, so maybe Leon had simply judged us on the numbers, and a detailed knowledge of what they might mean. Maybe he really did know more about football than the university coaches who sent us recruiting letters after watching us play.

Or maybe he just hated hearing us talk about plans for next year because he didn't seem to have any beyond playing dominoes in the Black kids' section of the cafeteria.

"Nobody's talking to you, Leon," I said.

"But *me* a tahk to *you*," he said. "Yuh nah guh do nuttin' nex year, star."

Leon was several kinds of guy.

He was the kind of guy who spoke standard English until tenth grade, then started talking almost exclusively in patois. We didn't share any classes, so I don't know how he spoke around white folks, but in the Black section of the cafeteria, he tried to sound like he just moved here from Montego Bay.

And he was the kind of guy who dominated middle school basketball because he'd been held back a year and stood six feet tall by eighth grade. In high school, everyone else grew and he wasn't special anymore. He might still have been a fine player, but he never joined high school teams because he wasn't the kind of guy who passed enough classes to stay eligible.

Sometimes Leon and I were friendly. One day before a football game, a bunch of us wandered into the gym and gathered near a basketball hoop, and Leon tossed me alley-oop passes that I tried to catch and slam dunk.

But we weren't friends. Kevin and Patrick and Andre and Mark were my friends; we had each other's phone numbers and socialized outside school. We talked about girls and sports and music and our futures, the way friends do. Leon and I were acquaintances, the way most Black kids at our school were. When we passed each other in the hall, we'd exchange a quick upward nod, that low-key greeting Black men often trade when we see each other in mostly white settings almost anywhere on earth.

We sat in the same section of the cafeteria, but we were very different kinds of Black kids. Leon smoked a lot of weed and code-switched into patois for months at a time. If your school had a decent number of Black kids, it might also have had a crew of guys like that, maybe in the deepest crevice of the Black corner of the cafeteria, playing dominoes at lunch.

I sat in the Black section of the cafeteria but, by my last year of high school, had carved out my own cultural lane—organically Black American.

Not that I had a monopoly on African American pop culture. It spilled over the border from Buffalo, beamed into people's living rooms via U.S. network TV, and before Toronto got its own Black radio station, almost every Black person I knew, regardless of their background, listened to WBLK. They heard Billy Howard in the morning and tuned in at night to hear DJ Huk-her and Dawn run through the top eight at 8. Most people tuned out before *The Quiet Storm* started at 10 p.m., kicking off four hours of smooth slow jams, but I kept listening.

And before BET came to Canadian cable boxes, we could all still watch *The Arsenio Hall Show* on CFMT out of Toronto, or *New York Undercover* on WUTV. Nobody besides my dad and my uncle Ken watched *Frank's Place* on CBS, but that show—both magnificent, underappreciated seasons—did, in theory, reach Canadian viewers.

We all knew who Gordon Gartrelle was supposed to be, because we all watched *The Cosby Show* until Rudy and Olivia outgrew their little-kid cuteness. And we all saw the step show episode of *A Different World*. "9-1-1 Emergency! Reconnect the community!" Within a week after it aired, seemed like every high school in the area with more than fifty Black kids had formed a step team.

But absorbing African American culture through the media is one thing. Growing up with it in your house is profoundly different.

A lot of Black kids we knew saw *Jason's Lyric* and *Boomerang*, but only my sister Courtney and I would show up at school in Grambling or Morehouse hoodies, or could tell the difference between spinach and collard greens. They had all seen *Malcolm X*, but nobody else had read *Manchild in the Promised Land,* which I borrowed from Uncle Ken's collection because I couldn't find it in the school or city librar-ies. I preferred it that way. That cultural capital set me apart, and I flaunted it the way guys like Leon exaggerated their Jamaicanness, and the other kids in the Black section of the cafeteria repped their parents' islands.

So, no, I never hung out with Leon, and didn't think much about him until that exact minute, when he made clear that something about me bugged him. He vented like he'd kept this resentment to himself for months.

"Yuh jus a tahk tahk tahk," he said, louder than before. "Nuttin next year, star. Pure bench yuh ride."

"Man, *shut up,*" I said. "Nobody's talking to you. If you don't like what we're talking about, be quiet. Nobody brought you into this conversation."

"Yo den *do something, star!*" he said, yelling now. "De-fenn it!"

"Defend what?"

"De-fenn dat big chat!"

"I'm not indulging this bullshit."

"Yo, shut up bout indulge. Big fookeen words."

He stepped toward me and motioned to a spot on the floor in front of him.

"*De-fenn it,* yuh *poosy*-ole!*"

"I ain't gotta defend shit."

"DE-FENN IT!"

"I ain't defending shit," I said. "You're just mad because I'm out of here in June and you'll still be here tryna graduate when you're twenty-two."

Kevin and Patrick laughed at that one. Even Leighton cracked up. Everyone laughed, except Leon. He walked toward me, drawing in a deep breath. When he exhaled, the spit came with it, splattering my glasses and my forehead and the bridge of my nose. I wiped it away with my right hand, but by then the fight was already on.

Leon threw wild punches; most of them missed. I took some glancing blows as I worked to get inside his reach. We fell together and tugged at each other's clothes and jostled for the space to throw more punches. My right shoulder slipped out of the socket and back in. Doctors call that a subluxation; I had heard that word a few times in the thirteen months since it first happened, when a big collision in football practice knocked me off balance and I landed with all my weight on the heel of my right palm. When my shoulder subluxed, numbness would radiate from the joint to my fingertips, and the next day I'd struggle to lift my arm above my chest.

If it happened during a football game, I'd head to the sidelines until the feeling and function returned. Against Chinguacousy, in the first game of the season, I sat out a few plays. Against North Park, in the last game before playoffs, I missed the whole second half.

But you can't call time out in a fight, or depend on coaches to intervene so you can regroup. So this time, when my shoulder joint clicked and that sickening but now familiar numbness flowed down my arm, I felt helpless.

Our school had guys who fought as their main extracurricular activity, the way other kids played soccer or saxophone. Leon wasn't one of them. He handled fighting like he did eighth-grade hoops—with more size than skill, which is likely why he chose me as an opponent. Faced with somebody in his weight class, he'd have kept his insults and spittle and fists to himself. But he looked at me, a guy half a foot shorter who wore glasses and made decent grades, and saw a mismatch.

Thankfully for Leon, I quit karate in sixth grade when I started football. I still possessed a decent right hand, but never sought opportunities to use it. I had the strength and stamina that came with being an athlete, but didn't use them to sharpen my knuckle game. I had sports: football and track. And I had hobbies: reading, writing, slow jams, hip-hop. Fighting was something I read about in *Sports Illustrated*, but only did once every three or four years.

In grade nine, I fought a pimple-faced, Black-acting white boy named Scott over some insult I thought he tossed my way, and I knocked him out with a crisp right cross to the jaw. A more skilled fighter would have lined up and landed that shot within thirty seconds. It took me what felt like a half hour but was probably closer to three minutes.

The year before the fight with Leon, I body-slammed Shane Jackson in the football locker room. He and I actually liked each other, but even Shane would admit he was a loudmouth. Imagine a voice as gravelly as Grover's, but at Luciano Pavarotti volume, and talking trash all the time.

Like, All. The. Time.

"HO-LEE! I LIT YOU UP IN PRACTICE TODAY!"

He didn't.

"OF COURSE I'M FASTER THAN YOU!"

He wasn't.

"THERE'S NO *WAY* YOU COULD BEAT ME UP!"

We'll see.

On that afternoon, post-practice, he brought his trash talk too loud and too close—like nose to nose. I told him to back up, but instead he pressed closer, even though he might have weighed 140 in his school clothes with a knapsack full of textbooks. When he bumped me with his chest, I dipped and put my right shoulder into his gut, then grabbed his legs and lifted and dumped him on his back. Like Leon, he had sized me up and seen a mismatch. I corrected his vision real quick.

But Leon had some size and strength. Even with fully functioning limbs, I couldn't have manhandled him like I did Scott or Shane, and with my right arm still tingling, I could only disguise the pain and my panic, then stall and survive until I could fight back. Leon threw wild lefts and rights, all of which sailed over my head as I ducked low and worked to stay inside his reach. I tucked my right arm close to my body and hit him with short left hands. Nothing big. A few shots up under the chin. Just enough to unsettle him.

Any of our friends could have stepped in to stop it, but instead they just watched. I couldn't blame them. This was mid-morning entertainment and worth missing class for. The longer it went, the better the story they'd tell the kids who missed it.

Leon swung and missed and cursed, like Ralphie's dad in a Jamaican-Canadian *Christmas Story*.

"Blood . . . claat . . . poosy . . . ole . . . bumba . . . ras . . ."

We grappled like bad dance partners as other kids stood back and gawked. We bumped into the wall, the Coke machine, the table where kids played dominoes. I ducked below another punch and stuck my shoulder in Leon's gut, just like I did when I form-tackled slow running backs or when I suplexed Shane that day. But I couldn't budge Leon. He had some ballast, and my right arm still felt disconnected from the rest of me.

To my right, I could see Leon's buddy, Leighton, crouched like a boxing referee delivering a ten-count to a fallen fighter.

"The knee, Leon!" he shouted. "Throw the knee!"

We all need a hypeman like Leighton. An expert martial artist might have timed my bobbing and weaving and cracked me across the forehead with his shin, or held me steady in a tight clinch and then kneed me in the ribcage. And it's cute that Leighton thought Leon could summon black-belt moves from thin air, but Leon wasn't trained. He was just a guy with hurt pride, lashing out at a classmate. He thought he'd land some free punches but now was engaged in a real fight.

Fighting is not fun, even if you're good at it. Most of us aren't.

Fights almost never end with clean, one-punch knockouts, and they rarely resolve the root conflict. Even winners suffer torn clothes or broken bones, and everybody endures the awkwardness. You sweat and tussle and grunt and, if you're not in shape, end up gasping for breath, because fighting is exhausting. Seconds earlier you professed to hate this person, and now you're embracing, clutching each other close enough to smell breath and cheap high school cologne.

I think Leon wore Cool Water or some shit.

By the time I sniffed it, I had straightened up and worked my left hand to the collar of his T-shirt and grabbed a handful of cloth. I could feel my right arm again. I drew my hand back to my hip and balled my fingers into a fist.

The only sensation that could have rivalled the satisfaction of smashing Leon's sneering face with my right hand was the relief I felt when a pair of teachers waded between us and pried us apart. Fighting sucks, and the part of me that preferred to emerge unscathed from a bout with no winner felt thankful, even if the part of me that would have accepted bruised knuckles as the price of raising welts on Leon's face went unfulfilled.

I stepped back and stared at Leon, who looked even more exhausted than I felt. He sucked air like he had just finished running wind sprints after basketball practice. I dropped my hands, satisfied the fight was finished. Leon did, too, then leapt forward and sucker punched me. His right fist met my left cheek, with all the strength he could summon, which, after a fight he hadn't prepared for, wasn't much.

I looked at him and smirked and shook my head.

"That's it?"

Leon looked drained and disappointed, the way we become when confronting the gap between expectation and reality. He expected to smack me around for fun, but couldn't land a clean punch until after the final bell. He expected to drop me, but didn't even make me flinch. The teacher placed one hand on Leon's shoulder, snatched the back of his shirt with the other, and guided him toward an exit. He skulked out of the cafeteria crestfallen, like most of us would be after learning first-hand how much more difficult it is to fight than to talk about it, to finish a fight than to start one.

When Leon tells the story, I'm sure he stresses how he bravely spat in my smug face for saying stuff I couldn't back up with my fists. He also probably tells people who didn't witness the fight that he bounced me like a basketball around the Black kids' section of the cafeteria, then ended the fight with a textbook right cross to my jaw. The picture his words paint of our fight probably resembles that classic snapshot of Rocky Marciano bringing a sudden end to his title defense against Jersey Joe Walcott—that right hand like thunder and lightning at once, distorting Walcott's features on impact, a split second before the lights went out.

But in my retelling, I can only report that I walked to the principal's office feeling light. I knew I'd get suspended, but didn't worry about explaining it to football recruiters or to my mom. They'd all have been more disappointed if I *didn't* hit some goon who spat in my face.

My shoulder throbbed, but I didn't have any visible cuts or bruises or welts. Not even a rip in my grey Bethune-Cookman College sweat-shirt. No sign I'd even been in a fight aside from the bloodstains, a trail of red droplets that had dripped down the back of my shirt, turning brown as they dried. But that didn't bother me, either. Blood would come out in the wash. Finding it back there made me happy because I knew it wasn't mine.

Full Speed Ahead

When the starter called us to our marks, I quit all my fidgeting and the manic pre-race pacing that my teammates said made *them* nervous, stepped out in front of my blocks, and gazed the length of the straightaway. Lane four, my favourite, and not just because the middle of the track was reserved for the fastest people. It also lined up with a brown-and-beige trash can at the foot of a grassy berm, at the south end of the stadium at Etobicoke Centennial Park, so it made focusing on my own lane easy. Just run to the brown steel drum.

I breathed in deep, then exhaled, mindful of the time. Every sprinter wants to cross the line first but settle into the starting blocks last. The bigger the event, the longer people take. This race, at the Blue and Gold Classic on the first Wednesday in May 1995, mattered. We knew, because the meet took place at the stadium, not the lumpy gravel track behind somebody's high school, and because almost every school in Mississauga and Brampton sent a team. Any meet that big would probably include future Olympians and would definitely feature races, like this 100-metre final, that felt like title fights.

Next to me, in lane three, Boyd Barrett dawdled on his way to the blocks. In a few years, the Winnipeg Blue Bombers would draft him as a cornerback, a position you don't play as a pro unless you can fly.

And on my right, in lane five, Elden Forskin ran through his pre-race ritual. Elden had serious wheels, too. He was the provincial champ in ninth grade and wasn't going to half-ass this final just because we were good friends. He'd probably run even faster just so he could talk trash next time we met up at LeVar Kelman's house to get our hair cut.

"Good luck, Den," I said as we slapped hands. "I'll save you the silver medal."

"See you at the finish line," Elden said. "I'll be waiting for you."

I chuckled and turned back to my lane, clapped twice, and did a tuck jump—launched myself into the air and drew my knees up to my armpits, as if bounding over a shoulder-high boulder. If anybody asked, I told them the jump primed my muscles for high output, but I actually did it for the other seven runners. They'd watch me leap and rethink whether they could beat me. Did you guys see how high I jumped? If gravity can't defeat me, what chance do *you* have?

I landed, eventually, then clapped again, dropped to all fours, and crawled backward into my blocks. Was my pre-race routine over the top? Only if you've never seen eight blazing fast eighteen-year-old boys, each one a Big Man on His Campus, line up for a 100-metre final. Ego and testosterone turn frayed nerves into live wires. You didn't want to wait for other people to line up; you wanted them waiting on you, so you postured to kill time. At the start line, preening like a peacock made you normal.

I strutted around that track meet like I was *somebody*, because, that spring, as far as anybody could tell, I was. High school glory? Check. In February, I had been named to Football Ontario's All-Star team. *The Mississauga News* wrote about it and ran a picture of me in my bright red Woodlands Rams football jersey. Wore that same shirt to the track meet, so folks who had seen the article would recognize me, and so everyone else would understand that track was just training for my main sport.

Future prospects? I had those, too. While most kids were still waiting on the yea or nay from Canadian schools, I already had acceptance letters from Williams College in Massachusetts, and Northwestern University, right outside Chicago. Williams was an objectively big deal. Exclusive, expensive school with a beautiful campus in the Berkshire Mountains. They recruited me for football *and* track, and offered me a healthy financial aid package. Not a full ride, but enough that, if I'd understood then how student loan debt hamstrings adults, I'd have appreciated more.

They faxed their offer to my guidance counsellor, and I still had it pinned on the fridge, next to my acceptance from Northwestern, where I really wanted to go. When I told people Northwestern's football coaches wanted me on the team next year, I was telling the truth. They just didn't want me enough to offer me a scholarship, and I was still figuring out how to become eligible for the kind of financial aid the school gave civilian students. And I would need a U.S. passport, and I didn't have one.

I had also just returned from campus, in Evanston, along the shore of Lake Michigan, first suburb north of Chicago. Arrived on a Saturday, crisp and sunny with a light breeze. Football weather in late April. Their stadium could seat nearly fifty thousand people, about half the capacity at Michigan, but still big enough to dwarf any place I might play if I stayed in Canada after high school.

I made friends with a running back named Tyrone Gooch and a wide receiver named Hasani Steele. Both stood about five-foot-ten and weighed in the 170s, so they didn't seem much bigger than I was. Cool guys, both set to enrol that fall on football scholarships. Possible future teammates. I watched the football team's springtime exhibition game and figured I could make the transition.

Northwestern had what I wanted. Strict admission standards, a journalism school, and big-time football. They had only won three games the previous season, but that was one more win than I had experienced in two years with the Woodlands Rams. At least they were losing in the Big Ten, against teams like Michigan and Ohio State. They were all just one big step from the NFL. Campus was far from home but close to family. I left Evanston bent on spending my next four years there.

Some big decisions loomed in the next few weeks, and they would have weighed heavily on a teenager willing to contemplate whether student loan debt the size of a small mortgage would snap an adult's spine. But that spring, I figured every detour and obstacle would just make an even more heart-warming backstory when my NFL contract made me a millionaire.

And at this track meet, I sprang from the starting blocks with a single-minded focus and a simple race model: be the first guy to 50 metres, then hang on after that. The strategy hadn't failed me yet this season. Every time I had lined up, I crossed the line first, including in my opening-round heat that morning.

Five strides in, I could already feel Boyd and Elden receding behind me. After ten steps, I was running alone, like I expected, opening a gap I figured even Elden couldn't close. But at 30 metres, I heard something unfamiliar. Footsteps in the next lane. Boyd Barrett's breathing. I could sense him with my skin, but I kept pressing, throttle all the way open, hoping to create some daylight before my late-race fade. Eyes on the horizon, I didn't notice the man kneeling on the infield, squinting into his camera's viewfinder, aiming his long lens at Elden, Boyd, and me.

—

If we placed all the Black Americans who have ever moved to Canada on a spectrum, Jackie Robinson would occupy one extreme. He spent 1946 with the Montreal Royals, dominating triple-A baseball. Robinson, the first Black player to sign with a Major League Baseball club, led the International League in batting average (.349) and on-base percentage (.468), and finished second in walks (92) and stolen bases (40). Montreal won one hundred games, lost only fifty-four, and claimed the International League title.

When Major League Baseball celebrates Jackie Robinson Day each year, some Canadian will inevitably point out on social media that Robinson played in Montreal before he suited up for the Brooklyn Dodgers. This framing portrays Canada as a colourblind country, and Canadians as inherently more progressive and less racist than their American neighbours. It's as if Robinson and Canada chose each other.

In reality, Robinson was always going to spend a year at triple-A, as a dress rehearsal for integrating the majors. Brooklyn's top farm team could have been in Toledo or New Haven or Havana. It happened to be in Montreal, so that's where Robinson played in 1946, an interloper with no long-term plans for life as a Canadian. He left his legacy in Montreal, and returned to the U.S. when the Dodgers called.

Rick James stayed longer. He didn't spend all his time in Canada, but was, on paper, a Toronto resident from 1964, when, at sixteen, he went AWOL from the U.S. Navy, until 1976, when he returned to the U.S. for good. James grew up in Buffalo, which is practically Canada's eleventh province, but by the time *Street Songs*—with its lead single, "Super Freak"—went platinum, his time in Toronto had become a career footnote.

By then, Canada's reputation as a safe haven for Black people fleeing racism in the U.S. was well established, thanks to the thirty thousand self-emancipated former slaves who, via the Underground Railroad, landed in Southern Ontario in the years before the Civil War. Thousands of them crossed back into the U.S. after the Union Army's victory, eager to reconnect with relatives, or finally experience freedom in the Land of the Free. For Robinson, Rick James, and the emancipated slaves who moved back south, Canada functioned as a place to exhale and regroup. A safe space to wait out untenable situations and plot future moves, but not a place to stay forever.

At the other end of the scale, we'd find Richard Pierpoint, the Revolutionary War veteran who settled in St. Catharines in 1780, under similar conditions to those that would bring Black folks to Nova Scotia en masse in 1783. Pierpoint, born in Senegal and sold into slavery in one of the Thirteen Colonies, fought for the British in exchange for his freedom, and was relocated to Canada West. When the War of 1812 broke out, Pierpoint again joined the Redcoats, part of an all-Black regiment that helped British troops repel the Yankees at the Battle of Lundy's Lane.

That Pierpoint leapt into this fight in his mid-sixties tells you he treasured his adopted country. American citizenship didn't even exist when he lived in the Colonies. After those jurisdictions became the United States and made war with Great Britain a second time, Pierpoint refused to spectate. Standing aside would have meant he chose peace against the nation that enslaved him, and the country that, had he lived there, would have minimized him as three-fifths of a human. Pierpoint chose war, on behalf of his new home.

But to the extent that Canadians learn about Pierpoint, mainstream narratives omit certain truths. They tend not to mention that he'd have encountered Black people in bondage and an active slave trade in Canada West; even when John Graves Simcoe outlawed buying and selling human beings in 1793, Black adults in the territory, which had been renamed Upper Canada, remained the property of their owners. Anyone born to enslaved parents stayed enslaved themselves until age twenty-five.

Or that, between the wars, Pierpoint petitioned the government of Upper Canada to grant land to him and other Black Loyalists. If they owned and worked adjacent plots, he reasoned, they could pool efforts and become more successful Canadians.

Petition denied.

Or that, early in the War of 1812, Pierpoint volunteered to raise an all-Black regiment of soldiers—Niagara-area locals who, like him, itched to keep the Yankees on the other side of the big river.

Motion rejected, though the Redcoats did end up organizing an all-Black unit—after finding a white person to lead it.

In his eighties, Pierpoint made one last plea to Upper Canada's government: to ship him to England, and from there he would travel back to Senegal, so he could die where he once lived free. He hoped the government would do him this favour as a thank-you for twice fighting on its behalf.

Request unsuccessful. Instead, the government found him a patch of land in Fergus, outside Guelph, one hundred kilometres west of Toronto. He died there in 1838.

Upper Canada granted him freedom but not equality, showing him his place and gently hemming him in, even though he had risked his own life, and maybe taken others', to defend the Crown. The subtle but unmistakable limits on his ambitions, the clear message sent with each petition tossed back in his face—it's all classic, soft-edged Canadian racism, with plausible deniability built in. Did Canada free him from bondage, or just hitch his collar to a longer chain? Some days, Pierpoint must have wondered.

But the details Canadians tended to learn about Pierpoint's experience in Canada came to us on leaflets, and cast his life's arc in typically patronizing Canadian ways. Canada as the colourblind meritocracy, in bold and righteous contrast to the rigid racial hierarchy of U.S. slave society. Pierpoint as the Black Canadian immigrant, rooted in his new country, and grateful for the chance it granted to restart his life.

That described my mom. Loyal to Canada, and thankful for the opportunity to start again. She didn't disown her first home, but she turned twelve in 1955, a year after the U.S. Supreme Court ruled unanimously, in Brown v. Board of Education, that racial segregation in public schools violated the constitution.

That year, Emmett Till—like my mom, a preteen from the South Side of Chicago—was lynched in Money, Mississippi, for whistling at a white woman—allegedly. In December, same year, Rosa Parks refused to surrender her seat to a white man on a bus in Montgomery, Alabama, kicking off the year-long boycott that forced the city's buses to integrate, and launched the modern Civil Rights Movement. Each event pushed sixth-grade Jeanie Jones closer to the decision she eventually made, as a twelve-year-old, to stop pledging allegiance to the flag of a country that felt no allegiance to its Black citizens.

The first time, in her classroom, before school started, she simply refused to participate. Sat out like Colin Kaepernick did the national anthem. Her teacher pulled her aside and lectured her, then threatened her with detention. Jeanie promised that, going forward, she would follow the rules and recite the whole pledge. The next morning, when the class rose in unison and began the routine, Jeanie mouthed the words but said nothing. She wouldn't swear another oath of loyalty to a flag until she became a Canadian citizen.

My dad? He lived closer to the middle of the spectrum, near people like Cito Gaston, who managed the Blue Jays to two World Series wins in the 1990s. Cito spent summers in Toronto, even after the team fired him, but he still had a house outside Tampa. Dad never had two-houses money, but his connection to Canada didn't negate his Americanness. My mom saw U.S. citizenship as a condition she could cure by becoming Canadian. My dad understood that U.S. citizenship might go into remission when you moved away, but it never disappeared.

You'd find my grandpa over near Pierpoint. He, too, felt liberated upon arriving in Canada. Toronto was the first place where, for him, racial integration seemed normal, and not forced or fitful or fleeting. He forged friendships with white people, and some would grow as close as family. Alexandre and Cathy Tremblay used to road-trip with us to Chicago, and would invite my grandparents to their cottage in Temiscaming, Quebec, the little milling town on the Ottawa River where Alexandre grew up. And the Tremblays didn't call my grandpa "Claude," rhymes with "pod." They called him "*Claude*," rhymes with "strode." Hearing his name *en français* sounded, to my grandpa, like music—another small pleasure that life in Chicago would never have bestowed.

The summer after my ninth-grade year, we took a family road trip to Chicago, timed to coincide with a late-July Blue Jays–White Sox series, so we could make some group outings to the ballpark. We agreed to meet outside Comiskey Park half an hour before first pitch, and, of course, Grandpa kept us waiting. He had driven separately because he said he had to run some errands. Five minutes to game time, he still hadn't arrived, so we all headed inside.

After about three innings, Grandpa ambled into the stadium and found us in the right field bleachers. He didn't apologize. He never did. For anything.

"Daddy, what happened to you?" my mom asked.

"Nothing happened," Grandpa said. "I got lost."

"Lost?" Aunt Peggy said, incredulous. "How do you get lost down here?"

"I just did," Grandpa said. "I've been gone so long. I'm Canadian now. This isn't my city anymore."

Granted, on the South Side of Chicago it's easy to drift into a neighbourhood where you don't belong. An outsider wouldn't know when they had crossed a gang boundary, or traversed the border between a Black neighbourhood and a white or Mexican one. But losing your geographical bearings is almost impossible. Lake Michigan, if you can see it, is east. The numbered streets tell you how far north or south you are, and State Street separates east from west. If you miss that signal, the Dan Ryan Expressway and the Chicago Transit Authority's Red Line train run like a seam down the middle of the South Side. If you knew the address or the intersection, you could usually get there by counting blocks.

In fairness, Comiskey Park had moved since the first Joneses left Chicago. It opened in 1910, and for eighty years anchored the north side of 35th Street, between Shields and Wentworth. Late in 1990, the stadium was demolished, and the White Sox opened the 1991 season in a *new* Comiskey Park, on the *south* side of 35th Street, between Shields and Wentworth.

And before you speculate that the lapse in memory signaled advancing age and cognitive erosion—no. A lifetime of making music had bulletproofed his brain. My grandpa stayed sharp deep into his nineties, and never forgot anything, except how he started or escalated every family fight. If he said he was, after twenty-five years in his new home, too Torontonian to navigate the South Side of Chicago, it's because he saw himself that way. He wore his Canadianness like a credential, and cultivated, performed, and projected his adopted, specific identity. American by birth but Canadian by choice, so Canadian above all.

—

"Yooooooo! Morgan! Long time, man!"

Here came Caliphe Buchanan, my old football teammate from the pee wee days and now an all-star running back at Meadowvale Secondary. We slapped hands and he sat down beside me on the bleachers in the northwest corner of Centennial Park Stadium. I should have spent the ninety minutes between my races someplace more comfortable than these hard wooden benches, but I wanted to see the 400-metre heats and watch pretty girls jog past.

"I saw you in *The Mississauga News* the other week," he said. "All-Ontario. Congrats."

"Thanks," I said.

The puffy white clouds overhead parted for a few minutes. Caliphe and I squinted in the sun as we spoke.

"You figure out where you're going to school yet?"

"Still working on it," I said.

We started football the same year, on the same team, the Streetsville-Meadowvale Colts of the Mississauga Football League. Damon Ealey was our superstar, a game-breaking tailback and an eraser at middle linebacker, and now was finishing his freshman year on a football scholarship at the University of Toledo. Caliphe and I anchored the defensive line—he played left end, and I played the right side. Neither of us had a future in the trenches. Puberty turns players into different athletes and football into a different sport. Caliphe grew into a durable tailback with good speed, and I became a fast cornerback who could play other positions.

By our final year in high school, we had both joined the scramble for football scholarships, and Caliphe had recently committed to Lehigh University, outside Philadelphia. Technically, it wasn't a football scholarship, since those were prohibited in the Patriot League, where Lehigh played. But those schools could offer need-based financial aid, with the understanding that a family's financial need was proportional to their son's football skill.

"Where you thinking of going?" he asked

"Williams College offered me."

"Where's that?"

"Massachusetts."

"Cool," Caliphe said. "Full ride?"

"Naw," I said. "They're a D-3. But it's a lot of money."

"So why aren't you taking it?"

"Mannnn . . ." I said. "I visited there in February. Too much snow and hardly any Black people."

"Ha!"

"And it's so far from everything," I said. "I had to take a train to Albany, and then drive another forty-five minutes. Nice campus, but man. I can't see myself there for four years. Football's only four months a year."

"I hear you," Caliphe said. "Where else?"

"Northwestern wants me to walk-on. And they have a journalism school, and I'm tryna be a writer when I'm done playing football," I said, as if a pro career was a given.

"Aren't they in the Big Ten?"

"Yep."

"Aw man, that would be so awesome," Caliphe said. "Our little MFL team lost to the Marauders in the championship, and we put three guys in Division 1 ball. Me, you, and Damon. I bet that's never happened before."

"Yeah, I know," I said. "I just gotta figure out about money. Northwestern ain't cheap."

"I bet," Caliphe said. "Hold up . . . Charles Allen is about to run. Watch lane five. Black singlet."

Caliphe and I watched Charles glide down the back stretch with the easy speed of a future Olympic finalist, widening his lead with each stride. He rounded the last curve and hit the home stretch looking unbothered. I had raced him back in eleventh grade but had never seen his face before, just the back of his head and the soles of his feet.

He crossed the line first. You could have fit a basketball court between him and the guy in second.

"And he's not even a 400-metre runner," Caliphe said. "He's gonna be trouble when he comes back to the one and two."

"I know," I said. "I don't have that kind of endurance. I just start fast and hang on."

"So when do these schools want an answer?" Caliphe asked, steering us back on topic.

"I dunno," I said. "Soon, probably."

I glanced at by black Timex Ironman wristwatch. Half an hour till my final. I stood and gathered my book bag. Almost time to warm up.

"Okay, man," I said to Caliphe. "Lemme go get ready for this race."

"Good luck, man," he said, slapping hands with me again. "Charles isn't running, so you have a chance."

"I know," I said, laughing as I hiked my knapsack onto my shoulder.

"But lemme know what happens with school," he said. "You need to make up your mind soon."

By then I had shaved my Canadian options to the University of Toronto, which I actually liked; York University, which I didn't mind; and the University of Windsor, my safety school. If I couldn't make anything happen in the U.S., I was ready to major in history and play football at musty old Varsity Stadium. U of T had won the national title in 1993, and stayed dangerous in 1994, largely because no defense could contain Glenn McCausland, their five-foot-six, 150-pound missile of a kick returner. He was graduating, and one night even called me to talk me into filling the void he was about to create. They also needed speed in their defensive backfield. If I wanted playing time straight out of high school, I would have it with the Varsity Blues.

But I was still fixated on the U.S.

Every Saturday afternoon, I had the option of watching Canadian university football on CHCH out of Hamilton—Western against Guelph or whoever, a few hundred fans in the bleachers, maybe a couple thousand for a big game. A light dusting of melanin on each roster, but mostly the teams were slow and white. And they looked even slower and whiter in contrast to the guys I saw when I flipped to the NCAA games on ABC and CBS, which were full of future NFLers performing in front of audiences the size of small cities: 73,000 in Lincoln, Nebraska; 100,000-plus at the University of Michigan. It all seemed so outsized and important. Canadian university football was a sport, but in the U.S. it was also a spectacle and, I would learn later, a business. At eighteen, I wanted the flash, and a straight path to a pro career.

I envisioned my future self in a sleek custom-fitted uniform—black cleats spatted with white tape, jersey tucked to showcase my abs—patrolling the defensive backfield someplace like Syracuse or Cal or, eventually, Northwestern. And as a Black person with roots in the U.S. and a growing awareness of the role race played in, well, everything, I saw myself, increasingly, as an American, edging toward my dad's end of the spectrum. A sort of hybrid citizen. Canadian, with an asterisk.

To be clear, I was Canadian enough to have cheered for Ben Johnson to beat Carl Lewis in 1988, but not so Canadian that I said "grade nine" instead of "ninth grade." I would have said freshman, sophomore, junior, and senior, but we had five years of high school, and I couldn't think of a fifth name that fit.

In the U.S., when people asked where I was from, I'd say Canada, because I was born and raised there. (A college football teammate named Chris Martin christened me "The Mountie" early in training camp my freshman year, and some people still call me that now, at forty whatever years old.) But when Black people around Toronto asked where I was from, I'd say the U.S., because the rules of multicultural Black Toronto dictated that you claim your parents' home territory as your identity. I grew up with Canadian-born kids who called themselves Jamaican or Trini or Bajan; even if you were eight generations deep on Canadian soil, descended from the Black Loyalists who landed in Halifax in the 1780s, you likely didn't, among other Black teenagers, identify yourself as *just* Canadian. You'd probably make plain that you were Scotian.

I was the son of two Chicagoans, descended from migrants from the Deep South, who themselves came from so many generations of U.S.-born slaves that it wasn't even worth asking where, precisely, we came from before that. No place we can pinpoint. The Campbells and Bonners and Joneses and Gaddises were all products of the New World. So, if you asked where I was really from—and a lot of Black people around Toronto did—I was American.

On the spectrum, I was creating space next to Elijah McCoy, the engineer and inventor who created high-quality automatic lubricators for steam engines that spawned a generation of less-reliable knockoffs. Legend says train operators seeking steam engine lubricators insisted on "the real McCoy," which, folklore tells us, is how the phrase entered the lexicon. McCoy and I were both first-generation Black American Diaspora, positioned to succeed because our parents had fled to Canada. I can't say for sure what I'd have become if I'd been the same type of troublemaking grade schooler in a segregated, big-city school system in the U.S., but I wouldn't have to exaggerate to imagine one final trans- gression taking me from the classroom to the principal's office to the Pipeline to prison. McCoy's parents escaped a Kentucky plantation and reached Michigan before crossing the Detroit River and settling in Essex County, outside Windsor; he became an engineer because he was born in Colchester, Ontario. He attended a segregated school in Canada, but at least he attended school. If he were born and raised on a plantation, he'd still have been brilliant, but not in a classroom. And he'd also have been somebody else's property.

McCoy also studied in Scotland, and ultimately moved to the U.S. to reach his full potential. When I pictured a career in an NFL or *Sports Illustrated*—or *SI* after a few years in the NFL—I saw an adulthood like his: Canadian by birth, and American because my talent won me a bigger platform. Black on both sides of the border, with success and a reputation that travelled.

I was born seven years after my parents moved to Toronto and a month after they became citizens. That detail didn't distinguish me from my sisters in my mom's eyes. All three of us were born in North York, and were just as Canadian as any Stu, Murray, or Doug who paired blue jeans with a blue denim shirt, and slathered ketchup on Kraft Mac & Cheese and called it dinner.

But viewed through the Canadian gaze of the immigration lawyer my mom called to help untangle the mess with Northwestern's financial aid office, my birth date made me very different. As the only Campbell kid born after my parents became Canadian, I was, in his reckoning, the only sibling without a claim to U.S. citizenship. This was his expert, and very Canadian, take on my situation, and my patriotic Canadian mom didn't consider that he might be wrong.

Early that spring, a flurry of phone calls and letters flew between Mississauga and Evanston. From my mom to financial aid and back. From financial aid to my mom and back. From my mom to the provost, who had been quoted in a magazine article, lamenting the challenges Northwestern faced in recruiting and retaining Black students.

My mom's letters went like this:

Morgan loves Northwestern and he really wants to attend, but we're broke. His dad just died, and he has two college-aged sisters. His dad and I were both born and raised in Chicago, and there must *be some way to qualify him for financial aid.*

The responses would arrive from Evanston, empathetic but unflinching.

Yes, we want Morgan here. And yes, he has a lot to contribute to the campus community. But no, we can't bend the financial aid rules for him or anyone else. We can't offer grants, but if you're open to an endowed loan for full tuition, at nine per cent interest, payable over ten years after graduation, let's continue this conversation.

What sober-thinking high school senior, with decent grades and real options, would choose to borrow 17,500 dollars at nine per cent interest? Anybody bright enough to get into Northwestern and Williams *and* U of T had to understand the power of compound interest. And someone pursuing a journalism career also had to know newspapers and magazines paid rookies a pittance, and that borrowing for a second and third year could bury you. Paying off more than sixty thousand dollars' worth of student loans on a journalist's salary? Might as well fight a forest fire with a garden hose.

In my eighteen-year-old brain, I figured I would accept the endowed loan, then use that money to buy enough time to prove I deserved a football scholarship. From there, I would land in the NFL, where I'd make enough money to pay that debt the way I paid bus fare: by grabbing some coins from my pocket and tossing them into the hopper. Big money to teenage Morgan, but spare change to an all-pro cornerback.

Under neutral circumstances, my mom and I could have played the schools against each other. "Williams has a lower admission rate, a higher ranking, and is giving us twenty thousand dollars a year. What are you going to do for me, Northwestern?"

And when the financial aid offers came in, you'd try to keep the money flowing by playing poor.

"We're down to one income here, but all the family's expenses are the same. Are you sure you can't do better? Northwestern just increased their offer . . ."

Except in my family's case, in the months after my dad died, we weren't playing. Somehow the lights stayed on, and we never starved; I had pocket cash because the federal government sent my sisters and me

150 dollars a month, our share of the pension my dad didn't live to collect. But we fell behind on the phone bill and lost service for a few days in December, right when I thought college recruiters might call. As a family we were, as my mom sometimes said, running on the smell of money.

And circumstances weren't neutral. One expensive school offered financial aid and the other didn't.

Maybe my dad would have fixed this problem the way he solved so many others, with pragmatism and fast thinking. Like the time Maclean-Hunter cut off our cable, so he dug up the next-door neighbour's cord and split it. Periodically during grade school, I'd ask my parents when we were getting TSN or MuchMusic, and their response was always "We'll see." The real answer: we'd get those channels when the Balas did.

Another time, my parents' friends Earl and LaVern Roberson drove up from Chicago with their five-year-old daughter LaTasha, who quickly developed a high fever and a sore throat and could barely swallow. My dad hauled her to Mississauga Hospital and explained to ER staff that his seven-year-old daughter, Courtney, had a high fever and a sore throat and could barely swallow.

Diagnosis: tonsillitis.

They gave her whatever short-term treatment you give to tonsillitis patients to bridge them to surgery, and she survived the rest of the trip in relative comfort, then had her tonsils removed back home in Chicago. If my dad could make LaTasha Canadian long enough to score medical care on a family vacation, would he have remembered what the 14th Amendment said about U.S. citizenship? Would he have figured out how simple it actually was to exercise my birthright? Just take three birth certificates—mine, his, my mom's—to the U.S. Consulate, fill out some papers, pay some fees, and wait for them to mail you a passport. My dad probably would have known.

But I didn't have my dad. Just a stack of documents promising I would pay back the endowed loan after I graduated, and a belief that football could solve my money problems. So I signed the papers, committed to Northwestern and some debt, confident I would earn a scholarship and, eventually, turn pro. That spring, I was willing to climb a wall to prove I belonged at Northwestern, when I really just needed someone to show me a door.

The photographer caught me at forty-five metres, half a step ahead of Boyd Barrett, flying down the front straightaway, intoxicated with the power of my body. In the picture, I was eighteen and confident, and bursting at the seams with muscle. Boyd, in green, had just hit the top of his stride. I wore red, white, and gold. Elden, to my right, cropped out of the frame but closing the gap fast. The photo showed me driving forward, brow bent with effort, thigh muscles rippling and biceps stretching skin.

Action shots made you look more jacked than you actually were. But I didn't complain. The photo reflected how I felt six weeks before the end of high school.

Strong enough to wrestle fate.

Fast enough to outrun iffy decisions.

The photo appeared in *The Mississauga News* on a Friday, two days after the track meet. When I arrived at school Monday morning, some staffer had pinned it to the bulletin outside the cafeteria. It replaced another picture of me, the one that accompanied the article about the All-Ontario football team.

I knew girls who clipped that picture from the paper and saved it in their scrapbooks. A decade later, the photographer recognized me; I was on assignment for the *Toronto Star*, he was still shooting for *The News*, both of us outside Carolyn Parrish's office on Central Parkway in Mississauga, waiting for her to emerge and explain why she had left the federal Liberal caucus.

The title above the caption read "Full Speed Ahead." I had a slim lead and figured I'd hold it for fifty more metres, but plans can unravel.

Two strides later, I ran into an axiom that governed 100-metre sprinting:

Moving fastest at fifty metres beats reaching fifty metres first.

I was first to fifty. Boyd was moving faster. He eased past me at fifty-five and inched away. My form, already ugly, faltered further when Elden overtook both of us at sixty-five metres and strode through the finish line.

He had confidence in his top speed and modeled his race around patience, peaking at the right time. Elden collected a first-place medal. I finished with a third-place ribbon, which I tucked into the front pocket of the book bag I used as a pillow during my midday nap, stretched out on the bleachers in the stadium's northwest corner.

I closed my eyes and visualized the near future. Relay at 3:30. District championship in a week and a half. Even stiffer competition, but the same game plan. Run to the brown steel drum. Full throttle from the gun. Full Speed Ahead, but faster next time.

The 90-Minute Slow Jam Tape

Kelly's family lived in a long tall townhouse half a mile from our school, and because we lived at opposite ends of Mississauga Transit's Route 44, getting there was simple. I rode the bus for twenty-five minutes, from stop 2424 on Falconer Drive to the corner of Dundas Street and Erindale Station Road, then walked a quarter mile east and arrived on her driveway a little after noon.

Ringing her bell meant scaling a steep set of stairs that rose from street level to the main floor of the house. It might raise a normal person's heart rate, or maybe cause a mild burning in the thighs, but I cleared two stairs with each stride as I bounded toward the porch, then pressed the doorbell and waited, breathing as easily as I had on the driveway, a full storey below.

At eighteen, I wasn't a normal person. I ran every morning and lifted weights most nights. In the six weeks since track season ended, I had put on five pounds of muscle, despite all that running in the early summer heat. I managed it because I treated eating like a part-time job, but also because my great-aunt Edith had given me one hundred dollars as a graduation gift that I put toward a YMCA membership, so I graduated from bicep curls in my bedroom to pumping real iron in a fully equipped gym. Fitness experts will tell you it's nearly impossible to build muscle while shedding fat, especially when you're already lean. But my eighteen-year-old body bent the rules of exercise science. I didn't just have abs. My abs had abs. No special diet. I just worked a lot, slept as much as I could, and tapped into the most powerful performance-enhancer on earth: late-stage adolescence.

I wasn't training for photo shoots. In six weeks, I was scheduled to start my first college football training camp, and the transition demanded a bigger *and* faster version of myself. I couldn't help my height. My mom stood five feet on a good day; my dad was six feet tall, but passed on his height to my five-foot-eight sister Courtney.

But I could train speed, which meant another summer sprinting up big hills, or bus rides to my school to run on the track. And I could build strength at the Y. In June, I stitched together a routine from the tips I gleaned reading magazines like *Muscle & Fitness* or *FLEX*, or watching *Body Shaping* on TSN. In July, I started lifting with my friend Andre, a star wide receiver at York University, and our buddy Mace, home for the summer from the University of Toledo. We followed the circuit Mace's coaches gave him—sixty minutes of torture, three times a week. Twenty or so exercises, back to back to back. Only rest was your walk between stations. Dre puked the first time he tried it. I would have cried but had already sweated out all my spare moisture.

I didn't skip a weight-room session all summer, and only missed my morning run twice. The first time, on a smoggy day in early July, the heat index hit 49 degrees Celsius. Ego told me to train anyway. So did anxiety, which had me thinking a lost workout might derail a summer's worth of progress. But good sense kept me home until the temperature fell.

The second time followed the phone call that led me to Kelly Charles's doorstep on an overcast Friday afternoon. Late the previous night, she called and told me she had a rare day off work, and the house to herself all day. I could have still squeezed in a quick sprint session, but made an executive decision to save my energy for whatever Kelly had planned.

So, I rang her doorbell, a book bag full of workout gear slung over my shoulder because Friday was Leg Day, and I figured I could still hit the weight room afterward. She answered the door wearing a full smile, wide and white and toothy, the one she rarely showed at school unless she passed me in the hall. Baggy denim overalls hung loosely from her shoulders and stopped just above her knee. Underneath, she didn't wear much.

"Hey, Morgan," she said, her voice dark and smoky like I imagined cognac tasted.

She wrapped her arms around my shoulders.

"Hey, Kells."

I hugged her around the waist. Slid my arm in the gap between her overalls and the small of her back. No shirt. This felt promising.

"Meet me in the kitchen," she said. "I'm just finishing lunch."

I took off my shoes—black-and-white Nike Air Icarus I'd still be wearing today if you could run in the same shoes for three decades—and placed them on the doormat next to her Filas with the thick red soles and white uppers. Then I followed her into the house.

"You hungry?"

Uh . . . in a sense . . . The word for my mood started with *H* and ended with *Y* and rhymed with "forlornly."

"Naw, I'm cool," I said.

I trailed her into the kitchen. She opened a cupboard and rose on her tiptoes to grab two clear plastic drinking glasses, then filled them both with ice and water. She handed one to me, then took a sip from the other.

"Follow me upstairs."

I followed, as if tethered to her belt loop, watching her bare skin beneath those overalls, her hips shifting with every step. We ascended a tight staircase, up so many steps I wondered if we were about to lose our virginity in the attic.

Finally, we reached a landing and made a right turn and headed into Kelly's room. Dim daylight trickled in through a small window crammed into a south-facing crevice of the house. It wouldn't have caught much sunshine on a clear day, but on an overcast afternoon like this, the room stayed gauzy.

She brightened the space with her murals, abstract with splashes of yellow and purple and fire-engine red. On a thin section of wall, in a tight corner of the bedroom, just above her slim twin bed, she had hung a poster depicting a handsome Black couple in a warm and deep embrace; they looked a little older than Kelly and me, photographed in black-and-white, amid a street scene, classic cars in the background. Across the room, art supplies and a small stereo rested on a desktop, alongside a shoebox full of cassettes. I sat on the edge of her bed, half-full glass of ice water in my hands, cool against my warm palms, watching her sort through the tapes, shoulders bare, navy-blue bra strap sneaking out from under her overalls.

"What are you about to play?" I asked.

"Just wait."

Kelly found the tape she wanted and freed it from its case, then pressed the eject button just before the tape deck's jaw eased open. She slid the cassette into the slot and snapped the deck shut, the rattle and clack of plastic on plastic. Then came the kind of keyboard riff that kicked off a lot of slow jams from the first half of the 1990s. Sometimes they came from a piano, but usually from a synthesizer on the "piano" setting. You didn't need perfect pitch to tell the difference. My grandpa had a concert-sized Steinway in his living room; my sister kept a seventy-three-key Yamaha on her desk in the basement. I knew which of those instruments made *this* sound.

From there, a not-so-subtle recasting of "Yearning for Your Love." Similar four-note bass line, and where The GAP Band's all-time classic slow jam has a rhythm guitar loop, this one played that same pattern on a keyboard.

> *Boy, I can't seem to get you outta my head*
> *But there's something about you that makes me smile*

Of course, I knew the song, "Always on My Mind" by SWV. I knew damn near every slow jam because I listened to *The Quiet Storm* on

WBLK almost every night when I should have been sleeping or studying. Slow jams were to me what hockey stats were to white kids: trivia, currency, and cultural capital. They could start a conversation with a new acquaintance or help me gauge character. Tell me some of your favourite slow jams and I can tell you something about yourself.

If you don't have any favourites, we don't speak the same language.

Maybe your preferred *Quiet Storm* cut was "As We Lay" by Shirley Murdock, where the singer spends a blissful morning with her lover, then clues in that his wife is coming for both their necks once she realizes where her man spent the night. If so, I would figure that you realized how complicated love can become. And if you wanted to dance to "As We Lay" at your wedding, like an early adult-hood girlfriend of mine did, I would know that you either didn't actually listen to the lyrics, or didn't care about fidelity. Either one is a check-engine light flashing on the relationship's dashboard.

Or let's say "Slow Dance" by R. Kelly was your song. If this was the 1990s, I wouldn't judge you. I would figure that you treasured the link between music and movement. Slow jams aren't just for listening. They're best experienced body-to-body and cheek-to-cheek, two step-ping in sensual rhythm.

In 1995, you probably ignored reports that grown-ass R. Kelly had married teenage Aaliyah, or at least dismissed them as rumours. After all, R. Kelly was deep into his twenties, old enough to be your big brother or youngest uncle. Years later, we all had to recognize R. Kelly for what he was—a grown man who was into teenage girls. If he had strolled into your friend's basement party, and the DJ threw on "Slow Dance," fifteen-year-old you and twenty-five-year-old R. Kelly would have been chasing the same girls, trying to bump and grind.

Back then, they were just slow jams. I had *Born into the 90's* on tape, and *12 Play* on CD, but I also built out my personal slow jam archives running that old Columbia House scam. If you grew up in the 1990s, you knew the drill. You signed up and received a bunch of CDs—Five? Eleven? Forty-seven?—for a dollar, then promised to buy more at full price. When your CDs arrived, you'd renege on your pledge and leave Columbia House waiting for more of your money. And when you wanted more music, rewind and repeat with a different name. Morgan Campbell wanted cheap CDs, but so did "Peter Campbell," "Campbell Peters," and "Pierre Morgan."

I used Columbia House to cop music library essentials, like Earth, Wind & Fire's two-volume greatest hits collection, and to buy entire albums I only wanted for one song, like Kenny G's *Breathless*. Yes, Kenny G, because he had that collaboration with Peabo Bryson, which they used to play on *The Quiet Storm*, and I loved the idea of me and some beautiful girl starting as friends, then becoming lovers By the Time This Night Is Over.

I actually paid full price for the Isley Brothers' *Beautiful Ballads*. Found it on a mid-winter visit to HMV at Square One Shopping Centre. Best compilation out there. Not their greatest hits, which might have included "That Lady" and "Work to Do" and other up-tempo songs I would have skipped. Just a collection of slow jams, which spoke to eighteen-year-old Morgan's priorities.

I listened to it every night for a month before I let Kelly take it home for a week. We agreed that when she brought it back, we'd each reveal our favourite track to see if they matched.

Mine?

Easy.

"Let's Fall in Love," because I still thought that's what I was supposed to do before I had sex, which I still planned to do, preferably with Kelly, before I left for training camp in August.

Romantic Ron Isley sang lead, his vocals an easy extension of his speaking voice: high-pitched and a little sweet. Sometimes he would let it drift almost sharp, but never too loud. The gap between his highest and lowest notes spanned *maybe* an octave—twelve notes on a piano, if you're including the black keys. But Ron Isley didn't need more. My uncle Jeff played bass guitar and made a living with just four strings; Ron Isley didn't need pipes or a wide range, because he had a

scalpel-sharp sense of how to embellish or rephrase a melody, how long
and loud to hold a note, and how to interpret lyrics to keep the listener
hooked.

"Let's Fall in Love" rests on a central truth:

Everybody needs someone to love

Then segues into a confession:

And I want to be the one you love

From there, a gentle suggestion that the woman does what the title
says, and falls in love.

Here, to Romantic Ron Isley, *love* meant love. A warm feeling and a
deep bond, something into which two people fall, crashing fast or with
a slow descent. You heard this same singer on the Isley Brothers' best-
remembered ballads: "Sensuality," "(At Your Best) You Are Love,"
"Make Me Say It Again, Girl." It's the voice of *Quiet Storm* staples that
reminded grown-ups how true love could feel, and prompted teenagers
like me to imagine how it might.

Kelly's favourite cut from *Beautiful Ballads*?

"Don't Say Goodnight (It's Time for Love)," featuring Romantic
Ron's sleazy alter-ego on lead vocals. They sounded almost identical:
same restrained longing, same mastery of melody and metre. But his
intent lent his voice an oily undertone. Where Romantic Ron sang of
commitment and fulfillment, and the broad foundations beneath
strong relationships, Sleazy Ron crooned with a pinhole focus on
sexual conquest.

Sleazy Ron didn't suggest, and he slid right past insinuation, greasy
as his late-career S-curl. *Love*, for him, in Kelly's favourite song, meant
sex. If you didn't clue in, he made it plain early, his slimy, slithery
singing voice snaking through the first verse.

I want to see, see what you're like
Like in be-eeehd

If your favourite slow jams opened a window to your character, I figured my top song and Kelly's top song off that Isley Brothers album spotlighted our objectives. I wanted to fall in love; Kelly wanted to see what I was like in bed. Sounded like an opportunity. Converging interests and common ground on the patch of carpet next to her bed as Coko from SWV sang another verse about the guy who was Always on Her Mind.

"This song tryna tell me something?" I asked.

"Maybe."

"Uh huh. Just maybe?"

"Just maybe."

In my bedroom, I'd have kicked this session off differently. Kelly went with a mixtape from an actual DJ, which let her avoid choppy transitions between tracks, and the slivers of commercials that snuck in after songs you recorded off WBLK. But you lost the intimacy of knowing the person making the tape chose each song because it meant something to both of you. It's like the transition from vinyl to CDs to digital. The new media were crisp and technically proficient, but the worn edges of sound made the old forms feel warmer.

Maybe I wouldn't even have picked a mixtape. I might have chosen something from my collection that followed the Early '90s R&B Album Template—side A full of upbeat songs to make edge-of-the-bed small talk less awkward, and back-loaded with slow jams to signify it's time for action. If you had a tape deck with auto-reverse, the click of the cassette changing directions signalled a shift in priorities, from conversation to kissing to whatever came next. If I played Keith Sweat, we could chat over "Keep It Comin'" and make out to "(There You Go) Telling Me No." By the time the tape rolled to "Give Me What I Want," we'd be half-clothed and horizontal.

Or given a week's lead time, equipped with a CD player, twin cassette decks, and a game plan, I could have made a tape for the occasion. I'd have led off with a love song—probably "Forever in Your Eyes" by Mint Condition—and raised the temperature track by track. Late into side A, I'd slide in a track that foreshadowed making love, like "50 Candles." Explicitly sexual, but with a veneer of innocence because Boyz II Men sang it.

From there, I could go in several directions. Sex songs that got radio play, like "Lay Your Head on My Pillow" or "Freak Me" or "Knockin' da Boots." Or slow jam gems buried deep on the B-sides of people's albums, like Jodeci's "Ride and Slide" or Joe's "Get a Little Closer" or Ralph Tresvant's "Last Night."

By the end of my final year in high school, trial and error had taught me the nuances of building a 90-minute slow jam tape. I learned, for example, not to cram Intro's "Come Inside" anywhere on the playlist. Thematically, it fits. A dude promising his girlfriend a long list of thrills if she lets him . . . "Come Inside." The double entendre is obvious from jump, and with some real-world experience, I'd figure out the third layer of meaning. But that song ran eight minutes and nine seconds, nearly half of it devoted to an outro that consisted of sex noises, a drum beat, and a refrain:

> I'll make you feel all right, oh baby, if you let.
> Me. Come. In. Side.

You couldn't include that song without crowding out another one. And you couldn't smooth over the three minutes of sex noises tacked on to the end of the track. Could make things awkward if the action hadn't started yet, or if it had, ruin the rhythm to which I imagined intercourse happened.

I also learned to keep two CDs with me whenever I started building a new 90-minute slow jam tape: Guy's *The Future* and Tony Toni Toné's

Sons of Soul. They didn't just make the cut for foundational grooves like "Let's Chill" or "Lay Your Head on My Pillow." If side A ran a few minutes short, you'd grab *The Future* and plug in "Where Did the Love Go?" It's a quick interlude that bridges the gap to halftime, and asks a question side B will answer. And if the flipside only runs forty-three minutes, take *Sons of Soul* and tee up "Castleers." Ideal soundtrack for afterplay. Eighty seconds long, with a hopeful ending. Piano chords, muted trumpet, and Raphael Wiggins, just before he became Raphael Saadiq, inviting some lucky woman to his "home, sweet home."

But the way I'd have done it didn't matter. This was Kelly's bedroom, her cassette deck, and her slow jam tape. She led with "You're Always on My Mind," and for a while I would have to follow.

I could have kissed her then, those posters overlooking us, SWV on her little stereo. But why? I had waited and worked since September to position myself right here. We had kissed in an empty school hallway at halftime of that basketball game back in November, but hadn't been one on one in person since then. Why not stretch this moment into a string of them, and let it all steep a little longer? I had gamed out dozens of ways this might happen. My place, her place, neutral site. Early morning, late night, overnight. Mourning, celebration, or random chance.

Now it was going down, just like this. I didn't want to rush. Kelly's folks would return home eventually, and I'd need to vanish early enough to let her clean up any evidence of my presence. As far as they'd know, she spent the afternoon sketching at the desk in her bedroom. We didn't have the whole day, but we had two sides of a 90-minute slow jam tape.

I stood and strolled across the room. Peered out the tiny window at the rest of the townhouse complex. Looked at her posters.

"You know I still have that picture you drew for me?" I said.

"Don't Disturb This Groove?"

"Yep. It's on the back of my bedroom door, next to Deion Sanders."

"I had to draw that one twice," she said. "I finished it, but it didn't look right. I stared and stared and stared. Then I figured out it said 'Don't Disturb This *Grove.*' So I had to start again."

"Ha! Well, it's coming with me to school."

"Really?" she said. "Who you gonna groove with down there?"

"You, hopefully. If you ever come visit."

Second semester we still circled each other, but in a wider orbit. I had enough credits to graduate but came back to package some half-decent grades with my university applications, and run some fast times during track season. Kelly was enrolled in a co-op program, working full time at a hair salon for class credit, and coming to school maybe once a week.

I had a girlfriend for a minute. Cool girl. Named Hope. Smooth dark skin. Short hair, long legs. Worked at the grocery store in the Valleys, near where my dad lived. We met in a YMCA youth group and started hanging out on the side. She was fun and convenient, but mostly convenient. We didn't have to schedule our meetings weeks in advance, or luck into each other in the Black kids' section of the school cafeteria. If we were free, we could meet at Square One—in front of the Burger King, where everyone met everyone in 1990s teenage Mississauga—and work from there.

And Kelly had some type of little boyfriend or something. I dunno. She mentioned him sometimes, but I didn't think much about him. Kelly's and my schedules were a bigger obstacle than I'd ever let that guy become. Listening to *The Quiet Storm*, I heard a whole sub-genre of slow jams devoted to finding honour in breaking up other people's relationships.

Me, under my covers, eyes closed but wide awake, little beige Casio clock radio tuned to WBLK. A keyboard riff and a bass guitar lick, and another rhythm guitar loop that echoed "Yearning for Your Love." Glenn Jones, that powerhouse of an R&B tenor, mewling, moaning, ready to let loose. Seconds later he's musing about seeing a certain look in somebody else's girlfriend's eyes.

Could it be the one you love just ain't been treating you right?

A rhetorical question for most folks, but loaded when it came from Glenn Jones in "Call Me." From there, a series of long-shot promises Jones knew he may never have to deliver. To fulfill her in ways her current man can't. To answer the phone *every time* she calls. To mend her heart the second this temporary boyfriend disappears.

"Put your *haaaaand* in my *haaaand*," he pleads during the outro ad-lib. "I've got what you *neeeeee-eeed*!"

When I'd arrive in Chicago later that summer, I'd hear a pre-pubescent Jason Weaver every time I turned on WGCI, serenading somebody he had never even met. He'd just seen her around the way, strolling local streets, running errands. Today we'd call it stalking, and call the cops or his parents, or at least his basketball coach. But in the summer of 1995, we just called it "Love Ambition" and treated it as normal.

"Don't even know if you have a man," he sang in the voice of someone young enough to collect allowance. "Don't even care, cuz I know one thing's for sure: you would love the way I do you, baby . . ."

Do, in this context, wasn't a synonym for treat or interact with. Weaver meant it the same way Prince did in "Do Me Baby," except that Prince was a grown man and Weaver barely sounded old enough to ride the bus alone.

A year later, Mint Condition dropped "What Kind of Man Would I Be," wherein Stokley Williams stood strong against a pretty young thing trying to pry him from his girlfriend. Because he was human, he was tempted. The video showed the band performing at a jazz lounge, with our girl standing next to the stage, front and centre. She wore a black dress with a low-cut neckline, and angled herself so that every time long-suffering Stokley took his eyes off the mic he could see straight down her cleavage. But she couldn't compel him to set his relationship aflame. Stokley had yearnings, but he also had principles and empathy and common sense.

Their very next single? "You Don't Have to Hurt No More," wherein Stokley sensed a female friend was unhappy in her relationship. Because he was sensitive and generous, he offered her an upgrade.

"I don't like the way he treats you," he said at the top of the song. "That's not the way that *I* would do you."

Here, *do* meant treat. Long term, Stokley almost certainly intended to "do" this woman in the Prince and Jason Weaver sense. But for now, if this lacklustre boyfriend was dragging her down, Stokley simply offered respect, and a soft spot to land if she ever made the jump.

Together, those songs provided a rulebook to messing around outside relationships. If you were thinking of easing between me and my woman because you're bored with your man, think of something else. That's cheating, and What Kind of Man Would I Be if I surrendered to you?

But if I sniffed that you were grumpy because your man took you for granted, it was my duty to lure you away. Ethically, it was justified. Like defying an immoral law. I'm Harriet Tubman, liberating women from unhappy situations. I'm actually racking up bad karma if I let you stay with that chump. You Don't Have to Hurt No More. Just do like Glenn Jones says, and Call Me.

Hope and I broke up early in track season and my life hardly changed, until my profile skyrocketed after *The Mississauga News* published that action photo of me. The attention had me feeling as confident as the picture made me look. Maybe I didn't think I could get any girl I wanted, but I thought I could snag the one I wanted most. By mid-season I felt like Glenn Jones, single and ready to unshackle Kelly from whoever that guy was.

But I didn't even need to intervene. When June arrived, her little situationship fizzled, and the path cleared.

By now, we all know that motivational bromide: "A Goal Is a Dream with a Deadline." I'm sure some NFL player has it tattooed across his bicep. My last year of high school, I couldn't even count the times I dreamt of winding up on the edge of Kelly Charles's bed, with nothing between us but a sliver of space and the rest of the day. The deadline settled itself when Northwestern's football staff told me to report to training camp on August 3. That meant leaving Mississauga by August 1, which meant whatever was going down between Kelly and I had to happen before then.

And Kelly? She was a week from turning eighteen. Maybe she had a deadline, too.

"What time does your brother get home?" I asked.

"Why? You have someplace to be?"

"Yeah," I said. "The Y. I already skipped my morning workout. Can't miss tonight, too."

"Really, Morgan?"

"Yeah. I'm tryna make the NFL."

"You can take *one* day off."

"No, I can't," I said. "For real, what time does your brother come home?"

"We have time."

Jodeci sang:

Baby, I'm beggin'! Baby, I'm beggin', beggin', baby!

We talked next year. My plans to go from a walk-on to an all-star on Northwestern's football team, and to learn how to write for real in journalism school. Her plans to keep working at the hair salon and, eventually, maybe, go to college.

Toni Braxton sang:

How . . . men-nee ways . . . I love youuuuuuu . . .

We talked the longer-term future. She wanted to build a business braiding hair. I planned to play in the NFL, and fantasized about buying a champagne-coloured Benz, like my aunt Peggy's but bigger, with glittering rims.

Wasn't much to discuss after that. We had spent the last ten months talking about everything: school, death, grieving, music, sex, sex, and sex. I kept one ear on the slow jam tape, trying to string the conversation along until I heard the right song.

I false-started at Blackstreet.

True love is so haaaaard to fiiiind.
And it's right between your liiiiips and miiiiine . . .

It almost fit, but I wasn't Dave Hollister begging for a single kiss. Kelly and I both expected more than that.

Another couple of songs rolled past. I stood and stepped toward Kelly's dresser, trying to borrow an extra minute until I could hear the next track. Kelly followed. She didn't seem as patient, but she played along.

"Wait, am I taller than you?" she asked, sidling up next to me as we both faced the mirror above her dresser.

"No, Kells."

"I might be," she said, easing onto her tiptoes.

"No."

"How are you gonna play in the NFL if you're not even taller than me?"

"First of all," I said. "I'll make the NFL because I'm fast. And second, I'm taller than you."

"Let's see."

We each did a half turn to face each other. I'd say we went nose to nose, except I stood half a forehead taller. We both knew that already. We each just needed a reason.

I recognized the next keyboard riff instantly, a sprinkle of notes on a synthesizer set to harpsichord. My cue.

I placed my left hand on her right hip as Kenny Greene, the lead singer from Intro, told the girl to sit back and enjoy the ride. "One of a Kind Love." Deep in the slow jam section of Intro's debut album. Best track on the whole CD, if you asked me.

That's how you do it, when you get right down to it

She was still talking as I pulled her into me. I kissed her mid-sentence, with my eyes open because I wanted to witness this moment as I lived it. I unhooked the straps and watched her overalls fall to the floor and puddle at her feet. Her shiny navy-blue bra matched her underpants. She pulled my Tommy Hilfiger golf shirt over my head and dropped it next to her clothes. Then went my undershirt.

I'm so in love, I'm at the point of no return

I slid my hands below her waist. She cupped the back of my head with one hand, and with the fingers of the other she traced my spine as we edged backward toward her bed. I lifted her and spilled her on to her mattress.

I realized I had never engaged in foreplay before today. Until then, on my luckiest days, horizontal and half-clothed was the main event. Today it was just a prelude. The tape deck clicked into auto reverse, Silk leading off side B. No more track-by-track cataloguing. Why obsess over the perfect song now? As long as the next track wasn't by Garth Brooks, we could keep going. It would take us where we needed to go.

So I zoned in on the moment.

Her body, taut and smooth. The sweeping curve of her thigh in the soft sunlight.

Her scent, faint and floral. The perfume she applied because she knew we'd wind up right here.

Her lips on my earlobe. My mouth. My neck.

She snaked her hands below my waist. If the male equivalent of sexy lingerie exists, I certainly didn't own it at eighteen. So when Kelly slid her fingers under my shorts, she ended up with two hands full of my newest and brightest Hanes tighty-whities. She circled her hands to the front of my waist and tugged at the elastic.

I tried to act calm, the way white football coaches would tell you to after you scored a touchdown. Don't celebrate. Act Like You've Been There Before. So I pretended to know my way around a situation I had never even sniffed.

My database of slow jams provided no guidance. Anytime anybody sang about somebody's first time having sex, the girl was the virgin. Betty Wright, Janet Jackson, Hi-Five—the dude is always the mentor, coaching the girl through a life milestone. He had already picked up experience somewhere, but nobody ever sang about where he started.

I kissed her cheek. Brought my lips to her ear and whispered.

"Do you have a condom?"

"No," she said. "You didn't bring one?"

"Nuh-uh," I said low, still kissing that spot where jawbone meets earlobe. "I thought you had some."

"What happened to the one I gave you?"

"I dunno," I said, still with my lips on her neck. "That was October. You didn't get more?"

"No."

I didn't have ten more months to wait for another opportunity like this one. Kelly and I might not have this much time alone together for the rest of our lives. I kept kissing her, as if the problem would solve itself.

Kelly wasn't just tugging on my waistband now. She wanted all my clothes off. Shorts, underwear, everything. One time. I stalled.

"Kells," I said. "We don't have a condom."

"I don't care," she said. "We don't have to finish."

That proposition. So tempting and fraught.

I knew the range of bad outcomes, but I could eliminate possibilities. We couldn't spread an STD because neither of us had a chance to acquire one. Two raw novices. She was as likely to give me the clap as I was to lose one million dollars on the stock market that week.

As for the other one . . .

The hell would I do with a baby? I had no money and no car. Not even a summer job; just a hazy plan to make the pros, which depended on me playing college football in Chicago—a move I could hardly justify if I had a kid in Mississauga who needed to eat.

That thought flashed through my mind in half a second, and pride says to tell you I weighed it all calmly, then made a principled decision to end the episode. Yes, I had spent nearly a year working toward sex with Kelly, but I also had a bigger plan for my life. I would have other chances to lose my virginity, eventually, somehow, I hoped. But I couldn't redo the admissions process, or balance school and football and a job that could keep a baby diapered and fed. So I'd love to tell you that, in that heated moment, level-headed Morgan stayed cool and chose his long-term goals.

Instead, I'll tell you the truth. I pondered those possibilities and froze. Panic made the decision for me. We know what happens when adrenaline kicks in and blood vessels constrict. Flag at half-mast. Slow leak in my inner tube. Choose your metaphor. Principle or not, it wasn't going to happen.

Kelly couldn't sense my terror. She lay there looking hopeful, her right hand cupping my elbow, and her left still clenching my waistband. She arched her spine and pulled me close. I leaned forward and kissed her collarbone, then her neck, then her earlobe.

"Kells," I said, choking back the fear trying to creep into my voice. "Let's just keep doing what we're doing."

This Is What Happens after You Die

After the funeral, after the drive out to the cemetery on the far South Side to grieve over Granny Mary's closed casket before the gravediggers lowered it into the frozen ground, after I hugged all the cousins and promised I'd stay in touch, I dashed back to her house before folks could start grabbing stuff.

I had seen several drafts of Granny Mary's will, so I knew the big things already had destinations. Ivory would get the car. St. James AME down the street would buy her house, the one she owned next door, and the strip of land in between, and we heirs would divide the proceeds evenly. Her cash would go into an escrow account to keep the bills and taxes paid while the sale went through. Whatever money remained would go to her grandkids, and my cousins from Grand Rapids, and my dad's half-sister, Julia, and Granny Mary's upstairs tenant, Darlene, and a few other folks I didn't know but who managed to land on the list of beneficiaries.

But anything inside her house would belong to whoever claimed it first.

Aside from her infancy in Pittsburgh, and the time she moved to an apartment when she and my grandfather separated for a few months,

Granny Mary spent her whole life at 9224 South Lafayette. At least eighty of her eighty-four years. Eight decades' worth of living. Eighty years of junk and trinkets and bowling trophies, but also heirlooms and tokens and family treasures, now orphaned.

So I snatched my dad's ashes.

I rose to my tiptoes and swiped the urn from atop a bookcase, then trotted outside to stuff it in the trunk of my rented Chrysler Sebring. Then I hurried back inside to see what else I could grab.

Mostly, I wanted photos.

I scooped more than one framed portrait of my dad, and I flipped through Granny Mary's bigger albums and lifted out the pictures I liked. I found a department store shopping bag made of sturdy paper and filled it with still more pictures. I felt a little like the Grinch in the Who family's living room, sweeping armfuls of their gifts into his burlap sack. But if somebody asked what I was doing, I wouldn't need to lie, or second-guess myself later. I had a claim to everything in that house, including the land beneath it. But I didn't have the time or desire to fight over money. I only wanted photos.

A snapshot of my dad and his best friend, Jimmy McGee, out in front of this same house, with Lafayette Avenue behind them and beyond that the Dan Ryan.

The studio portrait of Granny Mary in Pittsburgh.

The three-by-five of Granny Mary's mother, Lillie Donald, in a different portrait studio, stern-faced with her hands folded in her lap.

All of those pictures belonged to my sisters and me now.

But I didn't take everything.

I left the framed portrait of Uncle Ernest for my cousins from Grand Rapids.

Granny Mary also kept a painted portrait of her own grandmother, Lillie Mae "Handful" Gaddis, fair-skinned and unsmiling, staring out from atop the out-of-tune upright piano in her living room. I wanted that, too. Handful was from Sumter Carolina, while other Gaddises spread across the country. But I gave the painting to one of Handful's other grandkids, Granny Mary's first cousin from Syracuse, who explained the nickname: Lillie Mae was so small at birth that she fit into the palm of her daddy's hand.

By then, a few more friends and relatives had filtered into Granny Mary's living room. Ivory sank deep into a seat on the plastic-covered couch, appearing as overwhelmed as you'd expect an eighty-one-year-old to look when saddled with executing a will that now included a lifetime of possessions and more than a dozen people in line to inherit them. Ivory couldn't account for all those pictures, all that furniture, all those baubles, and he knew Granny Mary couldn't dispute anything he did now, so he turned the hours after her funeral into a free estate sale. Welcomed in folks who hadn't even attended the service and allowed them to help themselves. In case I hadn't figured it out, he summoned me to his spot on the couch.

"Morgan, if you see anything you like, mize well g'on head at take it," he said.

In this branch of this family, this is what happens after you die.

People don't wait for a will. They sift through your stuff and take what they like. Granny Mary showed us when my dad passed.

I thanked Ivory, then went looking for more photo albums. I had already seen too many fights over dead people's possessions. I didn't want money or anything I could sell for cash. These pictures, this history. That was enough.

Eight years earlier, I stepped off the train at the end of the Red Line and jogged up the stairs, through the turnstile and out the doors opening onto 95th Street. First time ever seeing the inside of this station, or even riding the train this far south. Strange, because my family only vacationed in one of two places: Chicago or Grand Rapids. We hit at least one of them every summer. Some years we visited both. By the time I finished high school, I had spent enough time in Chicago to know the Red Line ends at 95th Street—or, if you're from my dad's neighbourhood, begins there.

But when my sisters and I were teenagers, our parents never let us roam Chicago the way we did Mississauga. We stayed inside until an adult could shuttle us to Six Flags or River Oaks shopping mall, or another relative's place. We didn't travel without chaperones, and we never, ever took public transit. It's not that my parents thought my sisters and I would seek out trouble, but in the neighbourhoods we stayed in on the South Side of Chicago, they couldn't trust trouble not to find us.

By the time I enrolled at Northwestern, my folks couldn't micro-manage my travel anymore, and it didn't make sense to try to keep me off the El—so-named because the train tracks are elevated—or the city bus. I couldn't walk downtown from Evanston, and I couldn't call Aunt Peggy to pick me up every time I needed to visit the city. So before I even took my first college class, I had learned how to take CTA to Aunt Peggy's place.

If I was leaving football practice, I'd board the Purple Line at Central Street, then ride south to Howard, where Evanston ended and Chicago began, and where, if the Purple Line express wasn't running, I'd transfer to the Red Line. I'd hop off that train downtown, at State and Lake, then board the number 6 bus and head even farther south. The last white passengers always exited the bus by 57th Street, and I would keep riding to 67th and Jeffrey. Then I'd jump off and walk ten minutes east to Aunt Peggy's condo.

Granny Mary's place was farther south but easier to reach, if I ever wanted to visit. I could just stay on the Red Line and ride it to the end, then walk three blocks north. Her phone number hadn't changed since the Great Depression. If she wasn't out bowling or church ladying, she'd have answered the phone or welcomed me at her front door.

But I didn't visit or call. I pictured her wishing she could brag about me to the other grannies but shutting up because she couldn't explain why her only son's only son never spent time with her, even though he lived in the next city. Freezing her out couldn't bring back everything she stole from my dad's apartment, but I could feel satisfied leaving

Granny Mary hanging. Living so close and keeping so much distance between us, that was my revenge.

So, I didn't warn her before I parachuted back into her life. After I finished shopping downtown, I headed south before I could talk myself out of it.

I walked north on Lafayette, past St. James AME, where two generations of Joneses and Gibbses and Campbells worshipped, and where my sisters and I were baptized. And I passed the footbridge that spanned the Dan Ryan and let out at Gillespie Elementary, where my dad attended grade school.

One day in the mid-1980s, when I was about nine, Granny Mary let me play with some kids from the neighbourhood. She'd even lent me her Huffy ten-speed, on the condition that I only ride in front of the house or in the alley behind it and not to cross the footbridge. Of course, the neighbourhood kids dared me to ride to the schoolyard, and of course, I accepted and rode out onto the bridge. I stopped halfway, directly above the El tracks dividing northbound from southbound traffic on the Dan Ryan. Far enough to tell the neighbourhood kids I had ridden to the school, but if Granny Mary caught me, I could claim I had not, in fact, crossed the bridge.

So of course, she saw me, out above the southbound Dan Ryan. And of course, I never got to make my clever argument about not actually crossing the bridge. Granny snatched me off the bike, dragged me inside, and spanked me, but only with her hand and not a belt or a switch or some other weapon that could have left a bruise. Maybe this Granny Mary was softer than the Mary Campbell who raised my dad. Maybe her reflex for corporal punishment had dulled. She hadn't lived with a misbehaving kid since the 1950s, so she hadn't needed her arsenal for decades. Or maybe she recognized she couldn't beat another mother's child the way she had flogged her own.

I climbed the steps to her front door, rang the bell, and waited—longer than I would for most folks, because I knew this house and the woman who owned it. If she still spent most of her idle time on the back porch, the walk to the front door was at least sixty feet, and must have felt even longer on Granny Mary's arthritic knees. I figured she had slowed even more in the six and a half years since I had seen her.

The heavy wooden door eased open and Granny Mary peeked out at me through the crack. She looked like she did the week of my dad's funeral, but with less weight and more grey hair—subtle changes I might have missed if we'd stayed in touch, but glaring after so many years apart.

She looked like she was also trying to process what she saw. I had gained fifteen pounds, most of it as a freshman on the football team at Northwestern. And I had grown a goatee, for work. The previous autumn, when I started an internship with the *Toronto Star*, I would head out on assignment and tell people I was a reporter, and they would ask which high school's paper I wrote for. I figured facial hair would make me appear more grown up. But I still looked exactly like her son; she just needed a second to recognize it.

Granny Mary opened the screen door, and I stepped across the threshold. She turned away and walked into the living room. I could see her shoulders shudder as she sobbed. She turned back around and smothered me in a hug.

"My grandson," she said. "My baby."

She hugged me tighter.

"My baby," she said. "I've been praying for this. I've asked God so many times to bring you all back to me. Why did you come back?"

I didn't know. It was less a decision than a reflex. A compulsion. I couldn't explain any of that then, and barely can now, so I said what I could.

"It was time," I said.

She led me through the living room. I looked around as I walked, logging what had changed and what hadn't. New couch, same place— still against the long wall on the south side of the house, still covered in clear plastic. The upright piano still stood near the window across the room. The white keys still had gaps between them, like teeth needing

braces. I touched some. Still a little out of tune. Portraits of my dad
and his half-brother hadn't moved from their stand. I still didn't see any
pictures of their father. Her older brother, Sam, had died, but his
widow, my aunt Junella, still lived in the house next door.

But the house didn't smell like Lestoil and day-old cooking anymore. Now it smelled like sweet, damp tobacco smoke.

"You smoke pipes now, Granny Mary?"

"Naw, that's Ivory. Lemme introduce you."

She didn't have to explain. The name alone told me he was old;
you barely even saw Ivorys my parents' age anymore. And if he was
comfortable enough in Granny Mary's house to fill it with the scent
of his pipe smoke, he had to be her man.

"Hey Paw-Paw!" Granny Mary called toward the back porch. "Meet
my grandson. This is Pete's baby."

If someone had told me Granny Mary had a boyfriend named
Ivory, then asked me to envision and sketch him, I'd have drawn exactly
the man I saw. Flawless chestnut-coloured skin and a round balding
head; a cottony white beard framing his face; pipe placed between his
teeth to free up his right hand so he could shake mine.

He rose halfway to greet me, then sunk back into the blood-red
recliner that once sat in my dad's living room, and went back to
watching Maury Povich on my dad's TV, the sound amplified by dad's
three-foot-tall speakers. I don't know if Ivory knew how Granny Mary
had acquired all that stuff, but she knew that I knew.

We went back to her kitchen, which looked like it always did. Dirty
dishes in the sink, clean ones air-drying beside it. Small window over the
sink pried open to let in fresh air and sunlight. Tiny white gas stove where
Cousin Khadijah used to make me fried green tomatoes. A homemade
pound cake on the counter. She cut each of us a slice and we sat at the
small white table in the middle of the room. We cleared spaces for our
plates among the piled-up flyers and days-old copies of the *Sun-Times*.

She told me about her newest big red car—a Chevy Monte Carlo
this time.

I told her about my internship at the *Star*, and my hope that I could work my way to a major daily like the *New York Times* or *Chicago Tribune*.

She filled me in on the Grand Rapids family. Cousin Khadijah was back and forth between there and Chicago, in and out of jobs. But her daughter was a straight-A student about to have her choice of colleges.

I updated her on my sisters. Courtney was back home after a year in Seattle, in charge of desserts at a fancy steakhouse on Yonge Street, uptown. Dana was divorced but still singing, looking to crack the opera industry's glass ceiling.

What we didn't discuss was how my dad's death had wounded all of us. We didn't bring up what she had done after, even as she furnished her back porch with stuff from his apartment. And we didn't talk about why she did it, even though that heist was the only reason that, seven years later, we each needed all these updates.

I didn't ask and she didn't volunteer. I didn't know if I would even want a relationship with her after that day. I just knew I hadn't come there to fight.

———

Six-year-old Morgan loved Garbage Day. *Loved* it. So when Granny Mary motioned to me, I sprinted from her backyard to the end of her block and joined her in the alley, on the concrete beneath the passenger side door of the garbage truck. The big engine grumbled as it idled; Granny Mary shouted back and forth with the two-man crew, then asked if I wanted to ride with them for a minute. By the time she finished the question, I was already climbing into the cockpit and strapping myself into the passenger seat.

In Mississauga, the garbage trucks never actually entered our town-house complex, so they would pull up to the curb on Falconer Drive, where everybody on our street tossed their trash onto a huge pile. If we weren't in school or on punishment, the boys on our street would run to the trash heap when we heard the truck coming. Weekly garbage collection was our favourite spectator sport.

Those trucks were the most fascinating and powerful beasts I had ever seen. I couldn't stop watching that huge mechanical mandible, marvelling at how it pulverized everything the garbage man pitched inside it. And even though I hated seeing the garbage truck leave, I loved hearing the big diesel engine roar and burp out the black smoke that hung in the air above our street even as the truck disappeared around the curve, where Falconer Drive bent east toward Creditview Road.

And the men seemed so strong and fast and efficient. I couldn't even lug one trash bag to the pile, and here they were heaving two at a time into the belly of the big truck. Six-year-old Morgan didn't have a favourite athlete yet. My heroes picked up the trash every Wednesday.

Behind Granny Mary's house, the driver smiled at me as the big truck shuddered to life, and we lurched through the alley, a few yards at a time, stopping to let the man's partner hop off and empty somebody's trash cans into the back of the truck. I noticed the size of the gas and brake pedals, twice as big as the ones in my dad's Oldsmobile. The driver wore a toque and navy-blue coveralls and thick grey socks.

"Why don't you wear shoes?" I asked.

"I'm in this truck a loooong time," he said. "I gotta stay comfortable."

"Don't your feet get sore?"

"Naw. They get cold in the winter, but then I wear boots."

Granny Mary met us at the end of the block. She took my hand to help me descend the steps, and we held hands on the walk back to her yard. I thought of that ride in the garbage truck five years later, when my uncle Jeff took me to a White Sox–Blue Jays game at Comiskey Park. Afterward, we waited by the Jays' team bus, and I got George Bell and Lloyd Moseby and Kelly Gruber to sign a baseball that wound up in my hands after Gruber had fouled it into the stands. Riding in the garbage truck wasn't as exciting as meeting the Blue Jays—you could be the best sanitation tandem in the city, but you'd still never measure up to George Freakin' Bell, and that's not your fault—but it gave me a similar thrill, an up-close look at people and a process that had intrigued me. A moment with some grown-ups I admired. Some time to ask questions, to get them answered, and feel like I mattered.

I hadn't told Granny Mary about my obsession with garbage trucks and the strong men operating them, but she figured it out and flagged down the driver and talked him into letting me ride along. Just because she could, and because she thought it would make me smile.

My mind doesn't land easily on tender moments like those, but sometimes Granny Mary tried. When my dad would visit Chicago, she would send him back with care packages for Courtney and me, usually full of Chicago Bulls gear she bought from a friend at church who trafficked in non-licensed sports merchandise. The stuff was cheap, so Granny Mary bought it in bulk. And it was *cheap*. The portrait of Michael Jordan on the sweatshirt she gave me looked more like Terry Porter. And if the clothes didn't unravel the first day you wore them, they would the first time through the laundry. But at least Granny Mary was thinking of us, right?

When Granny Mary robbed my dad's apartment, though, she may as well have lobbed a hand grenade at my sisters and me. The memory spread like smoke in my mind, choking out nearly everything pleasant I might have even tried to recall about her.

Reconnecting with her seven years later was less a decision I made than a place I arrived. My mom told me to freeze Granny Mary out forever. Later, after the reunion but before Granny Mary died, whenever she would pull another stunt that left a loved one confused or crying or furious, my mom would remind me I should have left her alone till she died, then reappeared to contest her will. Those two houses were worth money, and my sisters and I deserved it.

But Granny Mary was also the oldest living Campbell, and so she knew things nobody else did—like my grandfather's hometown. Everybody else in the family came north from some specific location. Gram came from Ruston, Louisiana, and Gramps from Marshall, Texas.

My mom's mother was born in Bunn, Arkansas, and Granny Mary's family came from Sumter, South Carolina. My dad's birth certificate says that his dad was twenty-two years old, and from "Mississippi," same answer my dad would give when I asked about his father. Only Granny Mary could tell me her husband grew up in Tyronza, Arkansas, thirty-five miles northwest of Memphis, and close enough to the Mississippi River that his family could straddle state lines.

I needed those details. I might not always have liked Granny Mary, or my mom's father, but we were family, and I couldn't separate my fate or my history from theirs. I didn't just come from their genes but from their decisions, and from events they couldn't control but still shaped their lives. I needed to try to understand their stories if I hoped to know my own.

I also thought, and I still do, about people I've deceived or double-crossed or disappointed. They're usually people I've loved and respected and wanted to make proud. I know they remember what I did to hurt them, but I hope they don't forget what I tried to add to their lives. When they look at me, I don't want them to see the worst thing I ever did. I might deserve it, but I don't want it. None of us would.

So, when Granny Mary asked why I showed up on her doorstep and I could only tell her, "It was time," I didn't quite know what I meant. It wasn't time to forgive, because I knew she would never apologize. You can't bestow forgiveness on somebody who doesn't want or think they need it. That was Granny Mary. Always right, even when she knew she was wrong, and I wasn't about to fight that fight again.

And it wasn't time for the two sides of the family to reunite, because unity had never really existed.

But it was time.

To fill in some gaps.

To remind her, by my presence, of what she owed my sisters and me.

To try to view her through a new prism.

—

What I always knew about Granny Mary:

She was shrewd. Otherwise, she couldn't have come to own two houses and the strip of land between them in a society that placed so many obstacles between Black folks and home ownership. I still don't know what she did for a living besides homemaking and odd jobs, but she held the deed to those two houses—two more homes than my mom's folks ever owned.

What I learned about Granny Mary before she died:

She wasn't *from* Trenton, New Jersey. Just born there. Her father and big brother and very pregnant mother boarded a train in June of 1924, joining other Black South Carolinians in what history would later call the Great Migration, headed for Pennsylvania. Except Granny Mary couldn't wait. Grandma Lillie went into labour on the train. She and her husband hopped off in Trenton so Lillie could give birth. When mom and baby were strong enough to travel, they finished the trip to Pittsburgh.

Granny Mary spent her early childhood there, but then came the divorce and the move to Chicago. Or did the move precede the divorce? Some details, I have to accept never knowing. But we know her family went from Pittsburgh to South Lafayette Avenue, the house she would eventually own outright, and the place she would eventually raise my father.

What you can't understand about Granny Mary unless you survive it yourself:

The terror of seeing your drunken husband level his pistol at you, then diving to safety as he squeezes the trigger. The frightful knowledge that the bullet lodged in the china hutch was meant for your head. The sickening recognition that you owe your life to his bad aim.

The betrayal of learning that same husband had impregnated his mistress. The indignity of shaping the household budget to support your husband's other baby. The pride-swallowing that must have come when your husband's love child moved back to Chicago from

Yazoo City, Mississippi, and you had to introduce friends to your new "stepdaughter."

Or the helpless feeling of turning seventy, then learning you'll out-live your only child.

My mom kept telling me Granny Mary was simply a bad person—evil and selfish and ugly on the inside—and that I shouldn't waste effort fixing a relationship that didn't deserve to exist. But what if Granny Mary wasn't a pure villain? What if she and I had something worth saving? What if she wasn't just a product of her choices, but of all that trauma?

I stayed in touch.

———

At the end of the summer before I started seventh grade, my dad drove to Chicago in his off-white Hyundai Stellar. A week or so later, he rolled up to our house in a big red Cadillac with a white pleather roof and interior. Dad told us his car had blown up in Chicago. His words: "It blew up." Later, I learned the truth—someone had stolen it. In 1988, Hyundais were still rare cars in the U.S. That car thief probably thought rare meant expensive. Later, he learned the truth, too.

Granny Mary lent Dad her precious red Cadillac and he drove it all autumn. When he bought his Suzuki Swift, an undersized, overpowered pocket rocket of a car, Granny Mary bankrolled the down payment.

Dad wasn't broke. He finally had disposable income after three years of divorce-poverty, and had just moved to a new place. Still in somebody's basement, but now he had a separate entrance and his own parking spot—this place even had a kitchen and a bedroom. When he moved, he also bought a leather couch with a fold-out bed so my sisters and I—but usually I—could sleep over.

He just hadn't budgeted for a car theft.

Dad never told me Granny Mary had helped him buy that black Suzuki Swift. The summer after tenth grade, when Dad and I stayed at her place for two weeks in July, she couldn't stop reminding him of it.

"Glad to see you brought my car back . . ."

Or, "I like looking at both my cars in the driveway . . ."

Or, "If it worked like that, I'd have me a little black car, too."

A few days before my dad died, while my mom dealt with the doctors, Granny Mary parked in a chair at the foot of my dad's hospital bed and started rubbing his feet. By then, he was deep into painkillers, coherent when awake but unconscious most of the day. The whites of his eyes had yellowed already, and his legs swelled so much his kneecaps disappeared, like shallow islands in rising water.

Granny Mary rubbed the sole of Dad's right foot, and then the instep. Then she worked the left foot, bottom side to top. She smeared lotion on her palms, then put both hands on his right shin and worked with long strokes, ankle to knee and back down. Left shin, same motion. Then she moved on to his calves.

"I figured I'd lay on some healing hands," she said.

Dad couldn't answer.

"I had all of St. James praying for you, Pete. Lillydale, too."

No answer.

Granny Mary moved Dad's bed sheet to expose his right thigh. She rubbed more balm into her palms. She laid her hands on his leg and worked with long strokes, knee to hip and back down.

When Granny Mary learned her son was dying, she caught a flight to Toronto on short notice to comfort him. She had also spent the previous weeks plotting to rob his apartment, and in a few days she would follow through.

The Cadillac and the down payment and the constant reminders that my dad owed her something. The vigil, the healing hands, the heist. You can view Granny Mary through any of these acts, like lenses in an eye exam. To see her most clearly, you need to choose the right one.

—

Seven years after Granny Mary and I reconnected, here she came, tottering into the lobby of the Cage Funeral Home just before Aunt Edith's service, leaning hard on the cane clutched in her right fist. Ivory guided her with a hand in the crook of her elbow. These days, he was her pillar. Even before the operation the previous spring, meant to carve the cancer out of Granny Mary's pancreas, Ivory did all of the driving. He still had the strength to work the pedals and the reflexes to jerk the steering wheel. And in the five months since the surgeon sliced Granny Mary open, saw the cancer had spread, then sewed her back up because the disease had already won, Ivory did most of the cooking, too.

By now, in October 2008, Ivory walked and talked slower than he did when I first met him. So maybe he was less a pillar than a rickety wooden beam. But he still kept Granny Mary standing day-to-day, and supported her on this slow walk across the funeral home foyer.

I intercepted them before they could reach the Joneses. If she wanted one last stare-down with Claude Jones, I wasn't going to let her have it.

I kissed Granny Mary's cheek and shook Ivory's free hand. If Granny Mary didn't have cancer, my mom might have knocked her out. But if Granny Mary didn't have Ivory or that cane, she might have collapsed on her own from age and illness and bad posture. I steered Ivory and Granny Mary away from the Joneses and into a pair of aisle seats near the back of the chapel. My mom ignored them.

Granny Mary rarely travelled this far east within city limits. South Shore wasn't for Campbells, even when her son lived there as a young married man. It was Jones territory in 1961, when my grandpa moved his wife and kids there. And, to her, it was still Jones territory in 2008, when my aunt Peggy and sister Dana lived there, the neighbourhood almost all Black, but under the constant yet never fully consummated threat of gentrification.

But Granny Mary wasn't going to miss Aunt Edith's homegoing. However she felt about Claude Jones and his kids and *their* kids, she lost a peer when Aunt Edith died.

As kids, Aunt Edith and my grandpa and Granny Mary all attended St. James and graduated from Fenger when just a few Black kids went to school there.

And they both knew life on the wrong side of Claude Jones's ego and temper.

Granny Mary watched my parents get married in the living room of the Joneses' big apartment on Paxton, even though by then the beef between her and my grandfather was older than the bride and groom. Aunt Edith missed the wedding because Grandpa and her husband were feuding.

This one wasn't Claude Jones's fault. Aunt Edith's husband, Hugh, owned the house on Langley. He needed an upstairs tenant, but didn't want to splurge to get the apartment into shape. Enter Claude and the rest of the Joneses, who spent money and time and sweat renovating the upstairs apartment and lived there for a while. Then Hugh figured out he could fatten his profit margin if he weren't renting to his in-laws, He evicted the Joneses, which prompted their move to the big apartment on Paxton, and jacked up the rent for his next unwitting tenants.

Claude wanted Aunt Edith, stuck between her husband and her brother, to pick sides in this fight. More precisely, he wanted her to pick his side. When she didn't defend Claude with enough gusto, Claude banned her from his new home, and forbade his kids from talking to Aunt Edith. When he learned Jeanie and Aunt Edith still sent each other letters, he nearly cancelled the wedding. He relented, eventually, and told Aunt Edith she could attend—the reception, but not the ceremony. But Aunt Edith had her pride, and she wasn't crawling into her brother's apartment through the doggie door. Not even for her favourite niece's wedding . . . reception.

As seniors, Granny Mary and Aunt Edith lived a mile apart —Granny Mary on Lafayette overlooking the expressway, and Aunt Edith over on

Langley, across 95th Street from Chicago State University. When either of them needed yard work done, they each called on Percy or Hawk or another of the functional winos who gathered like day labourers in the parking lot of Foremost Liquors at 93rd and Cottage Grove.

So, she showed up at the funeral, her spine bent like a bracket, head bald beneath a silver wig. She came to grieve, but also to be seen and to compete. She and my grandpa both needed attention like normal people need air. She wasn't going to let him consume all of it just because he was the closest living relative to the deceased.

And she wanted to remind Claude that she had outlived his big sister, even if only by a few months. Granny Mary would die the following January. But today, if Aunt Edith's death made Claude Jones feel bad, Granny Mary hoped this fly-by would make him feel worse, because in this branch of this family, that's what happens after somebody dies.

Someone from the other side shows up to run a victory lap.

Granny Mary wasn't funny, but she used to tell this one joke. Before the cancer diagnosis, when she and Ivory would travel someplace, or visit the casino, or think about buying a new car, she'd justify it with this one-liner: "I'm spending you all's inheritance."

Hilarious.

It was also a warning because Granny Mary thought my sisters and I thought like she did, and figured we spent time plotting how to profit from her eventual death. I never counted Granny Mary's money or expected her to will it to me. She lied a lot, but when she said she didn't intend to leave any cash to inherit, I took that as truth.

But I treasured her property. Owning it, for Granny Mary, was an achievement. By the time she died, I was grown enough to know how structural racism walled us off from home ownership, and bled wealth from generations of Black families. I knew big lenders avoided Black neighbourhoods and Black buyers, so landlords kept us renting, or glorified loan sharks sold us houses on contract, all to keep us on a debt treadmill and away from the American Dream.

Yet here was Granny Mary, steward of property that had belonged to our family from the Great Depression of the 1930s through the Great Recession of the 2000s. I didn't want cash. This was ancestral land I wanted to own, if only for a few weeks until we could close the sale to St. James. That church helped both sides of my family gain traction in Chicago as fresh-out-of-the-South newcomers in the 1920s. My parents were raised in the church. My sisters and I were baptized there. To sell that land to St. James was to keep it in the family.

If we had lost that property to a shady lender, or eminent domain, or gentrification, I'd have understood. I'd still have hated the process and the feeling of watching it unfold, but it would have made sense given the forces arrayed against Black home ownership. But the thought of fumbling away the family land because Granny Mary's will was too convoluted to execute was a different kind of galling, and triggered a different kind of shame. But dealing with Granny Mary, it all made a different kind of sense.

She bequeathed us her land and her liens, and I'll cop to not understanding what happened in the eleven—yes, *eleven*—years after she died. For the first year or so, I'd receive a new set of documents in the mail every few months, which I'd sign and send back to the lawyer. When a new envelope would arrive, I'd open it hoping for something tangible— a cheque or a deed or a receipt from the sale of the land—to let me know it was done. But the envelopes always contained more documents, and an evolving list of co-signers. Courtney's name disappeared, but Dana had to sign. When the city got involved, Dana, because she still lived in Chicago, would have to head downtown and sort it out. But when the final, final, *final* estate got settled and the cheques went out—a whole $626.15 for me—I didn't see Dana's name on the list of recipients. I can't explain why this will needed so many signatures because I'm not a probate attorney; I can't explain how Granny Mary tinkered with it from beyond the grave because I'm not a witch doctor.

But we couldn't sell the house until the estate settled the lien, and we couldn't settle the lien because the lender was now defunct. Maybe the lawyers could have straightened it out with a few drama-free months and the cash still left in escrow, but then Ivory died, and then his kids scooped up his belongings, including his key to Granny Mary's house, and the bank card they used to drain his chequing account, swollen with Granny Mary's cash, which somehow never went into escrow. Then they vanished.

Because we couldn't find Ivory's kids to sign papers and hand over documents, the house sat empty. The pipes burst. The grass in the yard grew taller than the chain link fence. Scavengers stripped the house of copper wiring, plus anything else they could sell for scrap. The city sent threatening letters about the yard and the unpaid property tax. Whatever the estate could have done to head these problems off had to wait on Ivory's kids joining the rest of the heirs in signing, but since they never answered letters, nothing got done until the city condemned the building and applied its own lien.

I stopped even driving through Granny Mary's neighbourhood. If I had to leave the city on the southbound Dan Ryan, I'd fix my eyes on the road in front of me, or the footbridge overhead, but I'd never glance up the embankment at the houses overlooking the expressway from Lafayette. I didn't want to see 9224 devolve from a family home to a vacant house to an eyesore on an otherwise tidy block. Like a front tooth missing from a smile. Two generations of my dad's family had grown up there, in what was now a safety hazard, an anchor dragging down property values.

Now it's just a patch of grass. Type "9224 S. Lafayette, Chicago" into a search bar and you see it, bright and green and mowed low. The maple trees, thick with dark green leaves, and the shadows the houses cast on Lafayette hint that Google took this picture late on a summer afternoon. On the property's northern border, next to the fence that separates Granny Mary's yard from Uncle Sam's driveway, somebody has parked a white van, and it feels like a violation. Like coming home from a semester at school and seeing your sleazy new stepdad with his smelly feet propped up on your mom's coffee table. Or visiting your grandmother after seven years estranged and seeing her new boyfriend nestled deep in your dad's red leather recliner.

I used to see houses like that when cruising through South Side neighbourhoods and wonder how it happened. Who once owned those places and lost out when they crumbled? How much family history vanished when the house collapsed? What kind of people would let a proud home go derelict?

Now I knew.

My kind of people.

POSTSCRIPT:

I'm So Proud

PART I

When the emcee told the audience at the Ontario Science Centre that Claude Jones carried twenty thousand songs in his head, he wasn't exaggerating; the number might have even been an undercount. By the time Claude headlined this show at CJRT's Sound of Jazz concert series, March 3, 1986, he had been playing six nights a week for more than forty-five years. He needed songs for different venues, audiences, moods, and eras. And he kept them in his head because you can't lug it all around in a briefcase. Sheet music was for orchestras and amateurs.

And now the amateurs were trying to colonize his turf. Claude learned jazz by playing and listening and playing some more. He didn't transcribe his favourite players' solos—he memorized them, learning by immersion the way kids absorb language. But now they taught jazz in school. These new players learned from textbooks, and to Claude, it showed. They played a lot of notes but couldn't play the song. That's why he didn't listen to young players in clubs or at the annual jazz festival downtown.

"White boys with music stands," he called them.

But tonight, the people in the Science Centre's auditorium knew what they were about to hear. If jazz was a language, Claude Jones was a native speaker. And the new folks tuning in on CJRT? They were about to get an education. Professor Claude Jones, set to lecture with two hands and eighty-eight keys.

Claude steadied himself on the piano bench. Snapped the lapels on his gleaming white tuxedo jacket. Tonight, he wasn't playing a few sets to keep the mood bright and the drinks flowing at a swanky downtown lounge. And he wasn't playing opposite a bigger name, keeping the crowd awake and engaged between their sets. He had done that before the move to Toronto, for stars like Oscar Peterson and Sarah Vaughan.

Those folks filling seats in the auditorium had spent their money to see him. People at home turned up the volume on CJRT and set their tape decks to record. Claude Jones *was* the show. Centre of attention, centre of a big stage. First time in years. Maybe the last ever.

Claude smiled and nodded as the introduction continued, but forty-five years in the music business had burnt him out. At sixty-two, Claude was too old to expect a big break and a little too young to retire. The famous people he knew had been famous for decades, and this concert alone wouldn't turn him into Oscar or even Cedar Walton. It couldn't win him a JUNO or a record contract.

But for tonight, he had the energy that comes with a sold-out auditorium, and a sense of how deeply the people who heard his music appreciated it. Toronto's jazz radio station aired the concert live, so Claude had an even broader audience and a chance to make an impression. Didn't mean he would retire wealthy or well-known, but it meant something.

"He might be underappreciated," the emcee said. "But he's not under-talented. He'll show you tonight."

Applause rained down. Claude breathed deep and bathed in the ovation for a moment. Then he nodded at his bassist, Dave Young, and drummer, Terry Clarke, and leaned toward the black grand piano's keyboard. Claude waited until the applause stopped and savoured the silence a moment.

Then the music started.

—

As a toddler watching *Sesame Street*, I swore I saw Grandpa on TV at least once a month. Black man, white hair, playing piano, laughing and ad-libbing through scenes with Big Bird and the crew. I'd point at the TV and shout.

"Grandpa!!!"

"That's not your grandpa," the closest adult would say. "That's Ray Charles."

Sometimes we actually would see Grandpa on TV, either in the Cancer Society ad or the General Motors commercial. The Mott's Clamato spot didn't use his voice, just featured him in a tuxedo with a white jacket, seated at a white piano, the centre of a raucous party full of white people drinking Bloody Marys. Claude Jones, a pianist turned actor, playing a pianist.

Tonight, he wasn't playing. He was *playing*. His hands, the piano, all extensions of his mind. Riffing and improvising, but still playing the song. Claude's music, Claude's way.

The set list included pieces Claude knew people would recognize, reconfigured and infused with some jazz soul. Ever heard a jazz trio play *The Flintstones* theme? Let Claude and the ensemble show you how it sounds.

This concert was Claude's version of those albums from Oscar Peterson's *Exclusively for My Friends* series, recorded in a private studio, bankrolled by a wealthy aficionado who wanted to see what Oscar could produce if he didn't have to please fickle jazz fans and record company bean counters. One installment was titled *The Way I Really Play*, which also fit tonight's assignment.

Claude Jones pleasing the crowd, but playing songs he liked. Requests had their place, but this wasn't it. His favourite from the session? "Wee Baby Blues," the old Joe Turner song. Mine? "Lil' Darlin'," that Count Basie standard.

Of course, the trio stumbled. It happens when you perform live.

Late in "Shuffle Off to Buffalo," a mix-up in the transition from bridge back to chorus. Claude zigged and Young zagged. Quick eye contact and they fell back into rhythm. The detour lasted maybe two bars; a newbie jazz fan might not even have caught it.

Years later, after I had grown up and earned a degree and learned how to listen to jazz, Claude would describe that blunder with such pride. He had spent the twenty previous years as a solo act, playing piano and singing, tapping out bass lines with his left foot on that contraption he rigged from the pedals on an old Lowrey Organo, his right foot working the piano's sustain pedals. When he left Chicago, he stopped the daytime session work. In Toronto, he almost always played alone.

As for the Claude Jones Trio—the name overstated it. Clarke and Young were two of the Toronto scene's best-known veterans, and had collaborated before, but this group had never played together. A few hours before showtime, they met and talked, went over the setlist, and mapped out the changes in each song. Claude plunked out a few chords on the piano, and they talked some more. At night, they hit the stage.

For Claude, this was true musicianship. Pros didn't need much practice, and they certainly didn't need notes on a page. Playing a song with two other people, if you had all mastered the craft, should come as naturally as conversation with a trusted friend. Three people thinking with one brain, listening as they played, sharing ideas and energy.

By 1986, Claude had grown bitter and a little bored with music as an occupation, but sometimes he still missed the art and vocation—and, since the move to Toronto, this kind of teamwork. That night at the Science Centre, fronting a brand-new trio, he scrubbed off twenty years of rust in minutes.

"We only messed up that *one* time," he said.

Implied in the silence that followed was how much worse it would have turned out if he and Young and Clarke weren't such professionals.

That iteration of the Claude Jones Trio never played together again.

Young and Clarke returned to their careers, and Claude went back to his. The audience applauded and went home. Claude got paid, and JAZZ FM aired somebody else's show the next night.

That concert survived in Claude and Margaret's apartment on a cassette, and then as an MP3 on the hard drive of Claude's iMac, and finally on the CDs Claude would burn for any family member who asked. He didn't have a discography, or even a single album he could sign like a celebrity. But he had the concert, and the night Canada's flagship jazz radio station devoted its airwaves to him. A poster plugging the concert series hangs in a frame on a wall in the main hallway at Aunt Peggy's condo in Chicago.

Almost every note Claude Jones played in forty-seven years on the job vanished in a sliver of a second—something else he shared with famous folks. All musicians practice and perform more than they record. It's math and economics. Release one album, then tour a few months. Score a residency someplace, then play live every night.

But his peers built whole libraries of sound that would outlive them. Claude mostly left us fragments.

Piano on all eight tracks on side A of Eddie South's *South Side Jazz,* Chess Records, March 1951. If you know the name Eddie South, it's probably because of the time he spent in France, playing with Django Reinhardt. But by the late 1940s, he had returned to the U.S., set up a base in Chicago, and begun mentoring younger players, like Claude Jones, on the job.

Piano on "Leo's Blues" by Leo Parker, mustering all kinds of funk to bind the bass line to the melody, nearly stealing the show from the sax players up front, Parker on baritone and Eddie Johnson on tenor.

Betty Everett's "It's in His Kiss," whenever it crackled over the radio, or played on the PA system in the grocery store, my mom would interject, "That's your grandfather on piano," as if I hadn't listened the previous fifty times she reminded me, or the seventy-five times before that. If she wasn't with me, I'd still hear her in my head.

And, yes, the opening notes of "I'm So Proud," by Curtis Mayfield and The Impressions. Claude Jones on celeste. If I hear it when I'm with my teenage niece . . .

"That's your great-grandfather on this song."

A reflex.

One afternoon, driving my wife's car, Claude in the passenger seat, satellite radio tuned to Soul Town because they played music we both dug—R&B from the '60s, Motown acts, and all the sound-alikes. A song from Mary Wells came on. Claude saw the name on the monitor.

"I recorded with her," he said.

"This song?"

"Oh, I don't know," he said. "I did *so* many sessions back then. I couldn't keep them all straight."

By then, some more of his music was circulating among the family. A forty-minute set from Café des Copains, Wellington Street, down-town Toronto, in 1983, when Uncle Jeff showed up with recording equipment. He played "Take the A Train" by request and "Satin Doll" because he wanted to, and "Nina Never Knew" because Uncle Jeff had a stepdaughter named Nina.

And an hour-long session at the Scotch Mist, Rush Street, Chicago, early 1960s. He played and sang "They Can't Take That Away from Me," and hit a room-rattling low note when he said, "The way you sip your tea." Ended with "A Blues for Mag," a tribute to his wife, and the only song he ever wrote.

But I'm too young to have hung out at the clubs he played, and he would never touch the concert-sized Steinway in his living room. Not for fun or special occasions, and never because we asked him, which we did until we learned to stop. My mom resented it. Why couldn't he show her kids what he did for a living, and how well he did it? He always grumbled about how young people didn't recognize good music, so why not let his grandkids hear how a real musician sounded in person? Selfish, Mom thought.

Except Claude's gift was Claude's gift, his to use, squander, sit on, or apportion in small doses to the folks who heard him play in person. If he didn't regret recording so little, how could I regret it for him? He raised four kids playing jazz piano. Did some freelance photography, and a few commercials, but never needed a day job. Made a steady living in a boom-and-bust industry. Lived outside the spotlight, but comfortably, in a business that devours its middle class. Didn't matter if he never found the time or impetus to assemble a band and cut an album. Music brought him to Canada and changed the trajectory of a lot of lives. Made mine possible. That's success.

Do I think he should have done more?

Maybe *I'm* selfish.

Still, I sometimes imagine alternate outcomes. Claude Jones fronting his own trio and recording some albums, writing some songs and collecting some royalties. Passing on something besides anecdotes and snippets of sound to younger folks like me. Profiles on modern day streaming platforms, his music popping up alongside Ray Bryant or Bobby Timmons on my algorithm-generated, piano-heavy jazz playlists.

He would still have that signature sound—strong left hand, and a right so nimble you'd never suspect he was a southpaw. He could play loud, but defaulted to nuance. Fuse Erroll Garner and Red Garland into one pianist, and you have Claude Jones.

But if he recorded more, I wouldn't have to describe his sound. You would know it.

I wish you could hear it.

I wish I didn't have to imagine.

But maybe I'm asking too much.

PART II

I didn't trek to the indoor track at York University to chat with Perdita Felicien. The plan, on March 7, 2007, involved interviewing Andre

Durie, a football star making a comeback two years after destroying his left knee. He pushed our meeting back an hour, which bugged me. As a general assignment reporter, I didn't just cover one topic; I covered some of everything and could have used the time to scout another story.

As for me . . . my football scholarship never materialized, and neither did my NFL career. I graduated with a journalism degree, and a pile of debt best described as Himalayan. I worked a few internships and finally scored a full-time reporting job at the *Star* in 2004. First in news, and then finally in sports. By the time I was scheduled to meet Andre Durie, I had shrunk my debt from Himalayan to Laurentian to the size of one of those ski hills an hour north of Toronto. I even managed to buy a condo off Dundas Street in Mississauga, just south of my old high school.

I pushed through the doors of the indoor track, and as I walked toward the corner of the building where Andre warmed up, opportunity trotted past in black spandex and neon-green Nikes. I felt a flicker of recognition and a dawning curiosity. I stopped and turned to watch her jog to the end of the straightaway. Her butt didn't jiggle like regular people's did. It bounced as one solid, powerful unit. No extra fat on her frame. No superfluous movement when she ran. All power and precision, as if a Formula One car had assumed human form.

Of course, I knew of Perdita Felicien long before then. She was a world-class hurdler and Canada's brightest track star. After two world titles and a spectacular crash in the 2004 Olympics, her face—full lips and deep dimples and bright white teeth—had grown as familiar to Canadian sports fans as any hockey player's. In the twelve months since I had returned to the *Star*'s sports department, I'd never written about her, but as a fan of track and field and beautiful Black women, I had followed her career.

Plus, we had met before, briefly, on an airplane. I had seen her boyfriend on TV, so I knew she wasn't single back then. And I was taken, too, still trying to make myself happy in a draining relationship. After the plane landed, Perdita and I stood next to the baggage carousel at

Pearson and shared harmless conversation. I gave her my business card, just in case I might have to interview her, and went back to being her fan.

As she finished her workout and walked toward the exit, I figured we should meet again. I eased into a light jog, pushed through the glass doors and into the lobby, and found her on the steps leading to a viewing gallery, stretching and chatting on her cell phone.

Just then I realized the risk I had assumed. She was trying to finish her workday, and here came one more guy about to beg for her phone number. I didn't know how I'd distinguish myself from every other no-hoper who approached her. She probably turned away dudes like me all day. Even if she remembered our first meeting, it didn't guarantee a second conversation. When she snapped her flip-phone shut, I called out before I could stop the words, or at least devise a clever opening line.

"Perdita!"

She turned and eyed me from head to toe and back. I felt exposed, but thankful I'd worn pressed khakis and a red sweater instead of dressing like a sportswriter.

"Do we know each other?"

"Not yet," I said. "But we met on a flight from Chicago to Toronto a couple of Thanksgivings ago. Remember?"

If she didn't, I'd feel like a moron. I thought of ways to salvage some dignity if she had forgotten me or, even worse, remembered and just didn't want to talk. But then she flashed the smile I'd seen on TV hundreds of times since she won the world title in 2003, and I finally saw those dimples in person.

"Yes! You're the journalist!" she said. "Your name is Jason, right? You cover baseball."

"Almost," I said. "It's Morgan. And I don't cover baseball. That's above my pay grade right now. Wait . . . am I holding you up?"

"Nope. I'm just finishing. I don't even usually do calf raises, but my Achilles tendon has been bugging me and this helps," she said. "Now don't go reporting that."

"Of course not!" I said. "This is all off the record."

She smiled again and the fluttering in my stomach subsided. Perdita treated me like she sensed the confidence I hoped to project, and not the nerves I felt. When she told me about her sore heel, I took it as a sign she wanted to trust me. Our conversation fell into an easy rhythm, and my only goal was to keep it going.

I didn't know where it would lead. My last relationship imploded in the fall of 2005, and I'd spent the eighteen intervening months flipping through women like the pages of a magazine. But now, at thirty, I was ready to take somebody seriously.

Perdita didn't act like she had a man. I had met her previous partner through mutual friends, and sometimes rumours about them bubbled up through my network—breakups, reunions, possible engagements— but I hadn't heard anything recently. Nice guy, but he bathed in Perdita's fame as if *he* were the world champ, and it chafed me.

She never mentioned him, so I didn't either. And when she said she was late for a lunch date with her girlfriends, I grabbed my pen and opened my notebook.

"Well, at least give me your email address so we can stay in touch," I said.

"Absolutely," she said, taking my pen and pad. "We can go out to eat or something. I'll give you my number, too. You're the only person in Canadian media who has it."

She smiled and handed the notebook back, then picked up her gym bag and said goodbye. As she walked away, I admired the perfect round-ness of her behind. Envisioned it beneath that spandex. Wondered if it felt as firm as it looked.

When I lost sight of her, I opened the notebook to the page where she had written her name and number. Below them, she had drawn a smiley face with a wink, and not even my fear of screwing this up could blind me to a signal so blatant.

———

So of course we jumped the broom. Ten years, three months, and two days later.

I went with both feet, takeoff and landing, like a kid with rubber boots into a puddle. Perdita led with her right leg and trailed with her left, like she was clearing hurdle ten, en route to running 12.4.

Broom-jumping is another folkway Black folks in general picked up from Black Americans specifically, and I don't begrudge it. I save words like *appropriation*, and the resentment that comes with it, for white people who scavenge our language and fashion and music. But when other Black folks do it, it's because they admire us. Even if they won't admit it. If African Americans have an instinctive bias, it's toward inclusion. If you're Black and want to act American, for the most part, nobody will stop you.

Other varieties of Black people don't always reciprocate. Imagine me talking patois with a straight face, then imagine Jamaicans trying not to wring my neck. And they'd have a right to. Dialects are sacred in ways that languages aren't. There's value in scarcity, and in keeping your club exclusive. Otherwise, people who pay for luxury boxes at the stadium would just sit out in the bleachers with the plebes.

But Black Americans tend not to gatekeep or control borders. Any known blood makes you one of us if you choose, and if you're Black but not from the U.S., you can opt in. Even if you brand yourself a NotBlack—"I'm not Black, I'm from the Dominican Republic . . ."—you can still borrow our culture, interest free.

So, this wedding was all Black but multicultural, and very Toronto. The DJ at the reception cycled through sets of R&B and hip-hop and dancehall and soca, the way DJs have to when Black Torontonians gather. Mixed in some zouk for Perdita's St. Lucian family.

And for our first dance?

Something Black and American and particular to my family.

Grandpa jolted to attention when the DJ asked him to stand while he introduced the song. By then, he had been a widow nearly four years, long retired from his side job starting family fights. The following April, a failed kidney would land him in hospital. Four months and two facilities later, he would die. But before our wedding, he told us he had been saving energy for weeks, just so he could enjoy the night. He summoned the strength to stand and grabbed the back of his chair with his right hand for balance. He raised his left hand and waved it while the rest of our guests applauded, the way people used to clap for him six nights a week for his whole working life.

One last ovation.

Then we all heard him on the celeste.

And Curtis Mayfield sang:

I'm so proud

Then the rest of The Impressions echoed him.

And then the whole group:

I'm so proooooooud of you

I hugged Perdita's waist as we slow-dragged. She cinched her arms around my shoulders and squeezed. I brushed her neck with my lips. We danced some more. Our first married steps together.

As a slow-dance partner, I'm undefeated.

But as a husband?

Just trying to do the big things right, and remember that the little things also matter. Compliments. Filling and emptying the dishwasher. Waking up ahead of the toddler so Perdita can sleep late. James Ingram's estimate? Just a fraction of the number of details that can nourish a long-term romance or extinguish it. One Hundred? Try One Thousand Ways, James.

Most days, I succeed. Some nights, I sleep on the couch. Any night you find me there, I probably deserved a screwdriver to the neck, and if you ever see me with that screwdriver, assume I earned it. In the first few years of marriage, I've learned that the best way to become a great husband is to marry a patient woman who also draws a hard line against your bullshit. If it keeps you behaving, it'll save your marriage. If you keep crossing her, she'll drop kick you out the front door. Either way, you wind up with the life you deserve.

My mom would warn my sisters and me about thinking you could change a partner. For years, she could envision the best version of Pete Campbell, the way a master sculptor sees a statue in a slab of granite. She figured with enough love, he could learn to love himself a little better. Drop his bad habits and, maybe, his guard sometimes, the way both people in a strong partnership need to. He would mess up and she would forgive him, and love him some more, and hope it would trigger a metamorphosis.

Except that never works. People can change, but you can't make them. And you damn sure can't love their flaws away. Mom learned, after twenty-three years.

Yeah, I have flaws, too. I talk too much and communicate too little. If we're in a hot argument, I can shrink you from five feet to five inches tall with a single word. But if I want to shut you out, I'll treat you like you're not in the room. For days at a time. Learned from my dad. Like apprenticing from a master. The Michael Jordan of stonewalling.

Me as a father?

Terrified.

Our daughter, Nova, is a toddler right now. On days she doesn't look like Perdita, she looks like her aunt Courtney, which means she looks like our dad, and *his* dad. But in the right light, from the right angle, head tilted forward, concentrating on the doll in her hands, I'll catch her looking like my little twin, and it's chilling. I live with that responsibility all the time, her life and safety, but it hits harder in those moments. Closer to me than a clone would be, because she's just like me, but she's her own little person, and she needs me. She has a few friends and a lot of toys. She has her cousins and her favourite TV shows. But Perdita and I are her world right now. To feel so depended on . . . it's frightening. And I love it.

But I'm also within spitting distance of fifty. Middle-aged for most folks, but late life for a Campbell man. Uncle Ernest died in his twenties. My dad and his dad at fifty-two.

I was seventeen when my dad died—too young to expect it, but old enough to have to live with it. But if I die at fifty-two, Nova will still be in grade school, old enough to miss me and too young to function without her father. I don't obsess over it, but the thought does drift across my mind some mornings, while I'm making coffee or working out, or staring at my watch at 4:54 a.m., wrestling over whether to grab six more minutes of sleep or just start the day.

Still fighting, of course.

To keep my daughter safe and my marriage on track, and my career trajectory bending upward. Don't choose any of that stuff unless you're ready to knuckle up.

Doctors keep telling us that stress can shorten your life. I believe them, and try to act on what I know.

So I focus on what I can control.

My health, so cancer doesn't take me out.

My marriage, so Perdita doesn't put me out.

And opportunities.

To learn from other people's mistakes instead of regretting my own.

To see how good I can really be. Man. Father. Writer.

To follow through where other people never had the chance, or just never took it.

Acknowledgements

One last story about my grandpa:

November 1942, turning nineteen, a recent draftee set to join the U.S. Army.

Claude liked certain types of fights—arguments and battles of wills, mostly—but he wasn't built for violence. He was already a professional pianist, didn't want to risk injuring his hands in fist fights; firing rifles and lobbing grenades would fall well outside his skill set, too, even after basic training.

Also had a baby on the way: my mom, Jeanie, due the following March.

Didn't matter to the Army. The needed bodies in the European theatre, and Claude had one. They sent instructions to board a troop train at Union Station in downtown Chicago for the ride to basic training. Beyond that, Claude knew, loomed World War II, and, he feared, an assignment on the front lines in Europe.

At Union Station with Margaret, his pregnant wife, hugging and kissing and saying goodbye, Claude prepared to cross the street and head inside to find his train. As he stepped off the sidewalk, a passing taxicab ran over his foot and broke some bones.

That's the "what."

The "how" and "why" differ, depending on the storyteller.

Claude always framed it as a simple failure to look both ways before trying to cross a busy street—a bad habit meets bad timing. My mom suspects he saw that taxicab and made a decision—he was more likely to survive a broken foot than whatever awaited him in a war zone.

Two theories, one outcome. The Army wasn't shipping Claude Jones anywhere with a cast on his foot. The injury bought him some time, and eventually he landed in an Army office doing administrative tasks. This stuff, he could handle: filing, mailing letters, typing memos. Back at Fenger High School he had taken a typing class as a schedule-filler—now he used those skills every day, helping the U.S. Army keep up with paperwork. He said taking that class saved his life.

So if we're acknowledging people who helped bring these stories from experience to concept to finished product, we can start with the typing teacher and the cab driver. And then, my grandfather, obviously, for his bad timing . . . or quick thinking.

Also, my mom, for sharing the taxicab story with me, and filling in the gaps of so many of the others. Without her, my aunt Peggy, my uncle Jeff, and my sisters, Dana and Courtney, and even my niece, Mica, this book never happens. Uncle Ken and Aunt Cheeky, too. All of them, but especially the generation ahead of mine, are a bottomless source of the family stories that drive the first half of this book. I could have written another 100 pages, but I decided to spare all of us.

There are always more stories.

Granny Mary, for instance, claims she wrapped her newborn son, Prines Campbell Jr., in some blankets and smuggled him out of Provident Hospital in Chicago because, as an eighteen-year-old mother, she couldn't afford the bill. I have to thank her for being such a character.

I'm grateful to my dad—a difficult, beautiful man who did the best he could.

To my wife, the amazing Perdita Felicien, who embraced my fighting family as her own, and who supported me through a book-writing process I thought might never end—I love and thank you. Even before I signed a contract, when I had two weeks to write a proposal, she let me read the one she'd written for her first book, just so I could see how it was supposed to look. Saved me at least a month, which is like a decade in deadline-journalist years.

I also need to acknowledge Nova, our daughter, who was a year old when I signed the contract to write this book and is set to start junior kindergarten as I write these acknowledgements. Same age I was when I really started raising hell. Help.

I spent my adolescence at the Woodlands School, known for its windowless classrooms and lack of school spirit, but I met some incredible teachers during my five years there. Vicki Moore, Dave Ellis, Lori Morgan, and M. Dale Davis all invested time and energy in me and nudged me along the path from wisecracking teenager distracting his classmates to a grown-up who now gets paid for his wisecracks.

That last year of high school was heavy, but my friends lightened the load. Andre Batson, Mace Freeman, Kevin Gregory, Andre Webley, Mark Moore, Patrick Dottin, Elden Forskin, and the Kelman brothers, Levar, Quincy, and Ryan. They all held me down without feeling sorry for me.

The next year I enrolled at Northwestern and studied under some professors who made me a better writer—Pam Harkins, Susan Mango-Curtis, Michele Weldon, and the late Bob McClory in particular.

A huge thank you to Ashante Infantry, my ride-or-die colleague from the *Toronto Star*. She's the person who introduced me to Sharon Burnside, who ran the internship program through which I joined the company. Without Ashante, I would have remained just a name on a résumé for newsroom decision-makers, and I'm not sure how any of the rest of this plays out.

A few times during my eighteen years at the *Star*, my career wound up on life support, so I have to thank Irene Gentle, Doug Cudmore, and Jennifer Quinn for letting me resuscitate it. Each of them, as editors, could have placed a foot on my neck just to show me which of us had the power. Instead, they did the simplest, sweetest, smartest thing, and just let me work.

But journalism isn't creative writing, and writing features is a long way from penning memoirs. I needed help to make the transition, so *mil gracias a mi hermana Neudis Abreu, La Negra Primera de Sorocaima*, for directing me to the awesome writing coach Beth Kaplan, who taught me to write about myself.

A huge thank you goes to my editor, Jordan Ginsberg, who helped me stitch these disparate stories into a coherent *story*. And thanks to my agent, Martha Webb, for guiding me through the business of writing. If writing is like boxing, Jordan would be my trainer and Martha my manager. If they're not the two best in the business, they're the best for me, and for this project.

To take the parallel a little further, the copyeditor would be the cutman or cutwoman, swooping in on fight night to make sure things go smoothly and patch you up where you're leaking, so massive gratitude to the sharp-eyed Debbie Innes, who subtly, sometimes imperceptibly, but inarguably made this book stronger.

That would make Penguin Random House Canada the promoter, so thanks to Scott Sellers, VP, Associate Publisher and Director of Marketing Strategy, and a fellow trainee at Bang Fitness on Queen Street West in Toronto. On a Friday night in December of 2019, I made a series of posts on Twitter explaining that I was leaving the *Star* to start the next phase of my professional life. Except I had nothing lined up— just a fifty-four-week salary continuance and a promise to myself that if, after six months of working for myself it looked like I was about to starve, I would look for another job. Like, a real job, with a company and a boss and steady pay.

Saturday morning, Scott sent me a direct message.

"Morgan, let's connect in the new year. Would love to chat about what you're working on."

What I was working on were the essays that formed the spine of the book you just finished.

So shout out to Scott for believing in the project.

And, finally, thanks to you for taking the time to read.

MORGAN CAMPBELL is an award-winning journalist, currently a senior contributor at CBC Sports and a contributor to the New York Times. For over eighteen years, he worked at the Toronto Star where he established himself as one of Canada's finest sports writers. Morgan's best work highlights the places where sport intersects with off-the-field issues like race, culture, politics, and business.